A history of writing

A HISTORY OF
WRITING

Albertine Gaur

The British Library

To my husband
Denis Evelyn Hobbins Henning

© 1984, 1987 Albertine Gaur

Published by
The British Library
Great Russell Street
London WC1B 3DG

First published in 1984
First paperback edition (with corrections) 1987

British Library Cataloguing in Publication Data
Gaur, Albertine
   A history of writing.——[2nd ed.]
   with corrections
   1. Writing——History
   I. Title
   411'.09   P211

ISBN 0-7123-0145-3

Designed by Gillian Greenwood
Typeset in Plantin Light by Tradespools Ltd, Frome
Printed in Great Britain by BAS Printers Ltd, Over Wallop
Bound in Great Britain by Hunter and Foulis Ltd, Edinburgh

Contents

Abbreviations used in the text

AE	Arthur Evans, *Scripta Minoa, I*. Oxford, 1909
ALB	A.L.Basham, *The wonder that was India*. London, 1954
AS	Alfred Schmitt, *Entstehung und Entwicklung der Schriften*. (Herausgegeben bei Claus Haebler). Köln, 1980
DC	David Chibbett, *The history of Japanese printing and book illustration*. Tokyo, 1977
DC/MJ	Don Cassel and Martin Jackson, *Introduction to computers and information processing*. Reston, Virginia, 1981
DD	David Diringer, *The alphabet: a key to the history of Mankind*. London, 1953
DJ	Donald Jackson, *The story of writing*, London and New York, 1981
DML	D.M.Lang, *Armenia, cradle of civilisation*. London, 1980
EL	Ernst Lehner, *American symbols: a picture history*. New York, 1966
GB	Gustav Barthel, *Konnte Adam schreiben: Weltgeschichte der Schrift*. Köln, 1972.
GB/1	George Bankes, *Peru before Pizarro*. Oxford, 1977
GDP	G.D.Painter, *Gutenberg and the B 36 group: a re-consideration*. (Essays in honour of Victor Scholderer). Mainz, 1970
GGS	Gershom G. Sholem, *Major trends in Jewish mysticism*. 6th ed. New York, 1972
GM	Garrick Mallery, *Picture writing of the American Indians*. Washington, 1893
HJ	Hans Jensen, *Signs, symbols and script: an account of man's effort to write*. London, 1970
IJG	I.J.Gelb, *A study of writing: the foundations of gramatology*. Chicago, 1963
JB	Janet Backhouse, *The Lindisfarne Gospels*. London, 1981
JEST	J. Eric S. Thompson, *Maya hieroglyphs without tears*. London, 1972
JIW	Joyce Irene Whalley, *The pen's excellence: calligraphy of Western Europe and America*. 1980
MDM	M.D.McLeod, *The Asante*. London, 1981
ML	Murray Laver, *Computers and social change*. New York, 1980
PG	Peter Green, *A concise history of ancient Greece*. 2nd ed. London, 1981
RWBM	Ronald W.B.Morris, *The prehistoric rock art of Argyll*. 1977
SHS	S.H.Steinberg, *Five hundred years of printing*. 3rd ed. London, 1979
TQR	Thomas Q. Reefe, *Lukasa: a Luba memory device*. (African Arts. vol.10. p.49)
THT	Tsuen-Hsuin Tsien, *Written on bamboo and silk: the beginning of Chinese books and inscriptions*. Chicago, 1962
YHS	Yasin Hamid Safadi, *Islamic calligraphy*. London, 1978

Preface

Most works dealing with the history of writing look upon writing mainly as a means of reproducing language with the aid of graphic symbols. This attitude automatically imposes a hierarchical structure. If the aim of writing is the reproduction of language then the most satisfactory, and by implication the most advanced, form of writing, is the one which reproduces language most accurately, in the most economical manner — which inevitably leads to the alphabet. In the same way, if writing is based on the use of graphic symbols then the material most suited to receive and preserve such symbols is the material most suited for writing — which in turns leads to paper. Taking this attitude to its logical conclusion, writing can then be divided into three main groups: 'proper' writing, where a small number of codified graphic symbols reproduce, most accurately, the sounds of a particular language; 'forerunners of writing', where the sound element is still absent and symbols (or perhaps objects) reproduce whole ideas; and 'transitional' forms of writing where sound elements start to emerge. The alphabet thus becomes a Platonic idea towards which all forms of (proper) writing must by necessity progress.

Until very recently such an attitude was indeed perfectly justifiable, perhaps even self-evident. But during the last thirty years, especially during the last decade, the situation has changed dramatically. As we advance further and further into the new age of information technology, the storage, preservation and, ultimately, the dissemination of knowledge, depends no longer on the actual process of writing. Computers store information in an electronic memory by means of positive and negative impulses — the way information was once (during the age of oral tradition) stored in the human brain. With everything around us changing it is perhaps time to re-examine the concept of writing and look at it, not from the point of how effectively it can store language, but how effectively it can store information; information essential to the economic and political survival of a given society.

An extensive and in parts highly detailed literature exists on the various aspects of writing, the different scripts, their history and possible relationship to each other, and this study in no way pretends to compete with the work done by individual specialists in their respective fields. Its aim is of a more general nature; namely, to look upon writing from the late 20th-century concept of information storage, to examine the interactions between society and writing and to introduce the subject to a wider and more general audience. The story of writing is a tale of adventure which spans some twenty thousand years and touches all aspects of human life. It is important in universal, not just in scholarly, terms. Such an overall view of a highly complex subject must by necessity omit many details and invite speculations with which individual specialists may not always wish to agree. For those interested in a more detailed and perhaps more traditional approach there is a select bibliography at the end of this book (amended for the second edition) and there are abbreviated references in the text itself; the purpose of the latter is less to reinforce a particular opinion than to lead the reader to places where he or she can find more information of a factual and/or bibliographical nature.

While the opinions expressed in this study are of course my own responsibility, I am greatly indebted to colleagues inside and outside the British Library who have generously allowed me to share their time and expertise. I would especially like to thank my colleagues Ken Gardner, Frances Wood, Beth MacKillop, Yu-Ying Brown, Muhammad Isa Waley, Yasin Safadi, V. Nerssessian, Kathy van de Vate, Lama Chime, Patricia Herbert and David Goldstein, of the department of Oriental Collections (previously the Department of Oriental Manuscripts and Printed Books); Tom Pattie, of the Department of Western Manuscripts; Lotte Hellinga, of the History of the Book Group, and Annie Gilbert, of the Photographic Department of the British Library. Also Malcolm McLeod, Elisabeth Carmichael, Doroto Starzecka and John Mack, of the Museum of Mankind; Christopher Walker, of the Department of Western Asiatic Antiquities, British Museum, who generously provided the drawings on p. 66, and Morris Bierbrier, of the Department of Egyptian Antiquities, British Museum, who supplied those on pp. 62–63. My thanks are also due to V. A. Tatton-Brown, of the Department of Greek and Roman Antiquities, British Museum; Robert Watson and Robert Skelton, of the Victoria and Albert Museum; Tovia Gelblum of the School of Oriental and African Studies and Hilary Henning, for lending her computer expertise.

I should like to thank the following for permission to reproduce photographs in the book: the Trustees of the British Museum; Bodleian Library, Oxford; Mr Michael O'Keefe; American Tourist Board; Victoria and Albert Museum; John Rylands University Library, Manchester; University Library, Heidelberg; Bavarian State Library, Munich. The drawings on pp. 47, 49, 75, 76, 105, 167, 168, 187 and 192 are by John Ronayne.

10 March 1987   Albertine Gaur

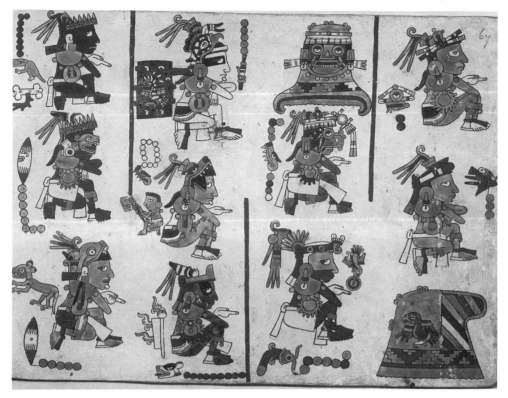

PLATE I Codex Nuttall *(made of deerskin); describes the sacred history of the Mixtec people, mainly in relation to events connected with the life of a great military and political hero, 8-Deer Tiger Claw, who lived between 1063–1101* AD. *The manuscript was probably completed shortly before the Spanish conquest of Mexico. (British Museum; Museum of Mankind; 39671)*

PLATE II *Traffic signs, notices and information; photographed by the author.*

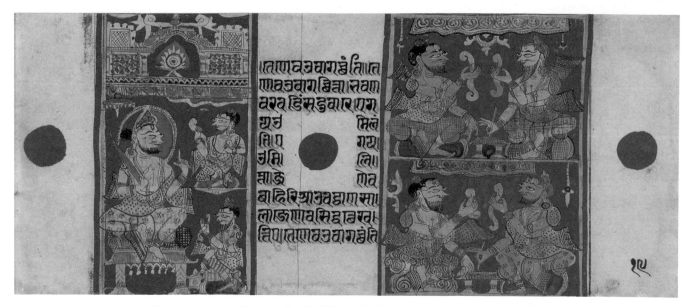

PLATE III Kalpasutra; *from Gujarat; dated 1502/1445. The soothsayers and astrologers consult their* *scrolls to determine the meaning of Queen Trishala's fourteen dreams and write down their opinion.* *(British Library; Oriental Collections; Or. 13700. f. 61)*

PLATE IV *Almanac written on cloth; the beginning is illustrated with signs of the zodiac; in the Rajasthani folk-style; 1844/45* AD. *(British Library; Oriental Collections; Or. 13489)*

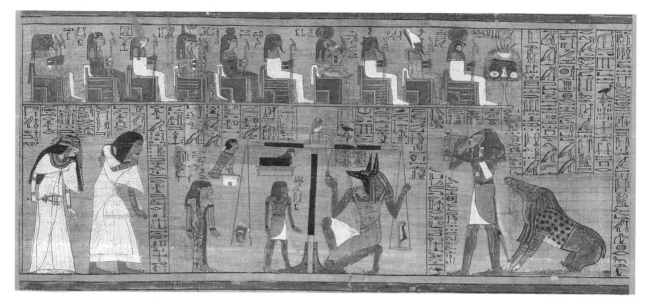

PLATE V *Among the Egyptian pantheon, the ibis-headed Toth acts as scribe and patron of letters. He is here shown noting down the answers given by the deceased royal scribe Hunefer in the course of the latter's judgment in the realm of Osiris. From Thebes, 19th Dynasty, c.1250 BC. (British Museum; Department of Egyptian Antiquities; 10470)*

PLATE VI *Page from the Lindisfarne Gospels; the main text (7th century) is written in insular majuscule (a script first developed in early Christian Ireland), with decorated initials, and the Anglo-Saxon gloss (added in the mid-10th century) written in insular minuscule. (British Library; Department of Manuscripts; Cotton MS. Nero. D. iv, f.15)*

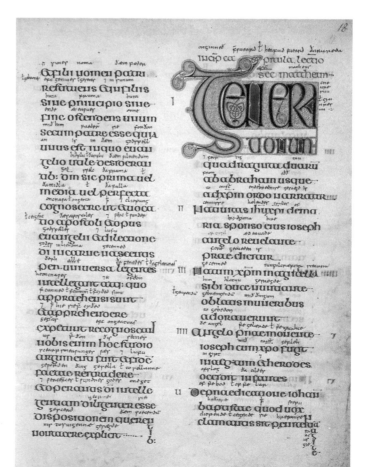

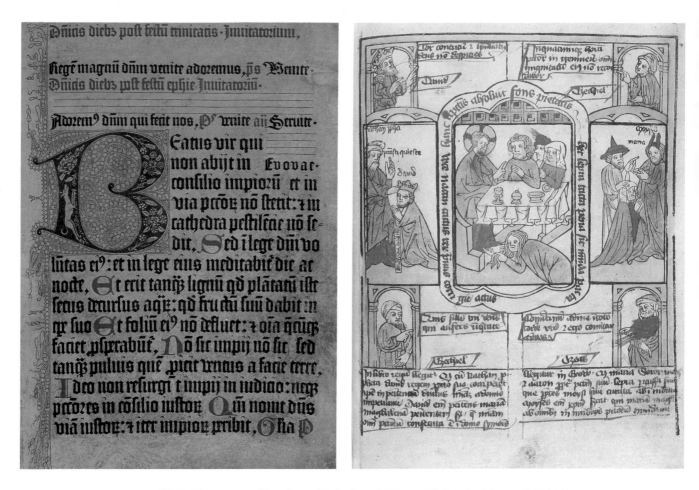

PLATE VII Biblia Pauperum; *chiroxylographic book; c. 1420* AD. *(University Library of Heidelberg; Cod. Pal. Germ, 438, f.117)*

PLATE VIII Psalterium cum canticis, *printed by J. Fust and P. Schöffer in Mainz, 1457. (British Library; Department of Printed Books; G. 12216, f.1r)*

I Origin and development of writing

What is writing and who needs it?

All writing is information storage. It is not the only form of information storage. Long before, and in many instances simultaneously with it, human memory served the same purpose. In most cases it was the memory of a specially trained and select group to whom society entrusted this task. Basic differences exist between these two forms of information storage which relate mainly, though not exclusively, to the transmission and the dissemination of information. Oral transmission needs personal, often (depending on the nature and complexity of the information) prolonged, contact between two or more individuals who have to be physically present at the same time and in the same place. Enough time has to be spent to satisfy (though never fully) the one who transmits the information that the other has effectively stored it in his memory, that he will be able to retain and eventually transmit it correctly. In the case of writing, the information is stored mechanically, on an independent object, and can be retrieved and used at any time, in any place (in the case of moveable objects such as books etc.) by all those who are able to consult and decode it. Here too, memory plays an important part, but only in the form of a one-time effort — that of learning the rules, however rudimentary or complex, of a particular form of script. Afterwards all information stored in this way is available to those who have mastered the rules.

Writing has other advantages, too. There are limits to the amount of data that human memory can retain. There is, in theory at least, no limit to the amount of information that can be stored in written form. In addition, being free of the often onerous task of having to assimilate completely (and perhaps permanently) some particular information, this information, consulted in written form, can be used as a basis for new speculations. Thus one generation not only acquires the knowledge of previous generations but can use this knowledge to make new discoveries, and to formulate new conclusions, which can then be added to the ever-increasing corpus of available data. In other words, written information can be manipulated. Learning by heart has the disadvantage that it does not encourage critical thinking; and it has indeed always been preferred for poetry (religious and secular), history (legendary, epic, semi-factual) or for secret knowledge not meant to go beyond the limits of a particular group.

If all writing is information storage, then all writing is of equal value. Each society stores the information essential to its survival, the information which enables it to function effectively. There is in fact no essential difference between prehistoric rock paintings, memory aids (mnemonic devices), wintercounts, tallies, knotted cords, pictographic, syllabic and consonantal scripts, or the alphabet. There are no primitive scripts, no forerunners of writing, no transitional scripts as such (terms frequently used in books dealing with the history of writing), but only societies at a particular level of economic and social development using certain forms of information storage. If a form of information storage fulfils its purpose as far as a particular society is concerned then it is (for this particular society) 'proper' writing.

Basically, all forms of writing belong to either one or the other of two distinct groups — thought writing or sound writing. Thought writing transmits an idea directly; the drawing of a leg means 'leg' or 'to go', the drawing of a tree means 'tree' (it could of course also mean 'fresh', 'green', 'life' etc.), the drawing of two trees can mean 'forest' and so forth, in any language. Sound writing (phonetic writing) is far more complex. It is not as we, on the basis of our own experience and training might be tempted to assume, more natural, nor even necessarily always more effective. In many ways it is a tortuous and somewhat unnatural process. An idea has to be translated first into the sounds of a particular word or sentence in a particular language, then those sounds have to be made visible in the form of engraved, painted or incised signs on the surface of a definite object, signs which more often than not bear no relation to the content of the original thought. In order to consult the information (and ultimately the whole purpose of information storage is communication) these visual signs have to be translated back into the sounds of the same language, and from this the word, the sentence and the original idea have to be reconstructed in the mind of the reader. And this is in fact exactly how primitive people without any writing of their own view the process.

Though the division between the two groups is absolute and basic, it would be wrong to assume that it is also clear-cut, that all forms of writing belong, wholly and exclusively, to either the one or the other group. As we shall see later, phonetic (sound) elements evolved early and often quite rapidly in almost all ancient forms of writing. Ideographic (thought) elements indicative of a concept or word are eventually left behind in most — though by no means all — scripts (see Chinese writing, for instance, but also signs such as 2, &, £, $ etc.), and phonetic elements become dominant and finally exclusive in syllabic, consonantal and alphabetic scripts.

The word 'evolve' has been used on purpose. A good number of scholars have been, and still are, of the opinion that phonetic writing in the full sense is the result of a definite, unique invention which took place only once; others, with a somewhat less fundamental-istic turn of mind, see in phonetic writing the result of several sporadic and often (semi-) historically documented inventions made by a number of definite persons (see *Invented Scripts*, pp. 130–134). The latter opinion has been revived by recent observations of how a number of people belonging to still basically tribal communities in Africa, North America and Alaska (AS, pp.15–219) made often temporarily successful attempts at inventing indigenous forms of writing. However in all those cases one can see, if one looks more closely, that the invention was in reality more a modification, stimulated by a close contact between the inventor(s) and an established system of writing, usually the Roman alphabet or the Arabic script. The history of writing is a long process of evolution — though, as in all historical and evolutionary processes, stimulated along the way by the contribution of especially-gifted individuals.

What kind of writing a society evolves, or chooses, depends largely if not wholly on the kind of society it is. (For once the chicken comes definitely before the egg.) The mere availability of writing does not transform a society. If writing is irrelevant to the existence and survival of a particular society, this society will, on coming into contanct with writing, either completely reject it or accept it in only a limited form, perhaps just for the use of a small and then often (but not always) privileged section. If a society has reached a stage of development where systematic writing becomes important for trade and administration (literature as such has always been able to manage perfectly well without it) — as happened in ancient Egypt, Mesopotamia and the Aegean — it will either evolve a script on the basis of already existing non-oral forms of information storage (such as memory aids, property marks, pictorial representations, tallies), or, often depending on the political situation, accept, adapt or modify the writing of another (not necessarily dominant) group; even if this form of writing might prove highly unsuitable for the linguistic peculiarities of its own language (Mesopotamia and Japan are two examples). But nowhere do we find a case where a society first developed a systematic form of writing and then increased its level of social and economic efficiency. Scripts do not create civilizations or new forms of society, but societies can create a new form of information storage.

Let us here briefly recount: what exactly are the advantages and disadvantages of the two main groups? We have already discussed the advantages of the first group — the thought or ideographic form of writing. They are, as we have seen, the possibility of communicating ideas and thoughts directly between the writer and the reader without the intermediary of language. In other words, this form of writing is independent of language; it can be understood and read in any language. An example, well-known and widely used, is the Chinese script, about which more will be said later. The disadvantages are the great number of different signs which have to be used (and remembered); in the case of Chinese as many as 50,000 for literary, and some 2,000–4,000 for elementary, use (and the Chinese language is particularly well suited for this form of writing). In the case of languages with a complex grammar and a large number of purely formal words (Japanese, for example), additional aids might have to be sought to accommodate all needs.

We have discussed the disadvantages of phonetic scripts, namely their dependency on one particular language, the fact that ideas have to be translated into sounds and that these sounds must then be made visible in the form of conventionalized (mostly abstract) signs which in turn have to be retranslated into the sounds of the (same) language and back into the original idea. Also, once a language has an established (written) form, any subsequent sound changes can only be accommodated by orthography, with the consequence that divergencies between the spoken and the written form can become considerable (English is an example). The same applies if an established phonetic form of writing is used for a language, or languages, with a different sound structure (see the Indian-derived scripts of Southeast Asia). On the other hand the advantages of a phonetic script — consonantal, syllabic or alphabetic — are considerable. In comparison to the 50,000 (or at least 2,000) Chinese characters, or the 700 or so Egyptian hieroglyphs, syllabic, consonantal and alphabetic scripts can manage with twenty to sixty signs. Information storage becomes thus more economic, less labour-intensive in relation to the time required to learn, read and write the script, and information can be stored in less space. In short, phonetic scripts are generally more cost-effective.

What kind of society can function with an ideographic form of writing (idea and thought transmission), using symbols and signs not yet fully codified or conventionalized, leaving a good deal to chance, individual imagination and an auxiliary background of commonly shared experience in both writer and reader? And what societies need for their survival and existence codified and economically usable systems which move towards and eventually reach a purely phonetic stage?

Scripts based on thought or idea transmission are perfectly adequate for societies with a pre-capitalistic structure of economy. Here much depends on individual effort, or group efforts based on loose and often temporary bonding such as happens among hunters, primitive herdsmen or simple agriculturists, who may, for mutual benefit, form groups (but not states) whenever the occasion demands it. This is the epic (some would say magic) stage where religion and society, history and legend are closely intermixed, with strong oral traditions helped perhaps by memory aids, notices or pictorial narratives.

On the other hand, societies which depend on coordinated labour efforts for irrigation, for example, which produce enough surplus to support a growing number of non-producing specialists, which assemble permanently in large and increasingly more densely populated areas (cities), need, sooner or later, some centralized form of organization; and centralized organization depends on an effectively functioning administration. One of the characteristics of this type of society is the high value it places on property, and the concept of property is by necessity interrelated with the idea of a state. Property may belong to an individual, a family or a group (as it did in the pre-capitalistic societies), but ultimately all property (producer, owner, the family and the group) must in one way or the other belong to the state — the state being the sum total of all goods, lands and persons. Since property, especially the surplus of property on which the new prosperity depends, can now only be obtained by communal efforts, such a state needs laws to coordinate and control property and those who produce it, and needs to provide protection from outside as well as inside disturbances. The yearly inundations of the Nile could only have been utilized by an efficient, centrally organized administration. If property is important, then the legalized transfer of property, namely trade, needs equal safeguards. Trade and administration are transient affairs which have to be carried out with a reasonable amount of speed and a reasonable amount of unambiguous exactness. For this purpose a small number of signs which can be quickly learned, written (perhaps on perishable material in a cursive hand) and read, offer definite advantages over the ambiguity and/or complexity of a script based on idea transmission.

Most codified forms of writing using (a varying amount of) phonetic elements developed in capitalistically-orientated societies with a primitive technology: between 4000–3000 BC in the Fertile Crescent, about 2000 BC in the Far East, and perhaps around 1000 BC in Central America. Indeed many of the early documents written in those scripts relate to property. In Mesopotamia, Egypt and the ancient Aegean we come across lists of goods sold, transferred or received, letters, contracts, administrative accounts and records. There are also (usually on permanent material and in a more monumental style) edicts of kings and references to deities — who are perceived as similar, often identical, to the temporary rulers of the land. Only gradually, and in many cases after a good deal of controversy, does the new codified form of writing replace oral traditions in the field of religious and secular literature.

How phonetic elements developed, how they were used, manipulated, differentiated, at times restrained, in their development, will be discussed later. Nowhere however was the evolution of writing truly linear; idea transmission does not lead automatically to the creation of a completely phonetic script. There are odd twists and curious retentions which may often look illogical and cumbersome, even unnecessary, but they always serve an overriding social need.

Idea transmission

The practice of representing data directly, without the intermediary of language, goes back to the dawn of human history. Ideas can be transmitted visually by various means: by objects, by abstract and/or geometrical patterns and designs, or by pictorial representations of human beings, animals, plants and objects. In many cases a combination of two or all three elements is used to store a particular piece of information.

Objects can communicate warnings (grass and leaves scattered over a side-track to indicate that it is best avoided); they can indicate direction (a branch stuck into the ground pointing to the direction where a person has gone or should go); they can be used to recall an event, a place or a person (stones piled over a grave). Herodotus tells the story of a Scythian ruler who sent the gift of a bird, a mouse, a frog and seven arrows to Darius, which were variously interpreted to the Persian king as either an offer of surrender (equating the mouse with the Scythians, the bird with their horses and the arrows with their arms which they were about to surrender) or a declaration of defiance (the Persians would be killed by the arrows if they did not fly away like birds, hide in the earth like mice and leap into the water like frogs).

By modifying or decorating objects (painting, carving, engraving) or by artificially creating (decorated) objects, an already remarkably high level of information storage can be reached. There are for example the message sticks of the Australian aborigines (fig. 1) — rounded wooden batons, sticks or tablets incised with marks, grooves or nicks. Often the incisions were made in the presence of the actual messenger and the importance of each mark was carefully explained to him. Message sticks were an essential part of aboriginal culture, linking together widely-scattered members of the community; and carrying such a stick would in many cases ensure safe conduct through hostile territory.

The Moche, a pre-Inca people from Peru (see p.78) used beans marked with dots, parallel lines, and/or a combination of both, for sending messages. Leather pouches filled with such beans have been found in Moche graves. They also feature quite prominently in scenes painted on pottery vessels, where runners are frequently depicted carrying them with exuberant determination (fig. 2).

The wampum belts of the Iroquois of North America (fig. 3) combined the use of patterns and colours for the transmission of messages; they were also used in ritual, ceremonial, as currency, and for personal decoration. Wampum belts were woven on a bow-loom in a manner analogous to other forms of weaving, and decorated with cylindrical beads made of sea-shells, winkles, whelks and clams. Most belts included designs in one colour on a background of another; no further colours were used. Dark colours signified solemnity and gravity, standing for danger, hostility, sadness and death. White stood for happiness, and red for war. More elaborate belts interwoven with coloured symbols could be used as declarations of war (a black belt with the sign of a tomahawk in red, for example), or as peace treaties (two dark hands on a white background), and so on.

Linguistic elements can already play a part, either by an association of ideas or an association of sound. Many of the decorations found on Ashanti houses, objects or utensils represent definite ideas expressed linguistically in the form of proverbs. For example, the

1 Message stick from the Murchison
District; Western Australia. (British
Museum: Museum of Mankind;
1901. 10-16.1)

2 Moche vessel showing runners carrying pouches filled with decorated
beans; Peru c. 200 BC–750 AD. (British Museum; Museum of Mankind;
1909. 12-1983)

3 Wampum belt from northern America. (British Museum; Museum of Mankind; 1906. 5-23-1)

4 Ashanti pipe showing a sankofa bird (right side of stem) turning its head backwards, representing a proverb: Shana, West Africa. Many images of Ashanti art are valued not only for themselves but for the verbal expression they call to mind. Proverbs are thought to summarise traditional wisdom and those aspiring to high office were expected to know hundreds of them. (British Museum; Museum of Mankind; Cb/B)

image (carved on a pipe) of a bird turning its head backwards can express the sentiment 'a person should not hesitate to turn back to undo past mistakes' (fig.4), and that of a crocodile grasping a mudfish in its mouth can stand for proverbs such as 'only a bad crocodile eats a creature which shares the same hole in the river bed' or 'if the mudfish gets anything it will ultimately go to the crocodile' (MDM, p.48).

An even more sophisticated way of conveying messages through objects is known to the Yoruba of Nigeria, who use cowrie shells for this purpose. One cowrie shell denotes 'defiance and failure', two placed together 'relationship and meeting', three placed apart 'separation and hostility'. Six cowrie shells mean 'attracted' because in the Yoruba language the word *efa* means both 'six' and 'attracted'. A string of six cowrie shells sent to a person of the opposite sex means 'I am attracted to you', and a string of eight shells returned to the sender stands for 'I agree, I feel the same' since *ejo* means 'eight' and 'agreed' (AS, p.16).

The ability to store numerical information has always been an integral part of writing (with the Mayas, for example, Hebrew script, and the Roman alphabet). Pebbles, shells, beans, beads or pieces of wood (fig. 5) can be used to store numerical data. On a more sophisticated level, tallies and knotted cords fulfil the same role. Tallies are usually sticks or rods of wood (sometimes also poles, house walls, doors etc.) into which notches or grooves have been cut to record the existence and memory of particular objects, numbers or events — such as the number of animals hunted, enemies killed, men or horses required in a particular camp, the days of a journey or the duration of an absence from home, the number and (depending on the type of individual marks) quality of goods sold, and so forth. The main purpose of the tally however has always been the recording of debts. Once a stick has been marked it can be split lengthwise, giving both the creditor and the debtor an incorruptible account of the amount of money or goods involved. Tallies have been used

*5 A tally (*kupe*) from the Torres Strait Islands. (British Museum; Museum of Mankind; 89 + 122)*

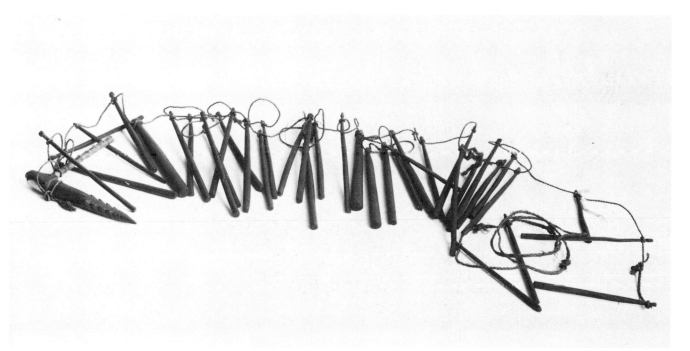

in most parts of the world and by nearly all societies. Some scholars have even suggested that the tally was important, if not instrumental, in the development of the Chinese script (HJ, p.27). In England the chief interest of the tally centres around its public use. Soon after 1100 AD tallies became recognized forms of receipt for payments into the Royal Treasury, a situation which continued until 1826 (hence such terms as 'tally clerk').

The use of knotted cords was equally widespread. Though normally a means of enumeration, a memory aid for the keeping of statistical records, knotted cords have also been cited in connection with the development of writing. In this context they are supposed to have been used in ancient China, Tibet, Japan, Siberia, Africa, California and the Polynesian Islands. In Hawaii they played an important role in the gathering of taxes; and in the Solomon Islands strings with knots and loops are still used for the exchange of news. The best-known and most accomplished version of the knotted cord is the *quipu* of ancient Peru. (fig. 6). *Quipus* were a highly efficient means of information storage, and Inca (see p.77) administration greatly depended on them. They may also have been adapted, at least in part, to the sounds of the Inca language.

6 A quipu *from Peru. (British Museum; Museum of Mankind; 1907. 3-19. 286)*

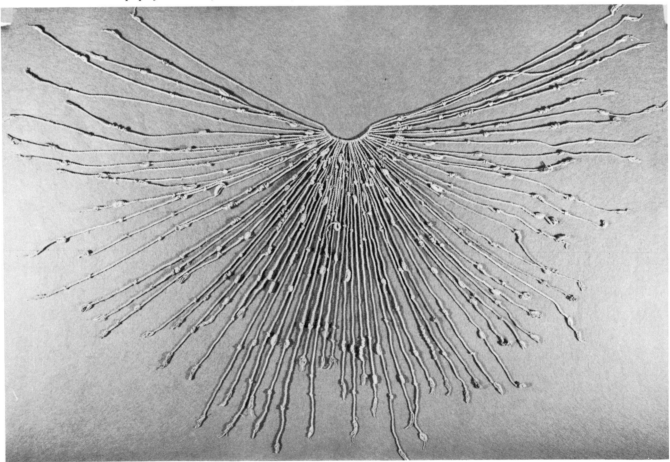

Geometrical and abstract symbols and signs such as circles, wheels, loops, combs, triangles, arches, spirals, zigzag lines etc. are already to be found — sometimes side by side with figurative representations, often alone — in a large number of prehistoric and later rock-drawings. Their exact meaning is still largely enigmatic, but they seem to have been a constant (archetypal?) feature, reappearing again and again in connection with property marks, marks of identification and distinction and (later) scripts. In the case of scripts, such signs are mostly, though not always, abstractions of previous picture signs, but attempts to interpret signs found outside the realm of systematic writing (the majority and the most ancient ones) remain largely speculative.

When, at the turn of the century, the French scholar Piette discovered in a cave near the Spanish border small pieces of flint dating from c. 12000–8000 BC which were decorated with signs painted in red and black, the outer appearance of some (though by no means all) signs tempted a number of scholars to speculate, not very convincingly, about possible connections with signs found in fully-established phonetic systems of writing such as the Aegean syllabaries, the Semitic consonant scripts and even the alphabet (HJ, p.37). But apart from the long time interval (some six to eight millennia) and the fact that similar signs have also been found on pieces of stone, on pebbles, beans, or rock-faces, in areas geographically (and historically) far removed from the Mediterranean, any comparison based entirely on the outward appearance of individual signs more or less chosen at random from two entirely different forms of information storage, one known (script), the other unknown, is usually quite meaningless. More plausible, but in the end equally uncertain, are attempts at an internal, representational interpretation — for example, circle for sun, comb for woman/spinning, spiral for womb/sun/water-hole and so on — which suggests that such signs are conventionalized simplifications of earlier pictures.

Geometrical signs, symbols and patterns are frequently used as property marks. Property marks are in many ways already a utilitarian form of writing; they can act as 'signatures', establishing authority, indicating ownership. They are closely connected with elements congenial to the development of systematic writing; a growing awareness of the importance of personal property, a realization that in a differentiated society property can bestow status, a desire to protect and/or exchange such property and the realization that property must be administratively identifiable.

In ancient Mesopotamia (see p.65) seals bearing personal patterns (fig. 7) which served as 'signatures' were already used in the 4th millennium BC. After 3000 BC, with trade and commerce rapidly gaining prominence, their importance increased. Writing had by then become well-established, but it was a complex art practised mainly by a professionally-trained class of scribes. Traders needed quicker and simpler means of identifying their belongings, authorizing their contracts, marking their property. The connection between seals, property marks and systematic writing is an interesting one. The still enigmatic signs on the seals from the Indus valley (see p.67) are a case in point.

Simple forms of property marks have been used in all ages and by nearly all people. Nomadic herdsmen and settled cattle-breeders alike have always used them, right up to the present time, for the branding of their livestock. Societies with an economy dependent on slave labour have similarly employed them. On a different and more rarefied level, branding and tattooing can be a voluntary indication of the complete identification between an individual and a deity, or an individual and a specific group. Into the same category fall clan and house marks, which have sometimes been used as signatures by people unable to read and write. The pottery marks from ancient Egypt have their modern equivalents in ceramic marks and in the hallmarks made on silver and other precious metals. There are furthermore the marks of masons from the ancient Aegean region, from Palestine, Anatolia

7 Seal impression marking property; Mesopotamia c. *3000* BC. *(British Museum; Department of Western Asiatic Antiquities; 1930. 12-13. 423)*

8 Staff recording the genealogical history of the Ngati-rangi-toke tribe; New Zealand. (British Museum; Museum of Mankind; 54. 12-29. 22) or medieval Europe, the various trade and inn signs, and the heraldic devices which proclaim identification with a particular (usually prestigious) family or lineage. Such signs and symbols (as indeed regimental badges, banners, national flags etc.) indicate proprietary rights, the belonging of a person, an animal, an object or a piece of land to a group, a clan, a family, a deity, a country or simply another human being.

Helpful to the communication and retention of data are mnemonic devices or memory aids. 'Memory aids' cover an exceedingly large area of information storage; indeed up to a point all writing is a form of memory aid. Memory aids hold a transitional position between oral tradition and writing, often being made legible only by skilled interpreters conversant with their own cultural heritage and traditional methods of explanation. Such interpreters can wield considerable power and influence, since it is left to them to decide how much of the information thus stored should be disclosed to which section of society. Often the interpretation of memory aids depends on additional, orally transmitted — perhaps even secret — knowledge.

Memory aids can be simple objects, decorations on objects, symbols, signs, patterns, single or narrative pictures. Some memory aids are highly sophisticated and already cross the boundaries between pure idea transmission, picture-writing, pictography and phonetic script. Memory aids can be important records and archives of tribal life, storing sacred and profane history, referring to legends and actual events alike.

The Maori of New Zealand for example used saw-shaped wooden boards called *he rakau whakapapa* (*rakau* – wood, *whakapapa* – genealogy) to keep their genealogical records (fig. 8) and youths were taught to recite the name of each ancestor with reference to each notch. The *churingas* (fig. 9) of the Australian aborigines (stone plaques or wooden tablets engraved with abstract line designs) relate to man's distant ancestors, mythical beings who

9 A stone churinga *from Central Australia. (British Museum; Museum of Mankind; 1935. 4112.1)*

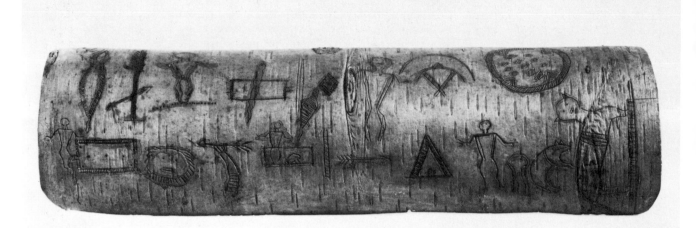

10 Mide scroll with pictures recording traditional lore. Collected from a Minnesota Ojibwa Chief, c.1850. Such scrolls relate to the Midewiwin, the Medicine Dance, which still exists in Ojibwa and other Great Lake communities. (British Museum; Museum of Mankind; 1949. AM. 22. 170)

11 Dakota winter count from northern America. (British Museum; Museum of Mankind; 1942. AM. 7-2)

had the characteristics of both man and animal and who, during 'dream time', moved about the as yet physically undifferentiated country. By their actions the 'dream time' heroes shaped the environment and set precedents which still govern human conduct. Each *churinga* tells a story connected with a particular totemic creature and the land on which the clan lived. *Churingas* were hidden in sacred places which women and uninitiated youths were forbidden, on pain of death, to visit.

North American totem poles record family (clan) history, legends and important events. Similarly much of the knowledge necessary to perform the *Midewiwin*, or Medicine Dance, of the central Algonquin peoples, as well as the memory of the dances and songs performed at the meetings of the Mide society, is inscribed on song-boards or birch-bark scrolls (fig. 10). The winter counts (fig. 11) of the Dakota Indians give a chronological account of the most recent history of the group and act as annals for the whole community. They can span a period of up to seventy years, each year being characterized by an outstanding and memorable event. For example, a drawing of the head and body of a man covered with red spots records the fact that many people died of smallpox; while three columns of ten parallel lines each drawn in black means that thirty Dakota were killed in the course of a particular year.

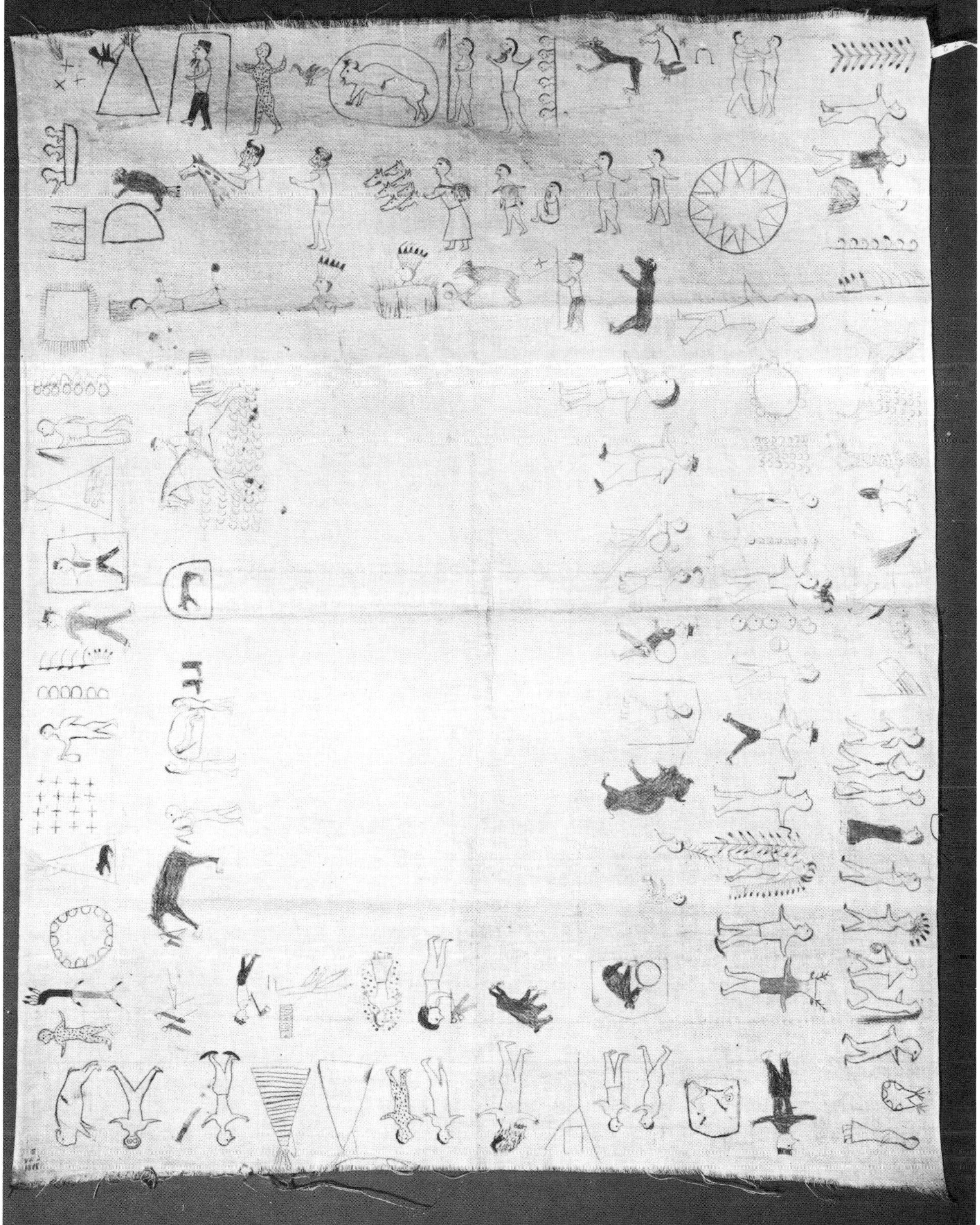

12 Lukasa, *a mnenomic device used by the Luba people of Zaïre in passing on mythological and moral lessons to initiates to the Luba secret society. The front of the board shows anthropomorphic carvings in high relief, the back depicts a turtle, an often used* mbudye *symbolism; from the northern Shaba region (formerly Katanga Province), Africa.*
(British Museum; Museum of Mankind; 1954. Af. 23. Q.)

Memory aids can also play a role in the secret and political life of the community. An example is the *Lukasa* (fig. 12), the 'long hand' (or claw), an esoteric memory device that was created, manipulated and protected by the *mbudye*, a once powerful secret society of the Luba people of Zaïre (Africa) (TQR, p.49).

As we have seen, objects (Yoruba love letters) and decorations (Ashanti proverbs) can already establish links, albeit tentative, with linguistic and phonetic forms of information storage; but the decisive transition from idea transmission to a more systematic and ultimately phonetic form of writing was probably made in the realm of memory aids. The usual picture-writing of the North American Indians, for example, is generally referred to as *kekewin*. There exists however a second form of picture-writing called *kekinowin*. The latter is known only to the priests who use it to memorize the correct order, and also the exact wording, of magic spells and incantations. Here the pictures represent not an idea or concept or event, but a definite sentence or verse, and in each case there exists only one possible spoken form to correspond with one particular picture. The pictures are read, in fact, exactly like a text. At an even more sophisticated level, memory aids can be integral elements of an already (partly) phonetic script. The writing of the Aztecs of Mexico (Plate I) was to some extent a form of memory aid which could be made legible only through the intermediary of trained interpreters (see p.76).

Memory aids are by no means a thing of the past. We tie a knot in a handkerchief to remind us of a task which must not be forgotten; devout persons use rosaries, where the size and position of the beads help to recall the correct order of certain prayers; children (and not only children) draw lines on calendars (or walls) to mark the days left until the start of the holidays or other pleasurable events.

Pictures have always been an important means of information storage. The paintings of animals, human beings and objects found on the walls of subterranean caves in places such as Altamira (Spain) or Lascaux (France) may or may not have been connected with magic, but they were certainly meant to store (and communicate) information — information essential to the social and economic life of the people who created them. Rock pictures, either painted (petrograms) or engraved (petroglyphs) can be found in most parts of the world, from Europe to Africa, America, Asia, Australia and the Polynesian Islands. Their dates vary greatly. Some, such as those of Spain and France, may date back ten, twenty or thirty millennia; the so-called cup sculpture of Scotland perhaps only some 4,000 years (RWBM, p.13). In North America rock pictures were incised (pecked) into stone until the advent of white settlers, and the drawings of the Bushmen of southern Africa are more or less contemporary. Some drawings are remarkably realistic representations of animals and/or human beings; others are highly stylized. Sometimes the figures and objects seem interrelated, giving the impression of a definite event (hunt? ceremony? gathering?); sometimes they stand in no recognizable relation to each other, sometimes they are superimposed one on another, obviously having been executed during different periods.

Pictures are highly versatile. They can express ideas, thoughts, sentences, words and ultimately sounds. The difference between a picture and picture-writing lies mainly in the fact that the former make a single statement (the picture of a buffalo simply represents the physical appearance of that animal), whereas the latter is narrative in intent (a group of buffaloes surrounded by armed human figures tells the stoy of a hunt). In both cases the elements of art and information storage are still almost totally merged, as they are in the case of some Southeast Asian picture-scrolls (fig. 13) where the 'reader' assimilates the

13 A folio for Captain James Low's (c. 1795–1852) Siam book depicting the Last Ten Birth Tales *or previous lives of the Buddha. (British Library; Oriental Collections; Add. 27370, ff. 11/12)*

information through the medium of art. The difference between picture-writing and pictography (Egyptian hieroglyphs and similar forms of writing), on the other hand, lies mainly in the fact that pictography has already reached a quite high level of abstraction, codification and conventionalization as far as the shape of individual (picture) signs is concerned. In pictography each sign has, at least to begin with, a definite meaning, corresponding in most cases to one word of a particular language. The signs used in picture-writing acquire meaning mainly through their combination with each other. They are meant to represent the whole thought-process as opposed to breaking the thought-process into the phonetic components of a particular language — words, syllables, consonants, vowels. In pictography the number of signs is more or less static; they can no longer be chosen or increased at random. In fact the tendency is for a move towards economization and a decrease in the number of signs (here Chinese is again the exception). In addition the order of the (picture) signs follows in most cases certain (syntactic) rules. In other words, linguistic (and eventually phonetic) elements are becoming an important component of information storage.

Picture-writing and idea transmission are still very much part of our everyday life. A person can drive from Edinburgh to Marseilles without understanding a single word of either French or English, and obtain all necessary information by way of pictures and symbols. Such a traveller will be kept well informed about which turning to take where, which road has the right of way, where it is advisable to drive more carefully because of roadworks, accidents, railway crossings, floods, bridges (or no bridges); where there are areas suitable for rest and recreation; where food, drink, petrol, perhaps even a bed for the night, are available. In addition to such notices and warnings, the traveller learns about the history and the most desirable features of the environment surrounding the vicinity of the main road; where there are abbeys, walled cities, a fortified castle, prehistoric remains worth visiting, a forest with rare animals (and what type of animals), the most important crops of the area, provision for sailing, boating, riding, pony trekking, fishing, golf, shooting, whether there is a beach nearby, a swimming pool or simply a very good vineyard which may make an overnight stop worthwhile (Plate II).

Pictures and symbols are important aids to international trade and commerce. A garment may have been made in Japan, Hong Kong, Korea, Taiwan, Germany, Brazil or India by people speaking no common language and unable to read each others' scripts, but somewhere inside it there will be a label with signs telling us whether it should be dry-cleaned, hand-washed, drip-dried, ironed (with a hot or cool iron), and whether it can be bleached. The weather forecasts on television can comfortably be understood by anybody, without any knowledge of the language used by the newscaster; a more or less internationally accepted series of pictures (a stylized black cloud for rain, a stylized white cloud with yellow or white lines radiating from it for sunshine, a cloud with suitably shaped symbols for snow) tell us what to expect for the next day or the coming weekend.

We are surrounded by picture-writing. Some of the signs and pictures have become internationally accepted by common usage. Others, such as those used for safety, engineering, in science, medicine, pharmacy or for computer technology have more or less been agreed upon.

As new technology diminishes the importance of writing (see p.210) the picture becomes again a favoured form of communication. International travel, international commerce and the necessity for cooperation in matters of industry, safety, defence and trade have created the need for easily-understood — that is, more or less self-evident — forms of communication and information storage which can transcend the boundaries of language. An interesting development in this direction is the increased popularity of 'coffee-table

14 Codex Mendoza (Pt. 3), written for Don Antonio de Mendoza, the first Spanish Viceroy of 'New Spain' (1535–1550). The drawings made by the Mexican, Tlacuilo, depict the daily life of the Aztecs; the Spanish 'commentary' is based on explanations supplied by local informants. Folio 60 demonstrates the strict way children were disciplined and taught. (Bodleian Library, Oxford; Ms Arch. Seld. A.1., f.60)

books' which are more or less picture books using photographs and a minimum of text. Equally on the increase is the popularity of strip-cartoons either in serialized form or in the form of books, where drawings are annotated by simple sentences (of dialogue or explanation) written more or less into the margin — a method similar to that used, for example, in some manuscripts produced after the conquest of Mexico by Spanish or native scribes and artists (fig. 14).

Picture-writing takes us right into the future: Pioneer 10, the unmanned spacecraft launched in 1972, which has already left the solar system on its journey into space, carries as a message from mankind a gold-anodized aluminium plaque engraved with the drawing of a nude man and woman, with the man's hand raised in a gesture of greeting (to show what we look like and to indicate that we are friendly towards any unknown life-form the spacecraft may encounter), and a series of symbols which testify to the level of scientific and technological development we had reached at the start of the journey.

Language and writing

In the previous section we have already met examples of an elementary interaction between language and writing. One is the *kekinowin* picture-writing of the North American 'medicine men', where pictures no longer stand just for ideas or concepts but for definite linguistic expression: a visual sign equals a sentence in a definite language. Another, that from Nigeria, brings us even closer to a phonetic form of information storage. Six cowrie shells mean 'I am attracted' because the Yoruba word *efa* means both 'six' and 'attracted'. We have here, in embryo, one of the most important principles in the development of phonetic writing, namely the principle of rebus transfer. By one dictionary definition rebus means 'the enigmatic representation of name, word etc. by pictures etc. suggesting its syllables' (*efa* – six is being represented by the six cowrie shells). Rebus transfer occurs if, once the phonetic interpretation of a particular sign has been established, this sign is then used to represent another word which means something quite different but which sounds at least similar (*efa* – six, represented by six cowrie shells, becomes *efa* – attracted, still represented by six cowrie shells). This process can be taken further; the phonetic unit (word, syllable or consonant group) can be used to form a component of another word, even that of a different language.

As has already been pointed out, the connection between language and writing is by no means as self-evident and fundamental as we, on the basis of our own background and experience, might be tempted to think. The primary object of all information storage is the preservation of knowledge. Knowledge can consist of thoughts, ideas, facts, concepts; it can be totally visual as in the case of art, acoustic as in the case of music, numerical as in the case of mathematics, physics, chemistry; in fact knowledge constitutes the sum total of all (up to date) human experience. It is only in so far as knowledge is expressed through the medium of language that information storage becomes identical with written language. Even on these premises written language and spoken language are by no means always identical, neither in the representation of sounds through script signs (there are at least five different ways of pronouncing the vowel sign *a* in English) nor in the use of words, or the way sentences are phrased. One language can also be written in several different scripts. The ancient Egyptian language, for example, used simultaneously three different forms of writing: hieroglyphic, hieratic and demotic (see p.63). From the 2nd century BC onwards it was also written in the Greek, and from the 4th century AD onwards in the Coptic, alphabet.

The most remarkable disregard for the writing/language connection shows itself in the way a script, designed for one particular language, is at times adopted for the use of another, totally different, language. A striking example is the cuneiform script (see p.65), originally designed for the agglutinative Sumerian language in which syllables and vowels played an important part. This script was taken over by the Semitic Babylonians to serve a language in which the meaning of words depended on the grouping of consonants, and where vowels played only a subsidiary part. Similarly the Chinese script, designed for a language with practically no grammar and a large number of homonymous monosyllabic words, was made to fit, with the aid of complex auxiliary additions, the agglutinative Japanese language, full of formal words and endowed with a very complex grammatical structure (see p.84). It could be argued that neither the Japanese nor the Babylonians possessed a script of their own, and that their choice was therefore limited and predetermined. But in our own more immediate past both the Russian Cyrillic and the Roman alphabet, being the scripts of economically and politically dominant groups, have been superimposed on a large number of Asian languages which already possessed perfectly serviceable forms of writing.

This of course does not mean that the connection between script and language is negligible or wholly arbitrary. As we shall see later, script, language and nationality (sometimes script and nationality alone) often become identified with each other, forming a strong and potentially powerful unit. During the long centuries of the Diaspora, the Hebrew script became a symbol of Jewish identity and was used for various languages in the countries of adoption. Thus Ladino (a Spanish dialect) and Yiddish (a German dialect) were both written in Hebrew characters, just as in Spain, during the period of Arab domination, the Jews spoke Arabic, but wrote it in the Hebrew script.

After the end of the Second World War a mission consisting of twenty-seven American educationists recommended to General MacArthur a drastic overhauling of the Japanese education system. They called especially for the abolition of the 'Chinese-derived ideograms', since otherwise Japan could never hope to achieve technological parity with the West (DD, p.174). Today Japan has not only achieved this parity, but seems uncomfortably close to overtaking the West, and this despite the fact that the Japanese still use their 'Chinese-derived ideograms', and that it takes Japanese schoolchildren two years longer than their Western counterparts to learn how to read and write. As we move towards the 21st century, the 19th-century concept of the alphabet as a Platonic idea towards which all writing (and information storage) must by necessity progress becomes less and less tenable.

The process of writing

The logistics of information storage necessitate objects on which this information can be stored: writing becomes writing when it is written down on some type of writing material. In the course of time (some 20,000 years if we take the concept of writing in its widest sense, nearly 6,000 years if we restrict ourselves to codified systems) any imaginable type of material has at one time or the other been used for this purpose: stone, wood, metal, animal skins, leaves, bones, shells, clay, wax, pottery, silk, cotton, paper etc. If we examine this list, and it is by no means complete, we can see that the materials named can be divided into two main groups — perishable materials and imperishable materials. And here we immediately come across one of the main difficulties in any study of the history and development of writing. Many ancient systems of writing, like those used in Egypt or India, seem to have appeared more or less fully-fashioned, simply because we encounter them first on imperishable material, mostly on stone. But as we know from later examples, writing on imperishable material is nearly always preceded (and accompanied) by writing on perishable materials: Roman-type wax tablets (fig. 15) for taking notes were still used in

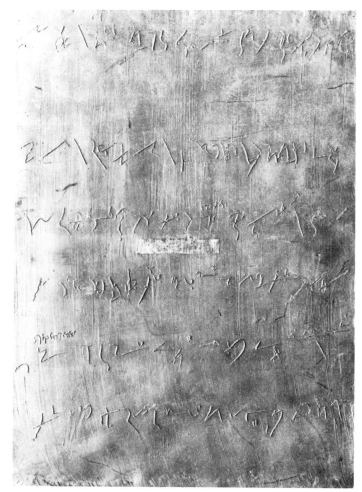

15 Roman waxed writing-tablets; 3rd century BC. The note-book consists of nine leaves, including those serving as covers, and is fastened together with leather laces. The notes are written in Greek longhand and shorthand, some of the latter evidently for practice. (British Library; Department of Manuscripts; Add. 33270)

16 A copper plate forming part of the so-called Velvikudi grant found at Madakulam, southern India; dated 769/70 AD. The grant is written partly in Sanskrit in the Grantha script (top lines), and partly in Tamil using Vatteluttu characters. (British Library; Oriental Collections; Ind. Ch. 4)

17th-century Europe; in India the title deeds of land grants engraved in metal (fig. 16) were first drawn up in draft form on palm leaves or perhaps bark. We know almost nothing about the structural and external development of the Egyptian hieroglyphics before we meet them, perfectly shaped, engraved on stone. Was Egyptian writing an independent development or a side branch of the (Sumerian) pictographic script of Mesopotamia? How exactly did the 3rd-century BC Indian Brahmi script evolve from its supposed Semitic prototype? What were the intermediary stages of this development? For that matter, how did the Semitic consonant script, using only twenty-two signs, abstract itself from the various highly complex systems of writing which prevailed in the Middle East between 3000 and 1000 BC?

Writing material is not neutral; it can shape and influence the development of scripts in matters of general appearance, the way individual signs are formed, and also as far as the direction of writing is concerned. It also frequently exercises a quite decisive influence on the shape of the 'book' (palm leaves used predominantly in South and Southeast Asia dictate an oblong shape, for example). Moreover, once a particular convention has been established it will often remain, even progress further in the same direction, long after it has been replaced by an entirely different type of material (the oblong shape of paper manuscripts or copper plates in India etc.). The material also predetermines to a large extent the instruments necessary for writing, and *vice versa*. The stone-cutter needs different tools and his tools create shapes different from those made by pen or brush on the soft surface of paper or papyrus. The connection between information storage and technology is not a 20th-century invention. It existed when Sumerian scribes first discovered that round curves did not always remain clearly visible on wet clay, and that therefore the shape of their (pictographic) characters would have to undergo further changes if information was to be stored effectively on the only material abundantly available in Mesopotamia — which was clay.

Types of writing material

Some writing materials suggest themselves since they can be used without, or with only a minimum amount of, preparation. Stone is perhaps the most obvious one. It is perfectly serviceable in its most natural state (the surface of rock or cave walls can be used for painting and engraving); or it can be fashioned into polished slabs. Stone has the added advantage of being very nearly indestructible (except by human hands), thus guaranteeing the permanence of the information recorded. This indestructibility has indeed made it throughout history the most favoured material for pronouncements issuing from the two central institutions of social, economic and political life: the Palace and the Temple — or, as we would call them today, the Church and the State. In Egypt and Mesopotamia, stone inscriptions in monumental form, on rough or prepared rock surfaces, on slabs, megaliths or buildings, date back to the 4th millennium BC. The ancient world, Asia from the Near East to China, Imperial Rome, and indeed all major civilizations right up to the immediate present have followed this example; we have only to think of the ceremonial unveiling of inscribed stone plaques to commemorate the opening of a bridge or building which are regularly reported by the media.

Equally accessible are leaves — which were no doubt used together with, and long before, stone. To paint or incise a figure or symbol on a dried leaf takes less technical skill than to engrave a carefully prepared piece of stone. Unfortunately leaves, especially untreated leaves, are also most easily perishable, and much that could help us to trace and understand the development of writing is therefore lost to us.

Other materials readily available and easy to use are wood, bones, bamboo, tortoiseshell and the bark of trees. Some of the earliest examples of Chinese writing appear on the so-called oracle bones from the Shang period (c. 1766–1122 BC, see fig. 17) which belong to the *jia gu wen*, the 'documents on tortoiseshell and animal bones'. Animal bones, especially those of larger species such as sheep, goats, camels or even horses, were used in many parts of Asia and Africa. Incised bones have survived from prehistoric Europe and from Central America where the Mayas (and others) made special use of them (fig. 18). The Arabs, well into the Middle Ages, considered bones a cheap and convenient form of material for the writing of documents, magical texts, even verses of the Koran. Indeed, according to some traditions the last will of the Prophet was taken down in this fashion.

Ivory from the tusks of elephants is a rare and therefore more expensive variation. It also requires a higher level of technical skill to write upon (especially if split into thin sheets as in Southeast Asia), and a society already conscious of status symbolized by the display of wealth. Ivory was used in Egypt and in the Middle East of Biblical times, but as far as the production of whole manuscripts is concerned it was mainly restricted to Southeast Asia.

A cheap and easy-to-use material, and one that was throughout history readily available in most, though not all, parts of the world, is wood (fig. 19). Egyptian inscriptions have been preserved on wooden statues and sarcophagi, the earliest surviving examples of a wooden writing-board coming from the Middle Kingdom (2134–1789 BC). Preparations for making it usable were minimal. Once boards or tablets had been shaped — a process that needs little technical skill — wood could be left in its natural state and the writing could be done with ink (or paint) either with a brush or pen. Alternatively the boards could be varnished, lacquered or polished to create a glossy, smooth surface. In some cases the script was incised with a sharp instrument, a stylus or a knife. Wood is still used in the form of blackboards by schoolteachers, and, until very recently, pupils too would write their exercises on small wooden boards, in both cases with white chalk on a blackened surface. Since the script can easily be erased with a cloth or a wet sponge, blackboards are highly

17   18   19   20

economical, especially for the purpose of taking notes or writing out exercises. They can also be re-used almost indefinitely.

The Greeks and Romans used waxed writing tablets (see fig. 15) for taking notes, a habit they probably acquired from the Near East where such tablets, dating from the 8th century BC, have been found in the Assyrian city of Nimrud. Greek and Roman writing tablets consisted of thin rectangular boards with a slightly hollowed-out surface filled with black wax. They were used together with a metal stylus, pointed at one end (for writing) and flattened at the other (for erasing the script and smoothing the wax surface). A number of tablets laced together formed a book, or, as it was referred to, a *codex*.

Equally easy to handle but more dependent on availability were bamboo (fig. 20) and bark. Whereas bamboo and wood can be used in their natural state, bark needs a certain amount of processing to render it suitable for writing. The most sophisticated and accomplished use of bark comes from Central America. Maya and Aztec manuscripts (see p.76) are made either of deerskin or of long sheets of *amatl* 'paper' manufactured from the fibre, roots and inner bark of the wild fig tree. Their surface is covered with a fine coat of white varnish which contrasts pleasingly with the text painted in a wide range of colours on both sides. The term 'paper' is of course strictly speaking a misnomer, but the finished product does indeed look very similar to paper and it is equally durable. Some Aztec manuscripts were made of coarser material derived from the fibre of the *agave americana*.

In the northern parts of India two varieties of bark enjoyed considerable popularity; the Himalayan birch tree (*betula utilis*) and the aloe (*aquilaria agallocha*). The earliest extant birch bark folios, cut, polished and oiled, are fragments of Buddhist works written at the beginning of the Christian era, but there is reason to believe that birch bark (sometimes in scroll format) was already in use at the time of Alexander's invasion (326 BC). In Kashmir birch bark manuscripts, the folios cut in *codex* form and bound between leather covers,

17 *Chinese oracle bone from the Shang period; 1766–1122 BC. (British Library; Oriental Collections; Or. 7694/1554)*

18 *Carved bone from Monte Albán engraved with signs relating to ritual and calendric calculations; Mexico 700–1000 AD. (British Museum; Museum of Mankind; 1949. AM. 16–57)*

19 *Wooden slip inscribed with Chinese characters, from the Han period; 206 BC–220 AD (British Library; Oriental Collections; Or. 8211. 449)*

20 *A 19th-century Batak manuscript from Sumatra. Four pieces of bamboo have been welded together to form a hollow cylinder. The writing has been incised with a sharp knife and then blackened to make it more legible. (British Library; Oriental Collections; Or. 5309)*

21 *Birch bark manuscript of a ritual text written in Sanskrit; from Kashmir, 16th/17th century. (British Library; Oriental Collections; Or. 13300)*

22 *A book of invocations and divination as used by the Batak medicine men of Sumatra. The inner bark of trees has been fashioned into long strips, folded accordion-wise and put between protective wooden covers. (British Library; Oriental Collections; Add. 19379)*

23 *Chinese bronze vessel from the Western Zhou period (1050–771 BC. Inscriptions in sunken characters could be cast into bronze vessels by inserting a section in the mould on which the characters were shown in relief. (British Museum; Department of Oriental Antiquities; 1936-11-8-2 (11))*

were still used in the 16th and 17th centuries (fig. 21). Birch bark can be rather fragile, and in the north-east of the sub-continent manuscripts made from the bark of the aloe were at times reinforced by wooen boards to increase their durability. An interesting variety of bark manuscripts are the *pustahas*, the private notebooks of the Batak medicine-men which can still be found in Sumatra. Long sheets of thick, coarse bark are folded accordion-wise into squares and protected on both sides by strong wooden covers (fig. 22).

Many materials were primarily designed for a different purpose and for different use. These are silk, cotton, linen, metal, ostraca (pieces of broken pottery) and various utensils and objects such as swords, glass lamps, bronze vessels (fig. 23), furniture, fans etc. In terms of information storage, the status of metal, in particular that of bronze, is very similar to that of stone: both guaranteed permanence. The Roman laws are supposed to have been kept on the Capitol, inscribed in bronze. In India and Southeast Asia, where until very recently the main writing material was the highly perishable palm-leaf, important legal documents, especially entitlements to land, were usually engraved on specially fashioned copper plates (see fig. 16). Occasionally Jain, Buddhist and Hindu scriptures were accorded similar treatment.

22

23

Lead, a rather soft metal which could easily be beaten into thin sheets, inscribed, and then rolled up for storage, was fairly popular in the ancient world. Pliny and Pausanias both refer to lead sheets used for writing. Lead was also used by the Hittites; and the Mandaeans, a gnostic sect speaking an Aramaic dialect, used lead for inscribed amulets. Precious metals, gold and silver, were mostly employed to stress the value of a particular text, to show respect when sending a letter or message to a person of exceptionally high rank, or, last but not least, to draw attention to one's own wealth and social standing.

The use of textiles such as silk, cotton and linen is well documented. Silk, first cultured in China (supposedly at the time of the legendary Yellow Emperor *c.* 2640 BC) and for long a prized export article, is mentioned in a number of early 5th–4th century BC documents in a manner which implies frequent use. By the time of the Eastern Han (25–220 AD) silk was widely used for letters, literary compositions and official documents. It was however an expensive form of writing material, and already by the beginning of the Christian era a method had been developed which allowed old silk rags to be pulped, and the resulting mixture thinly spread on a frame to produce a paper-like material. Cotton, a product of India (cotton yarn was found on the site of Mohenjodaro) is frequently referred to in classical Indian literature. A firm yet flexible material (well suited for letters and drafts of documents), it was turned into writing material by being treated with wheat or rice paste, dried, and rubbed smooth with a cowrie shell or a stone (Plate IV). In Southeast Asia, pieces of cotton were sometimes cut into the oblong palm-leaf shape and stiffened with black lacquer, a slow and labour-intensive process during which the letters of the text were inlaid with mother-of-pearl. The third textile, linen, was much in evidence in Dynastic Egypt; mummy wrappings dating from the 6th Dynasty (*c.* 2345–2181 BC) have been found inscribed with passages from the Book of the Dead. Linen was also employed by the Copts and Arabs, and Livy (59 BC–17 AD) speaks of the *libri lintei* (linen books) used in contemporary Rome.

Finally there are the materials specially devised for the use of writing: clay, parchment, papyrus and paper. Clay tablets, the writing material of ancient Mesopotamia, though unassuming in appearance, were the first reliable form of writing material produced by artificial means. In addition, the script impressed on them represents the earliest systematic form of writing. Their invention — or better, the realization that bricks, sun-dried or baked in a kiln, could not only be used for building temples, palaces, houses or irrigation channels, but also for information storage — was no doubt inspired by necessity, for Mesopotamia is poor in wood and stone resources. Clay tablets have a long and distinguished history; they were in use for thousands of years, from about the middle of the 4th millennium BC until, eventually, papyrus and leather gained in prominence. The size of individual tablets varied: the most popular formats were the many-sided cylinder (fig. 24) and the oblong brick with convex sides (fig. 25). Because of their importance to the social and economic life of ancient Mesopotamia, clay tablets were stored in special libraries attached to temples and palaces, where they were foliated, indexed (according to the first sentence), cross-indexed (rather like a modern library record) and arranged on shelves in appropriate order.

Animal skins have been used since prehistoric times, first for shelter and clothing, later for information storage. Without undergoing curing (smoking) and processing (manipulation with oil) skin decays quickly, but once so treated it can be converted into one of the most durable and flexible of all writing materials. By a process of tanning (using tanning agents such as oak bark or acacia pods), which renders it non-putrescent and impervious to water, skin can be turned into leather. The earliest surviving leather documents come from ancient Egypt (*c.* 2500 BC), but leather was equally popular in western Asia, Persia, Iraq

24 An octagonal cylinder with inscriptions in Assyrian, recording the campaigns, hunting expeditions and building activities of Tiglathpileser I, king of Assyria (1114–1076 BC). In 1857, the Royal Asiatic Society used this text (then still unknown) to test the validity of the decipherment of the cuneiform script. (British Museum; Department of Western Asiatic Antiquities; 91003)

25 Account of barley issued as loans to workmen attached to various temples and as pay to other hired men. Dated the 47th year of Shulgi, king of Ur (2048 BC). The text is written in Sumerian, in the fully developed Neo-Sumerian cuneiform script. From Girsu (Tello), S. Iraq. (British Museum; Department of Western Asiatic Antiquities; 14318) and later, Turkestan. Only one side of leather is truly suitable for writing, and in consequence the scroll format evolved.

Despite its many advantages, leather was however clearly inferior to papyrus, and attempts towards an improvement led to the discovery of parchment. Traditionally the credit for this invention is given to Eumenes II of Pergamum in Asia Minor (197–158 BC) — and the term parchment is derived from the name of the city of Pergamum. Parchment is the result of an already fairly complex manufacturing process: the whole skin has to be treated with lime, dehaired and defleshed, stretched, scraped on both sides, and treated with hot water, scraped again and rubbed with pumice, and then dried. Stretching is important; the thinner the parchment, the finer its quality. Recto and verso are clearly recognizable: the outer (hair) part is tougher, more yellow and in general better able to retain ink; the grain of the inner (flesh) part is smoother and easier to write on, but has a tendency to cause certain types of ink to flake. Fragments of parchment have survived from the 2nd century BC, but it was not before the 2nd century AD that it began to rival papyrus in the Roman world, and two more centuries passed before it was used for the best books. More or less simultaneously, the *codex* form began to replace the old scroll format, since it was no longer necessary to write on one side only. In Europe parchment remained the most popular writing material until well into the Middle Ages, when it was gradually supplanted by paper. The Arabs began to use paper in the 9th century but they still used parchment for copies of the Koran. Parchment was never used in India, Southeast Asia and the Far East. Hindus and Buddhists alike would have viewed with horror the idea of writing their sacred texts on the skin of slaughtered animals; and by the 2nd century AD the Chinese in any case had already invented paper.

Much has been written since the days of antiquity about the use and the production of papyrus (fig. 26). As an invention, papyrus seems to be as old as the hieroglyphic script, for an uninscribed roll was found in the grave of a 1st Dynasty (c. 3100–2890 BC) noble at Saqqara. The earliest inscribed examples are fragments of temple account books from the 5th Dynasty (c. 2494–2345 BC). For over four thousand years, papyrus held a dominant position in Egypt and in the countries of the Mediterranean world. Though other materials were simultaneously in use, none was as serviceable, as pleasing and, even more important, none could be produced as readily in equal quantities. The production of papyrus was (like that of silk and paper in China) often a highly profitable state monopoly, first of Egypt and later of Rome and Byzantium. To manufacture papyrus, carefully-cut pieces from the inner stem of the plant, laid one on top of another on a special table, were pressed or beaten together and then dried in the sun. Some simple form of adhesive was no doubt necessary, perhaps some glue made of (Egyptian) flour, hot water and vinegar, or perhaps the properties of the muddy Nile water sufficed. At the beginning of the Christian era papyrus became increasingly scarce, and in consequence more expensive (the traditional Egyptian society and traditional Egyptian economy which had fostered its use and production were disintegrating) and the *codex* form, where both sides could be inscribed, began to take precedence over the scroll format.

According to Chinese records paper was invented by Cai Lun, a eunuch at the court of the Han Emperor Wu Di, in the year 105 AD. In actual fact Cai Lun seems to have been more of a supervisor than an inventor (he was charged with collecting information and reporting on various experiments in paper-making that were taking place in China) and the invention of paper was in all likelihood the outcome of an evolutionary process based to no small extent on the knowledge of making silk 'paper'. Cai Lun's paper had the advantage of being considerably cheaper than silk, having been made, according to contemporary records, from tree bark, fish-nets and old rags; botanists who have examined the earliest

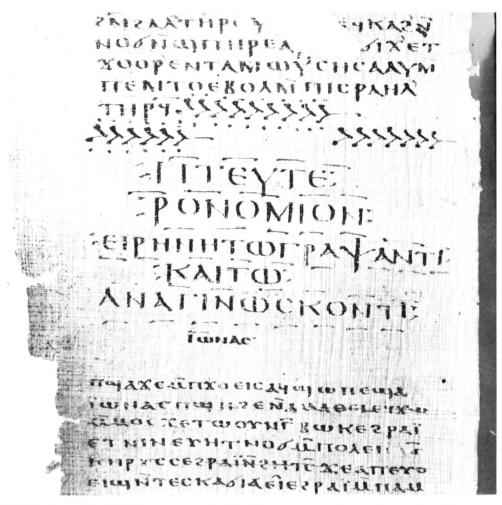

26 Folio from a Coptic Bible written in the Sa'idic dialect on papyrus showing the beginning of the Deuteronomy; *from Upper Egypt, early 4th century* AD. *(British Library; Oriental Collections; Or. 7594, f. 53)*

available (2nd century AD) paper fragments pronounce it a mixture of raw fibres (mulberry, laurel and Chinese grass) and rags.

One can reconstruct the earliest techniques of paper-making as follows: tree bark was cut into pieces and soaked in water for a considerable period of time (100 days). The pieces were then pounded in a mortar to separate the inner from the outer bark, which was then removed. The remaining pulp was mixed with either lime or soda ash, heated over a fire to boiling point for at least eight days and nights, and washed repeatedly until the fibres were completely softened. This mixture was then strained and pounded into a soft doughy substance, and bleached. The bleach was removed by further soaking and the mixture was placed in a large vat and some starch added to prevent the finished sheets from sticking together. To make sheets a frame was dipped into the vat, the sheet drained (fig. 27) and eventually lifted from the vat, and then well dried on heated wood or brick walls (DC, p.19).

Paper reached Europe a thousand years after its invention by a tortuous and not always easily verifiable route. Originally the manufacturing process had been a closely guarded state monopoly and during the first 600 years the technique of paper-making was known only in China, from where it did not spread much farther west than Chinese Turkestan. In 751 AD the Muslim governor of Samarkand took captive a large number of Chinese prisoners, some of then adept in the art of paper-making. According to one verison those men voluntarily set up paper-making shops in Samarkand; another version claims that they betrayed their secret only under torture. For the next hundred years or so Samarkand paper (which used linen rags instead of mulberry bark) was as highly priced an export article as Chinese paper, but the social and religious structure of Islam is averse to localized exclusiveness and soon paper was being made in the Middle East; Baghdad, Damascus, Tiberius, Hamah, Tripoli and later Cairo became important manufacturing centres. In the 12th century the Arabs introduced paper to Spain and Sicily, and a century later to India. Rags remained the most important ingredient; in the laws of Alfonso X of Spain (1236 AD)

27 Paper making. The frame is dipped into the vat to drain individual sheets. Peking 1929; a reproduction of a 17th-century edition. (British Library; Oriental Collections; 15258. cc. 13 (vol. 1))

paper is referred to, rather fittingly, as *pagamino de paño* (cloth parchment). In 1492 the Muslims lost Spain and the art of paper-making passed into the hands of less skilled Christian craftsmen. Almost immediately the quality of paper declined. During the following centuries paper established itself firmly in the Western world. In 1338 a paper-producing factory was established in France (Troyes); in 1390 paper-making reached Germany (Nuremberg), in 1498 Austria (Wiener-Neustadt) and in 1690 America (Germantown near Philadelphia). Until the 19th century the manufacturing process remained basically the same; then, for economic reasons (the spread of general education caused an increase in demand), wood was introduced as a substitute for rags. This guaranteed supplies of paper but irrevocably diminished its quality, durability and appearance.

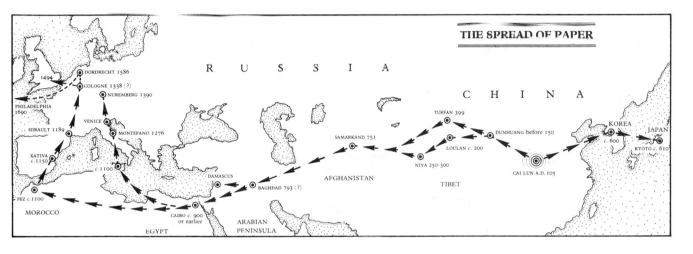

The influence of paper on western civilization has been enormous. The quick spread of printing, the popularization of education, our whole industrial society depending on administration not only at government but also at office level, is in retrospect unthinkable without easy access to almost unlimited quantities of cheap paper. By the beginning of the 20th century nobody would have been in any doubt that paper was here to stay, that it was the most important, efficient and totally irreplaceable medium of modern information storage. Economically and intellectually our society had become a paper society. But this faith has already been badly shaken. Computers, the quick advance of information technology, television, the varied uses of video displays, microfilm, microfiche, electronic information storage, have during the last decade heralded the advance of a totally different approach, a complete revolution in the field of information storage as far as methods as well as media are concerned. The supremacy of paper has been irrevocably challenged. Even if the electronic library, the paperless office and the bookless society have not yet arrived, the position of 'writing' material has changed fundamentally.

From the point of information storage, and from the point of material used for information storage, we can distinguish three distinct stages: oral traditions, where information is stored in memory to remain available in unaltered form; writing, where information is stored independently of the human mind to be retrieved and manipulated; and information technology, where the 'material' on which the information is stored manipulates the information for the user and by so doing creates additional, new information (see p.208).

28 *Inscribed clay tablet of the Late Proto-literate (Uruk IV) period, c. 3000 BC. Probably a list of names. At this early stage in the development of cuneiform writing, many of the signs are still drawings of everyday objects. Some have acquired a separate phonetic use, and this use indicates that the language of the scribes was Sumerian. The deep circular impressions represent numerals. Probably from Jemdet Nasr, near Kish, S. Iraq. (British Museum; Department of Western Asiatic Antiquities; 116625 (1924-5-21-1))*

The development of forms of writing

Some materials have decisively influenced the development of certain forms of writing. To begin with, the Sumerian script seems to have been largely pictographic. The material and the implements most commonly used in ancient Mesopotamia were clay and the reed stylus. Wet clay, it has been argued, is not particularly well suited to retaining soft lines, circles and curves (neither, incidentally, are stone, wood and bones). Originally, two different types of stylus seem to have been used: one with a sharp point, for incising the line pictures, the other ending in a flat round point for writing the numerals (fig. 28). By holding the 'numeral' stylus in a certain way, a mark closely akin to a wedge-shaped impression can be made, and it may well have been from this point that the later triangular (or half oval) pointed stylus developed. It is not absolutely clear whether the cuneiform style (from *cuneus*–'wedge'), where each sign consists of a number of unconnected strokes or impressions, developed solely because of the need created by the writing material used, or whether it was simply a stylistic development, fostered, in part, by a desire for greater speed. In all likelihood more than one element contributed to the change.

Theoretically, wedges could be impressed in eight different directions. For practical reasons, however, 5, 6, 7 and 8 were seldom used, and were soon altogether abandoned. 1, 2, 3 and 4 eventually remained the only wedges in use, 4 being relatively rare. By slightly altering the position of the stylus, the wedges could be made shorter or longer, while two more wedges could be obtained by changing the position of the stylus still further. Thus the Mesopotamian scribes had at their disposal the following double row of wedges with which to fashion the whole range of the cuneiform script:

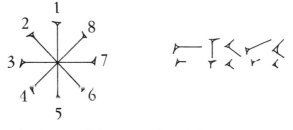

The cuneiform script (see p.65) is written from left to right, but there are reasons to believe that it was originally written from top to bottom, in columns running from right to left. For practical reasons a rectangular tablet has to be held differently (with the fingers instead of in the hollow of the hand) from the way the earlier (square) tablets were held. At first the rectangular tablets were turned 90° to the left for the purpose of writing only, but eventually the new position was used for both reading and writing (AS, p.242) and in consequence the top-to-bottom columns became left-to-right top-to-bottom lines:

The evolution of the cuneiform script

URUK UPRIGHT	PICTOGRAMS c.3100 B.C. JEMDET NASR TURNED 90° TO LEFT	c.2800 B.C.	'CLASSICAL' SUMERIAN c.2400 B.C. LINEAR	CUNEIFORM	OLD-AKKADIAN c.2200 B.C.	OLD-ASSYRIAN c.1900 B.C.	OLD-BABYLONIAN c.1700 B.C.	NEO-ASSYRIAN c.700 B.C.	NEO-BABYLONIAN c.600 B.C.	Picture	Meaning
										NECK + HEAD	HEAD FRONT
										NECK+HEAD + BEARD or TEETH	MOUTH NOSE TOOTH VOICE SPEAK WORD
										SHROUDED BODY (?)	MAN
										SITTING BIRD	BIRD
										BULL'S HEAD	OX
										STAR	SKY HEAVEN-GOD GOD
										STREAM OF WATER	WATER SEED FATHER SON
										LAND-PLOT + TREES	ORCHARD GREENERY TO GROW TO WRITE

According to available evidence the new direction of writing began to establish itself firmly from about 3200 BC onwards as far as clay tablets are concerned. Monumental inscriptions however continued to be written in vertical columns.

The theory has been put forward that the shape of bamboo canes, one of the most widely used writing materials of ancient China, determined the vertical direction of the Chinese script. Wooden slips (see fig. 19), often with notches on one or both ends for binding them together, may in fact have been imitations of the earlier bamboo models, a switch made necessary when Chinese administration moved to areas where bamboo was less readily available. The perishable nature of bamboo makes such assumptions difficult to prove, but there are certain indications which point in this direction: the pictogram for 'state archive' (*ce*) for example, authenticated at least from the 14th century BC, seems to portray narrow bamboo slips laced together.

A material which had a decisive influence on the shape of characters and the development of a large number of scripts in India and Southeast Asia is the palm-leaf. As writing material it was probably used from very early times (tradition claims that Buddhists and Jains committed their Scriptures to palm-leaf, wood and bamboo slips in the 6th century BC), but, being highly perishable by nature, no definite examples seem to have survived prior to some 2nd-century (AD) fragments found in central Asia and Japan. In India few palm-leaf manuscripts pre-date the 16th century, but the characteristic oblong shape of the palm-leaf appears in a number of other writing materials, such as metal (fig. 16), paper (Plate III) or bark (fig. 69).

Palm trees which produced leaves suitable for writing were the talipat palm (*corypha umbraculifera*), the palmyra palm (*borassus flabellifer*) and, especially in Southeast Asia, the lontar palm (*corypha utan*). Palm-leaves are usually broader in the middle, gently tapering off toward the ends. To make them suitable for writing a simple process is necessary; each leaf has to be separated from the central rib, cut to size, boiled and dried, usually several times, and finally rubbed with a stone or cowrie shell to create a smooth surface.

Indian scripts (see p.106) are generally thought to have developed from a 3rd-century BC prototype called Brahmi. This script produced, at one point, a variation characterized by a pronounced wedge at the top of each character (see p.111). In the case of north Indian scripts this wedge developed eventually into one long horizontal stroke connecting all characters of a word or even a whole line. No problems arose in the north of India where the scribes used ink and pen (Plate III), but in the south and south-east of the sub-continent a method developed by which the characters were incised with a sharp metal stylus (fig. 29).

29 A palm-leaf inscribed in Sinhalese script; and a metal stylus. (British Library; Oriental Collections; Or. 6600 (72))

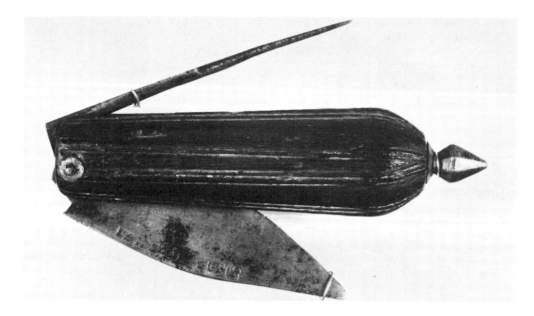

30 Knife and stylus from India. By courtesy of Mr Michael O'Keefe

Long horizontal strokes, following exactly the lines of the palm-leaf fibre, could easily have split the palm-leaf lengthwise and destroyed it. In consequence South Indian scripts began to take on a more and more rounded shape, with no interconnecting lines between individual characters. When the South Indian form of writing was brought to Southeast Asia in the course of the first millennium AD (see p.114) this element seems to have persisted, despite the fact that the materials used (gold, silver, paper, bark, bamboo, lacquered cloth etc.) no longer warranted such precautions.

Writing implements and writing materials are closely interconnected. To engrave characters, the stone cutter needs tools different from those the scribe uses on the soft surface of paper, leather or papyrus. Pen and brush have usually encouraged more cursive hands; stone, metal and other imperishable materials tend to favour monumental styles. Writing implements have also influenced and guided the development of certain calligraphic styles, as will be discussed later (see p.165).

Broadly speaking, the actual process of writing can be executed in two distinctly different ways. The script can either be scratched into the surface of the material with a sharp instrument, such as a stylus, knife, or stone cutter's tool (figs. 29, 30), or it can be applied onto the surface with a pen (quill, reed, wood or metal) (fig. 31) or a brush, using ink, paint or lacquer. The process of transfer, when a rubbing is taken from a stone or metal inscriptions (see p.195), represents an intermediate stage which, taken to its logical conclusion, leads to printing (see p.194). It is certainly no accident that in many languages the word used for 'writing' is in some way derived from verbs meaning 'to paint', 'to cut', 'to incise' or 'to scratch'. Ink has been used since antiquity and a variety of recipes for its preparation have been handed down to us. Most of them have lamp black as a basic constituent, combined (according to the effect desired) with resin, gum, honey, borax, burnt almonds or cow's urine, and — in the case of coloured inks — a colouring agent (sometimes gold or silver).

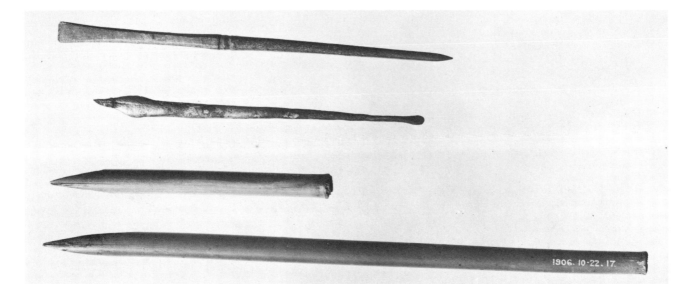

31 Two Roman bronze pens; a reed pen with a split nib from Egypt, Roman period; a stylus for incising letters into waxed tablets, with a flat end for erasing. (British Museum; Department of Greek and Roman Antiquities: GR 1900.6-11.4; GR 1968.2-12-1; GR 1906.10-22.18; GR 1893.11-2.1)

Writing directions and word divisions

Anybody brought up within the confines of western civilization might be tempted to regard the direction of writing which runs from left to right, and where the lines follow each other from the top to the bottom of the page, as the most logical and normal one. However, one soon discovers that there are a large number of scripts (Hebrew and Arabic, for example) where this 'natural' order seems to be reversed and where the writing runs from right to left with the lines still following each other from the top of the page to the bottom, but where the book (or manuscript) is actually read from what to us may seem back-to-front. A person with a more inquisitive mind will eventually realize that Chinese and Japanese are written in vertical columns from top to bottom, but after this may feel that the range of possibilities as far as directions of writing are concerned has been exhausted.

Nothing could be further from the truth. To begin with, our left-to-right direction is by no means so self-evident and universal as we might think. It is in fact a rather late development; even the alphabet was, to begin with, written the other way round, namely from right to left. In addition, there exist a large number of possibilities which have been used by different civilizations at different times. Sometimes these have been governed by the type of materials used for writing, but often there is no other reason than the fact that what is regarded as normal and logical differs considerably from place to place and from civilization to civilization.

The following directions of writing have been used:

(1) From left to right with the lines following each other from top to bottom; in fact the way our own alphabet is written —

A B C D E F G

H I J K L M N

(2) From left to right but with the lines following each other from bottom to top —

H I J K L M N

A B C D E F G

(3) From right to left, with the lines following each other from top to bottom (the common direction of all Semitic scripts) —

G F E D C B A

N M L K J I H

(4) From right to left with the rows following each other in an upward direction —

N M L K J I H

G F E D C B A

(5) Boustrophedon, or 'the way an ox-drawn plough moves'; a popular and widely used writing direction of antiquity —

G F E D C B A   *or*   A B C D E F G
H I J K L M N   N M L K J I H

(6) In a circle, in either direction —

```
        A                       A
   G         B             B         G

  F           C           C           F

     E    D                   D    E
```

(7) In a spiral, again in either direction —

```
     F  G                        G
          H               F           A
    E                         J    H
      A       I          E              B
   D                         I
      C    B                D       C
           J
```

(8) From top to bottom in vertical columns, with the columns following each other from right to left —

H	A
I	B
J	C
K	D
L	E
M	F
N	G

(9) In vertical columns following each other from left to right —

A	H
B	I
C	J
D	K
E	L
F	M
G	N

(10) In vertical columns following each other from right to left, or left to right, but with the direction of reading in each column running upwards —

G	N		N	G
F	M		M	F
E	L		L	E
D	K	*or*	K	D
C	J		J	C
B	I		I	B
A	H		H	A

(11) A further possibility is to have vertical columns, either read upwards or downwards, but with the columns following the boustrophedon mode —

P	I	H	A		A	H	I	P
O	J	G	B	*or*	B	G	J	O
N	K	F	C		C	F	K	N
M	L	E	D		D	E	L	M

(12) 'Shark-toothed', which means that the writing material has to be turned upside down after completing a line—

ИWꓶꓘſIH
ABCDEFG

(13) Sometimes, as in the use of the Maya glyphs, the script may be arranged in pairs of vertical columns (JEST, p.26) —

A	B	I	J
C	D	K	L
E	F	M	N
G	H	O	P

(14) Finally there is the meandering form of writing direction. A good example is to be found in the Aztec manuscripts (see p.9) where red lines indicate the place where the next group of symbols has to be read. Somewhat similar elements manifest themselves in the painted screens which the professional story-tellers of Rajasthan

32 Section of painted cotton cloth (125 × 72 cm.) depicting the exploits of Bagrawat, a celebrated tiger killer. Marwar, 1933 AD. (Victoria and Albert Museum; 1:S.13-1968)

(India) carry from village to village (fig. 32). These screens are vividly painted with representations of the key scenes in the narrative, and only the story-teller knows the correct order in which the scenes follow each other, pointing them out while reciting his tale to the audience.

Connected with the direction of writing is the direction of individual signs — pictographs as well as letters. This too can vary. Egyptian hieroglyphic signs, for example, face mostly towards the beginning of the line, as do the majority of pictographic or pictorial forms of writing. Alphabetic signs look towards the end of the line. In cases where the direction of writing changes, the direction in which the individual signs look may change too. For example in early Greek documents where a boustrophedon direction of writing was used, the individual signs looked alternately in one or the other direction in the same inscription:

A B C D E F G H
ꟼ O И M ⅃ Ʞ I I

The division of words and sentences, which we take so much for granted, developed only gradually. The majority of ancient scripts — Egyptian, the cuneiform script of

33 Meroïtic inscription from Nubia, c.50 BC. (Not yet deciphered).
(British Museum; Department of Egyptian Antiquities; 1836)

Mesopotamia, the syllabic script of the Aegean, at times also some Indian scripts
(especially the two classical languages of the sub-continent, Sanskrit and Tamil) — did not
divide words and/or sentences. In those societies writing was done by specialists who were
completely immersed in writing conventions and who could therefore dispense with such
aids to legibility. This lack of word division is also a feature of early European manuscripts,
no doubt for similar reasons; the monastic scribes knew not only the intricacies of their
script, but, since most manuscripts dealt with religious matters, they also knew the text.
Word divisions, when they do occur — and they can occur quite early, as for example in the
case of the Meorïtic (fig. 33) or the Cypriote script (see p.70) — can take a variety of forms:
one dot, two dots, three dots arranged in triangular form; one, two or three vertical strokes
or an oblong stroke; or more ornamental variations of what was originally perhaps just a
simple dot. The practice of joining letters together to form ligatures becomes noticeable
quite early on and is mostly associated with handwriting and the use of perishable
materials. In an elementary form ligatures are already a feature of the demotic script of
ancient Egypt (see p.64).

Positions for writing

There is, finally, the actual position assumed for writing. This can vary considerably. We frequently come across representations of Egyptian scribes sitting cross-legged on the floor, the kilt stretched tightly across the knees to support the papyrus used for writing (fig. 34). Others are shown kneeling with one knee raised and the writing material placed upon it. Equally popular in the ancient world was the standing position (Plate V and fig. 35).

34 Pes-Shu-Per, Chamberlain of the Divine Votress of Amun, Amenirdis, depicted as scribe. (British Museum; Department of Egyptian Antiquities; 1514)

35 Details from a palace relief of Tiglathpileser III, king of Assyria (745–727 BC), showing two scribes registering the spoils from a city in Babylon. (British Museum; Department of Western Asiatic Antiquities; 118882)

There are variations to these postures. On the whole, Eastern scribes preferred to sit on the floor, or on a cushion (see fig. 94), with the writing material either in their lap or on a small table in front of them (see Plate III). In Japan and China calligraphers would kneel on the floor, the paper spread before them, holding the brush unsupported in the right hand. European scribes favoured table and chair. Medieval manuscripts depict them sitting on a chair or bench, the *codex* (or scroll) in their lap or on a small, usually steeply sloping, table in front of them (fig. 36). If a standing position was assumed, the manuscript was placed on a tall, often steeply sloping table.

36 Basic to the illustration of manuscripts of the gospels are representations of the four evangelists, often portrayed as scribes. St Mark is here shown dipping his quill pen into his inkhorn with one hand while in the other he holds a long-handled pen-knife; 11th-century manuscript from the Benedictine abbey of Les Préaux in Normandy. (British Library; Department of Manuscripts; Add. 11850, ff.61b/61)

II The main groups:
their characteristics, history and development

Writing in the Fertile Crescent

For the purpose of this study the term 'Fertile Crescent' does not refer only to Mesopotamia — the arc of arable land stretching from Palestine through Syria to Mesopotamia — but also to Egypt and the Indus valley (now Pakistan). Sometime in the 3rd millennium BC, neolithic agriculture, which had been evolving slowly over the previous 2,000 years, took a revolutionary leap forward, resulting in changes as far-reaching and irreversible as those produced by the industrial and scientific revolutions of the 18th and 19th centuries. This new, improved type of agriculture, which depended largely on irrigation, not only supported a steadily increasing population but also an ever-growing number of non-producing specialists such as craftsmen, architects, administrators, priests, soldiers, artists and scribes. With specialization and population growth came the establishment of urban settlements alongside the banks of navigable rivers (Nile, Euphrates, Tigris and Indus), the exchange of surplus goods by trade which introduced a new concept of property, and a definite need for a centralized form of administration (religious, secular or both) to control, synchronize and if necessary protect the framework of what were becoming cooperative political units.

This new type of society, which derived its identity from the Palace and the Temple — institutions depending on each other and more often than not identical — soon outgrew the use of memory aids, property marks and pure ideograms, and made the decisive step from idea (thought) representation to language (sound) representation in order to record laws, contracts, edicts, histories, astronomical calculations and eventually also literary traditions. Nearly all writing as we have known it for the last 2,000 years, with the exception of Chinese and pre-Columbian scripts, originated in the Fertile Crescent during the latter part of the 3rd millennium BC; and, in the opinion of some scholars, in Mesopotamia itself. Thus Mesopotamia has often been referred to as the cradle of civilization and the place where literacy as such developed. This, however, does not mean that the Fertile Crescent was the only place where phonetic elements evolved. Such elements can be observed, not only in the writing conventions of people possessing a similar level of civilization, as for example the Aztecs of Central America (see p.76), but also in simple forms of idea transmission (such as memory aids) used by tribal societies (see p.21).

Egyptian scripts

Much has been written about the conservative character of the Egyptian people, who during the 3,000 years of their recorded history maintained almost the same way of life, based on barely changing social, economic, religious and political concepts. This conservatism did not lack dynamism, however, since it was largely based on observable natural phenomena.

For 3,000 years Egypt enjoyed an almost unparalleled level of secure prosperity. The Nile automatically revitalized the land with its yearly inundations. It was easily navigable, made more so by the fact that the wind blows almost continuously from the north up the river, and that during the annual floods, flat-bottomed barges could transport goods, and if necessary building materials, far inland. After each inundation the land was rehabilitated, irrigation channels were cleared and marks re-established — all tasks which called for cooperative and centrally organized labour, and in one or another way involved the whole population. As for outside invasions, Egypt was well protected by deserts on both sides, the cataracts in the south, and the marshy delta in the north. Indeed what tensions arose, with the exception of some relatively short-lived intervals, were less the results of outside threats than disturbances caused by interactions between Upper and Lower Egypt, or by rulers of the provinces, who occasionally acquired more power than the centre, represented by the 'Lord of the Two Lands', the Pharaoh. Until the beginning of the Christian era, when Egypt became a Roman province, such tensions invariably balanced themselves in due course and life continued much as before. Similarly Egyptian writing remained a national script, serving one language and one people, introducing no basic changes, only modifications to serve internal needs. It was also from the beginning an extremely complex and highly sophisticated system, mixing ideography and sound writing with elements of a well thought-out consonant script. The more or less sudden appearance of a fully-fledged writing system at the end of the 3rd millennium BC has led some scholars to speculate about the possibility of Sumerian (Mesopotamian) prototypes serving either as actual models for the Egyptian script or at least stimulating the development of writing in the Nile valley; but no proof exists for either speculation.

Recorded, or Dynastic, Egyptian history begins with the unification of Upper and Lower Egypt by Narmer (Menes) in *c.* 3100 BC. This event seems to have coincided with a remarkable number of new inventions and practices — such as the import of timber from Syria (wood suitable for building was not available in Egypt), monumental architecture in brick and stone, roal graves (at first only of the *mastaba* – house type) and, most important from our point of view, hieroglyphic writing. Nothing that can definitely be identified as writing has so far reached us from pre-Dynastic times, but there are many examples of painted pottery decorated with well-executed pictures of birds, animals, symbols of deities, and abstract designs which already show the characteristic ability of later Egyptian artists for observing nature and their strong tendency towards codified abstraction (fig. 37). The place of decorated pottery in the history and development of writing should perhaps in any case be more closely investigated.

37 Pre-Dynastic decorated pottery vase; from El Amra, c.3100 BC. (British Museum; Department of Egyptian Antiquities; 35502)

We are fairly ignorant about the way hieroglyphic writing developed. Some scholars believe (HJ, p.56, and others) that phonetic elements are already discernible in objects such as the palette of Narmer and the plaque of Akha or Akhai (DD, p.58), both relating to the beginning of the First Dynasty.

To understand the complex, yet at the same time flexible and also logical, way the Egyptians manipulated their seven hundred or so hieroglyphic signs, an examination of the inner structure of the Egyptian writing will be useful. Pure pictography, or logography, where one sign equals one word, is exceedingly rare, partly because of the large number of signs this would necessitate, partly because of the way most languages are constructed. In the case of the Egyptian language the large number of purely formal words (prefixes, suffixes, etc.) — so different, for example, from Chinese — would have made such a solution even more difficult. But the Egyptian language had another characteristic which was fully exploited by the hieroglyphic script. It bore affinities to both the Semitic and the Hamitic group of languages; that is to say, its word structure, in common with other Semitic languages, depended predominantly on consonants. Basically, Egyptian writing consists of a mixture of ideography and phonography, idea and sound writing; but a more detailed breakdown of its internal structure leaves us with five different components—

(1) The drawing of a particular object could stand for one particular word denoting this object.
(2) A concrete visible action could be represented by its most characteristic elements.
(3) A word, or better the two consonants (more rarely three) of a word, could be expressed by the picture of an object which contained the same consonants, in other words by means of a rebus (see p.33). This allowed for a high degree of flexibility; for example, if we transfer this idea to the writing of English, the drawing of a sun disc meaning 'sun', and containing the consonants s–n could be used for writing *sun*, *son*, or in combination with other signs *Sun*day, *sun*ny, *sin*ging, *sun*g etc. Because of the consonant-dominated structure of the Egyptian language, a relatively small number of double consonant signs (*c.* eighty) was needed; but this advantage was partly lost again by the ambiguity such a script would create (even our English example indicates this).
(4) In addition, the Egyptians had twenty-four single consonant signs which could quite adequately have been used to form the basis of a purely phonetic — that is, consonant — script, eliminating the need for all other conventions. Why the Egyptians failed, or perhaps better, refused, to take this step has been the subject of much discussion.
(5) Finally, to eliminate ambiguities which arose in connection with the use of phonetic signs the Egyptians employed determinatives, sense signs which were added at the end of words to indicate the sphere to which a word belonged (to return to our English example, the sign of a man added to the sign of the sun disc representing *s–n* could only mean *son*).

(1)	⌡ = leg	⬭ = eye	
(2)	⌃ = to go	☂ = to weep	
(3)	⌑ = p-r (house)	▽ = n-b (basket)	
(4)	⌒ = r (the mouth)	⌠ = s (folded cloth)	⬭ = h-t-p (a loaf on a mat)
(5)	⚘ = (identifying) plant (sphere)	≈ = (identifying) water (sphere)	⬬ = (sign for book roll identifying abstract ideas)

When writing a word an Egyptian scribe could choose between various methods. He could, for example, simply write the appropriate ideogram followed by a vertical stroke —

 ⌐⌐ = p–r (house)

More frequently he would use single consonant signs followed by a determinative —

 🦅 ⌡ ⊙ = w–b–n (rise/shine)

 🦅 = w   ⌡ = b   〰 = n   ⊙ = determinative (sun)

Or he could use a double consonant sign, followed by two single consonant signs, repeating the two consonants already expressed in the double consonant sign, followed by a determinative —

 ⌐ 🦉 △ = m–r (pyramid)

 ⌐ = m–r   🦉 = m   ◠ = r   △ = determinative (pyramid)

In addition to hieroglyphic (from the Greek *hieroglyphika grammata* – sacred carved letters) the Egyptians employed two more scripts – hieratic (from the Greek *hieratikos* – priest) and demotic (from the Greek *demotikos* – popular). Both were descendants of the hieroglyphic script. By the time that Greek names came into existence (*c.* 200 AD) hieratic was used only for religious texts (although in earlier times it had also been used for literary texts, business documents and private letters), whilst demotic was reserved exclusively for secular purposes. Hieroglyphic writing (fig. 38) was ideally suited for the carving of inscriptions on royal, religious and funerary monuments made of stone; it conveyed

38 Hieroglyphic inscription. Stela of Tjetji; limestone. From Thebes, c. 2100 BC. (British Museum; Department of Egyptian Antiquities; 614)

beauty, dignity and, above all, permanence. The Egyptian economy, with its dependence on administration, record keeping and labour control, needed an additional form of writing which could be executed with more speed on less valuable material. Already between the 1st and 3rd Dynasties (*c.* 3000–2600 BC) there appeared sporadic examples of writing on papyrus, potsherds, flakes of limestone or wood, done with a rush pen. This form of writing encouraged a rounding of the angular signs and eventually a loss of detail to encourage greater speed, in short a development towards a more cursive form of writing. In contrast to hieroglyphic, which could be written in either direction or in vertical columns, hieratic (and later demotic) was always written from right to left, at first still in vertical columns. During the 12th Dynasty (*c.* 1999–1786 BC) scribes began to write in horizontal lines, which allowed the writer to adopt an even more cursive hand, and by the end of the 8th century BC demotic began to establish itself as the new alternative (fig. 39). Speed became the dominant factor; too elaborate hieroglyphs were substituted by an

39 Demotic document written on papyrus; 270 BC. (British Museum; Department of Egyptian Antiquities; 10077)

oblique stroke or (more rarely) by some new signs, whole groups of hieroglyphs were amalgamated into one single sign, and abbreviations came into use. Although, as far as the internal structure is concerned, no difference exists between hieroglyphic and demotic, visually they look like two entirely different scripts. The demotic script was if anything more difficult to read; it was not, as its Greek name might suggest, a tool for spreading literacy over a wider spectrum of society. For well over 3,000 years the art of writing was mostly practised by a privileged class of professionally-trained scribes.

An interesting level of development seems to have been reached by the (so far only partly deciphered) Meroïtic script (see fig. 33). After *c*. 850 BC an independent kingdom arose to the south of Egypt. Though the spoken language of the people was in no way related to ancient Egyptian, the script, and the language of official inscriptions, was at first entirely Egyptian. After *c*. 560 BC the capital was moved from Napata to Meroe and Egyptian influence began to decline. During the 1st century BC a new national script developed which used two different styles: a monumental style based entirely on the model of Egyptian hieroglyphs, and a written style based on the Egyptian demotic — at least as far as outward appearance was concerned. Internally however the two scripts differed radically from the Egyptian way of writing; they were both purely phonetic scripts, using only twenty-three different signs, which consisted of consonant signs, two syllabic signs and some vowel signs, though the latter were not always used consistently (there were, it appears, no signs for *o* and *u*). The phonetic values of the Meroïtic hieroglyphs do not always match their Egyptian models, and the 'demotic' signs do not correspond to the phonetically equivalent (Meroïtic) hieroglyphs, but seem rather to have been selected at random from the Egyptian script. Words are for the first time separated, by three dots in the hieroglyphic, and by two dots in the 'demotic', style. The direction of writing is more or less consistently from right to left.

The cuneiform scripts

Unlike Egypt, Mesopotamia, the 'land between two rivers', was during the whole course of its long and often violent history subject to almost constant internal and external pressures. Irrigation was not a matter of course; rivers, especially the Euphrates, were unpredictable. They could erupt into catastrophic floods or change their courses altogether, so that whole villages and, later, prosperous cities had to be abandoned. There was never any durable political or racial hegemony; individual cities, each the estate of a different god, led their armies against each other, and foreign invaders appeared with periodical certainty. Whatever cultural hegemony existed began to crumble with Alexander's march through Asia in 330 BC. By then cuneiform writing had already begun to lose its place to the much simpler Aramaic script. Finally, in the 13th century AD, the army of another great conquistador, Chingis Khan, destroyed the irrigation system and returned the once fertile land to the desert.

The people generally credited with the creation of the cuneiform script were the Sumerians, who in the middle of the 4th century BC established a dominant position in southern Mesopotamia. Neither they nor their language have so far been clearly classified. All we know with any certainty is that they were a non Semitic group speaking an agglutinative language. To begin with their writing was pictographic, but unlike the Egyptians, whose pictograms convey a codified elegance, the Sumerian drawings show a marked tendency towards abstraction: in keeping with their whole attitude to life, utility was more important than artistic beauty. The impetus for the development of writing was an apparent need for a more advanced form of property marks (see fig. 7). Indeed the carefully executed seals of later periods basically still fall into this category. As the economy (closely connected with the Temple which together with the Crown acted as a major market force) and the socio-political life grew more sophisticated, writing too advanced from a means of marking goods and keeping records to a tool for expressing the phonetic intricacies of the Sumerian language.

At first the Sumerians used a great many (about 2,000) signs (GB, p.54). These signs were never clearly codified in the Egyptian manner and could thus, by a process of simplification and conventionalization, move towards a more linear script (see figs. 25, 28). The striking change from still-recognizable pictorial signs to the abstract cuneiform (from Latin *cuneus* – wedge, and *forma* – form) and the change in the direction of writing (from vertical columns running from right to left to a horizontal line running from left to right) was however, as we have seen, at least partly caused by the material and the implements used for writing — soft clay tablets and the reed stylus. The cuneiform script introduced elements of economy, for by around 3000 BC, instead of the original 2,000 signs only about 800 were used. The Babylonians reduced the number to about 570 of which only about 200–300 were in constant use (DD, p.48); the Assyrians, however, somehow extended the range again by re-introducing many older signs.

The internal structure of the script consisted of three basic elements: pictograms, phonograms and determinatives. A pictogram, that is, the drawing of a particular object, could either represent the object in question (i.e. the Sumerian word for the object), an action associated with this object, or an idea associated with this object. All this is already familiar to us. The phonetic principle, the question of sound, had to be solved in a different way. The Sumerian language is rich in monosyllabic (verbal root) words, but, unlike ancient Egyptian, vowels are important. Therefore phonograms represented syllables which could either be used directly or like a rebus. Thus the drawing of a particular object could stand for the (word of the) object it depicted or for its homonyms (a sun disk for *sun* and *son*), and also for any other homophonous syllables (to return to our English example: the drawing of a bird's bill could stand for *bill*, the name *Bill*, or it could also be used in words like *buil*–ding, a–*bil*–ity, etc.)

a - na   na - bi - ì - lí - šu   qí - bí - ma

um - ma   ᵈEN.ZU mu - ba - li - iṭ - ma

25 ŠE.GUR i - na GIŠ.MÁ ṣe - na - am - ma

a - na   KÁ.DINGIR.RA.KI   šu - bi - lam

The above sample gives both phonetic signs and ideograms (ŠE – barley, GUR – a unit of capacity, MÁ – a boat). Determinatives are d (god), GIŠ (wood), and KI (town). There is also the very complicated 'ideogram' KÁ.DINGIR.RA for Babylon, and the ideogram for the name of the moon-god Sin is the Sumerian form Suen written typically in reverse — EN.ZU. The ideograms are all Sumerian but the basic text is Akkadian (specifically Old Babylonian). Two different signs each have been used for li, bi, i, and ma; and the same sign serves for both i and li in the first line.

TRANSLATION:

> To Nabi-ilishu say,
> 'Thus (says) Sin-muballit,
> "Load 25 hectolitres of barley onto a boat and
> send it to me in Babylon."'

Visually, Sumerian cuneiform may look difficult to read, but it was still a relatively simple script. Problems arose when after *c.* 2800 (or 2600) BC the Semitic Akkadians (Babylonians/Assyrians) began to establish their dominance in Mesopotamia. Culturally less advanced, they took over the more dominant features of Sumerian culture, among them the Sumerian script and the Sumerian language. Eventually Sumerian ceased to be a spoken language and receded into a position similar to that of Latin in medieval Europe. The Sumerian cuneiform script however retained its position, but was now used to express the entirely different structure of a Semitic language, a task for which it was ill-suited, and which could only be achieved by a number of complex compromises which (at least to begin with) made reading and writing rather difficult. Thus the Akkadians took over the Sumerian ideograms or word signs, but substituted for the Sumerian word the Semitic equivalent. (If we transferred this situation to English and German, for example, the drawing of a bird's bill could now be read as *Schnabel*.) In addition the Sumerian phonetic value of the word signs did not disappear but was used to express a syllable (to return to our English–German example: the drawing of a bird's bill could also be read as *Bield*, *bil*–lig, *Bil*–dung etc.). Special signs were made available for syllable-forming vowels such as a, e, i and u, but just as the Egyptians had never used their twenty-four single consonant signs to develop a consonant script, so the Babylonians did not move towards the development of an alphabet, nor did they try to replace their entire and undoubtedly cumbersome system of writing by a purely syllabic script. They simply relied on the use of determinatives, which could be placed at the beginning or the end of a word to overcome problems of ambiguity.

Nevertheless, during the 2nd millennium BC Babylonian–Assyrian written in cuneiform script became the language of international diplomacy and was used as such from Persia to Anatolia, from the Caspian Sea to the banks of the Nile. The cuneiform script was also transmitted to various foreign peoples such as the Elamites, Hittites, Chaldeans and Hurrians, and the technique, though not the system, of the cuneiform script, formed the basis of Old Persian and Ugaritic (which used the cuneiform signs in a consonantal manner).

The Indus script

The third, and in many ways most enigmatic, literary civilization of this period — we are still unable to identify language, script and ethnic affinities — flourished in the valley of the River Indus (Pakistan) around two large cities, Mohenjodaro and Harappa, with outposts as far south as Kalibangan in Rajasthan and the seaport of Lothal in Gujarat.

There were similarities with Egypt and Mesopotamia: the artery of the life-giving river, the use of copper, of the plough and of bricks, well-planned cities with areas reserved for secular or perhaps theocratic administration, domesticated animals, trade and commerce (reaching as far as Mesopotamia and perhaps Oman). Above all there was the existence of an apparently indigenous script, schematic and rather linear in appearance, consisting for the major part of what could perhaps best be termed stylized picture signs.

There were however also differences: a far less definite form of irrigation (ALB, p.18), with floodings of the rivers less regular and benevolent than those of the Nile. The cities were comfortable, with a drainage system far superior to that of contemporary rural India; but they were unimaginatively laid out. The conservatism of the Indus civilization far surpassed that of ancient Egypt; town planning, the layout of the houses — and the outer appearance of the script — did not change for almost a millennium. Documentary evidences, as far as they are available, date the Indus civilization between c.2800–1600 BC, with a peak period lasting from 2500–2000 BC. The end seems to have been caused by a combination of floods, the silting up of rivers and port(s) and shockwaves announcing the coming of barbarian invaders some centuries before their actual arrival.

The script, which despite many determined and imaginative attempts has remained undeciphered (see p.146), appears mostly in the form of short inscriptions on seals (fig. 40). As such it could hardly have been more than an advanced form of property marking, a tool for identification in relation to commercial and administrative needs, mixed perhaps with phonetically or symbolically represented proper and/or place names. Scholars — and there are many — who call it proto-Indian, see in the variation of basic signs an indication of a syllabic vowel-marking in the manner of contemporary Indian scripts. But speculations of this kind are extremely tenuous since there exists a complete hiatus, as far as writing is concerned, between the end of the Indus civilization and the first written documents using the characteristically syllabic Indian form of script (Brahmi — see p.106) in the 3rd century BC. Moreover the Indo-Aryans who moved into India in about 1500 BC possessed a civilization, and above all a social structure, which at this stage had no need for writing and was indeed by necessity hostile to it.

40 Seals and sealings from Mohenjodaro; c.2500–2000 BC. (British Museum; Department of Oriental Antiquities; 1892-12-10-1; 1912-6-29-1; 1947-4-16-2; 1912-5-7-1; 1917-4-16-1; 1947-4-16-3)

Ancient Mediterranean scripts

Cretan

For most of the second millennium BC, until the focus of power shifted towards the Greek mainland, ancient Crete was the home of a brilliant civilization which drew its vitality from a successful combination of Palace economy and sea trade. It seems that the first Cretans were immigrants from Asia Minor who kept goats and sheep, cultivated olives and stored their grain in large earthenware jars. By 2300 BC they began to show signs of a growing prosperity but it was only after 2000 BC when the island's political and economic gravity polarized around Knossos and Phaistos that the highly original Palace civilization we associate with Crete, and which still astounds us with its sophistication and elegant affluence, began to evolve. Trade, based on a powerful fleet, further increase in prosperity and a flourishing Palace bureaucracy seem to have stimulated the development of an indigenous Cretan script (influenced perhaps by a knowledge of the Egyptian way of writing) out of earlier cult symbols, and/or property marks. In fact three different forms of writing, two of them still undeciphered, were used, mostly for commercial purposes, between 2000 BC and 1200 BC.

The earliest script, using pictorial signs, survives in various stages of development in the form of short inscriptions on seal stones, or (rarely) scratched in clay. Most of these inscriptions come from Knossos and have been ascribed to the period between 2000–1500 BC. Sir Arthur Evans lists about 140 different signs representing human figures, parts of the body, domestic animals, religious symbols, ships, wheat, olive sprays and some purely geometrical signs. The number of signs is too small for a pictographic script, and phonetic — most probably syllabic — elements seem to be indicated. Whether some of these pictures were ideograms, used perhaps as determinatives, (AE, p.49) is a question for debate. The direction of writing seems to have been left to right, or right to left, as well as boustrophedon.

Around 1700 BC linear forms of writing appeared. The first of the two linear scripts, Linear A, is documented in the form of short inscriptions, written mainly on square fields with four to nine lines in each field (GB, p.129). The majority of these inscriptions were found at Knossos, some also in the course of excavations around Hagia Triada and at Palaikastro, and a few were discovered on at least two Greek islands. The number of signs is greatly reduced; not more than seventy-seven (eighty-five according to some scholars) have been counted, which suggests even more clearly a syllabic form of writing. There are still a number of seemingly pictorial signs.

Between 1450 and c. 1200 BC Knossos came under Mycenean influence and the Cretan scribes seem to have adapted their syllabic script for the expression of the new ruling class language, namely Mycenean Greek (PG, p.30). Linear B (fig. 41), the only Cretan script fully deciphered (see p.144), was mostly used in Knossos and has in consequence often been referred to as 'Knossian court calligraphy'. The texts deal mainly with accounts rendered, lists of goods, statements of weight or delivery and other elements of commercial life. It has been suggested that half the signs are the same as in Linear A, and about twenty

41 Clay tablets with Greek inscription in Linear B. The smaller one records an inventory of ewes and rams at Phaistos, the larger one an offering of oil to a goddess; from Knossos, Crete, c.1400 BC. (British Museum; Department of Greek and Roman Antiquities; 1910. 4-23 (1 and 2))

of these signs seem to have developed from the old picture signs (HJ, p.125). After 1100 BC, when the Cretan civilization finally vanished in a series of cataclysms caused by invasions of Greek-speaking Dorians and a number of disastrous earthquakes, the skill of writing was lost.

Cypriote

The first Cypriote script, known as Cypro-Minoan, has about eighty-five syllabic signs. It is still undeciphered but is evidently related to the Linear A script of Minoan Crete. The earliest document dates from about 1500 BC but the script only became firmly established from the 14th century and remained in use until the 12th century BC. The Cypriots had no close links with Minoan Crete at the time of the script's adoption and it therefore seems likely that they learnt it from Cretans in Syria, perhaps at Ugarit where both countries had colonies. To the 11th century BC belongs the first document, a bronze spit recently found at Kouklia (Old Paphos), with a Greek inscription in the Cypriote syllabic script. This script was in regular use from the 7th until the end of the 3rd century BC (fig. 42). It was related in some way to the Cypro-Minoan script and was used to write both Greek and Eteo-Cypriote, a still unknown language. It has fifty to sixty different signs each denoting a syllable; words can be divided by raised points or short strokes. No distinction is made between long and short vowels and the same sign is used for voiced, unvoiced and aspirated forms.

42 *Terracotta tablet with Greek inscription in Cypriote script; from Akanthou, c.600–500 BC. (British Museum; Department of Greek and Roman Antiquities; 1950.5.25-1)*

43 *Syro-Hittite (hieroglyphic) inscription from Carchemish; c.900 BC. Dedication of the temple of the goddess Kubaba by Katuwas, king of Carchemish. (British Museum; Department of Western Asiatic Antiquities; 125002)*

Hittite

The picture script of the Hittites is generally included in the (eastern) Mediterranean group. The Hittites, an ancient people of differing ethnic and linguistic affinities, began to move into Mesopotamia about 2000 BC; by the 18th century BC they had established a home around the river Halys. They seem to have had contacts with Babylonian culture from an early date, and between 1500–1200 BC (when their political fortunes began to decline) they used, mainly in the area around Boghazköy, the capital of their empire, for purposes of commerce and administration, a cuneiform style of writing obviously borrowed from Mesopotamia. Simultaneously however (and up to c. 600 BC), they also made use of a picture script for a perhaps similar though not necessarily identical language. Most pictorial inscriptions were chiselled in stone or on rock walls, the earlier ones in raised characters (fig. 43), the later incised; some have also survived in the form of seal impressions on clay or on lead scrolls. The underlying objects are no longer always recognizable, and alongside true picture signs, and often in the same inscription, more cursive forms appear; these may however be technical simplifications and not necessarily a later stage of development (HJ, p.146). The script is generally written boustrophedon, with the heads looking towards the beginning of the line (as in hieroglyphic Egyptian). Inscriptions are normally divided by clear horizontal lines and the signs within each section are read from top to bottom. The total number of signs so far established has been estimated as c.220 (DD, p.57) or 350 (HJ, p.148) — too few for a true pictographic or word picture script. Although we are still largely ignorant of the actual language of the inscriptions, a syllabic script mixed with some word picture signs seems to be indicated. The normal Hittite syllabary consists, according to some research, of about sixty signs (IJG, p.83), each representing a syllable beginning with a consonant and ending with a vowel. In accordance with the principle of economy which we have already encountered in the case of the Cypriote script, no distinction is made between voiced, unvoiced and aspirated consonants.

This still leaves the question of the origin of the Hittite picture script. Was it an indigenous invention (DD, p.85) or merely the further development of an original borrowing? So far the question has not been convincingly answered either way, but Cretan influence, or at least an adherence to some common ancestry, is being advocated.

Lybian

Apart from the mysterious Phaistos disc which will be discussed later (see p.144), another group of scripts, referred to as Lybian, existed (towards the end of the first millennium BC) in the western region of the Mediterranean, namely northern Africa (Tunisia) and southern Spain. The North African group consists of the so-called Numidian script which has a modern offshoot in the Berber script still used by the nomadic Tuaregs. The Spanish group is generally referred to as Turdetanian. Lybian scripts do not however fit into the predominantly syllabic orientated Agean cycle of writing. The fact that they are consonant scripts, using in most cases a right to left direction, suggests Semitic connections.

Pre-Columbian American scripts

It is generally accepted that the American Indians are the descendants of Mongoloid immigrants who moved from Asia across the Bering Straits more than 20,000 years ago. Gradually this movement became self-perpetuating and extended over both American continents, creating tribal communities whose economy depended mostly on hunting or a simple form of agriculture. Many of these communities developed effective and original forms of information storage, but only in three areas did urban and literate civilizations similar to those of Egypt, Mesopotamia and the Aegean arise: among the Mayas of Yucatan, the Aztecs of Mexico and the Incas of Peru. Many elements congenial to the development of writing were present in those areas: an advanced agriculture which could support non-producing specialists, an architecture in no way inferior to that of ancient Egypt which obviously depended on some sort of organized labour, a trained priesthood closely connected with the (elected) ruler (thus interaction between Palace and Temple), widespread trade, and a centralized and efficient form of administration. But there were also puzzling differences. The level of arts and crafts was high, but the skill for handling metal was mainly confined to the jeweller's art — working in gold and copper. In Mexico the tools used for warfare (and by the sacrificing priest performing the ritualistic cardiectomy) were mostly stone-age flints and obsidian. Technically the wheel was known, but it was not used, except for toys. The domestication of animals was negligible (the llama for transport in Peru, for example, and a small dog bred for food in Mexico). The various writing systems which developed have at times been labelled primitive or transitory; in the case of Peru, the existence of a 'proper' form of writing is still largely denied. Yet those systems effectively supported complex religious, political and economic organizations, and were indeed vital for the welfare and the survival of the community.

Central America

Writing in Central America was closely connected with the creation and development of a sophisticated almanac based on a remarkably high level of mathematical and astronomical knowledge. The calendar was made up of two cycles operating concurrently. One cycle, the sacred year of 260 days, determined the pattern of ceremonial life. It was formed by joining twenty day names to the numbers 1–13. Another cycle of eighteen 20-day months ran concurrently. To designate a particular day, the positions in both cycles would be indicated. The combined system (which did not repeat a single date) divided time into self-contained (fifty-two-year) cycles, with the uncomfortable possibility that the end of each cycle could mean the end of the known world if proper ritualistic precautions were not observed. To indicate dates beyond the span of fifty-two years, another much larger cycle was used. Dates from this cycle, called the Long Count, were inscribed on monuments. These dates recorded the number of days which had passed since a day in the year 3113 BC; and we are indeed able to correlate dates in this system with our own calendar.

For a long time the Maya civilization, which lasted from 500 BC–1200 AD, with a classical period of some 600 years between 300–900 AD, was credited with the introduction of both the almanac and writing. But it has now become more and more apparent that much had been handed down by the Olmec, whom native tradition names as the earliest inhabitants, and who were supposed to have overcome the mythical giants and founded the first sacred cities. Indeed, certain design elements on Olmec clothing, accessories and body may represent embryonic script signs (JEST, p.20). It is not known whether the names and signs for the twenty days (see fig. 18) were already known to the Olmecs, but they are in evidence in the Mont Albán I period (*c.* 500 BC).

Except for calendar signs and notation symbols, Maya writing has still not been fully deciphered. No doubt the religious fervour of the Spanish conquistadors and their accompanying Jesuit priests who indulged in wholesale destruction of carved images and written documents, and who did much to erase the old beliefs from the memory of the people (their dictionaries carefully omitted ritual and ceremonial terms), played its part. But in pre-Columbian America, as indeed in most parts of the ancient world, the knowledge of writing was never democratically shared among the people; it was predominantly in the hands of the priesthood and/or consecrated interpreters.

The Mayas used two styles of script, a monumental and a written form. The monumental script (fig. 44) was hewn in stone, or incised in jade, or moulded out of a kind

44 Lintel 25 from House 'G', at the ancient Maya ceremonial centre at Menche (Yaxchilan), Guatemala. The inscription shows the calendar round date 5 Imix 4 Mac (c.681 AD). (British Museum; Museum of Mankind)

45 Troano Codex. *Madrid. (By courtesy of the Museum of Mankind)*

of stucco. It bears no resemblance to any other form of writing and is characterized by an element of inherent dynamism, a combination of restrained abstraction and pure fantasy. The earliest surviving Maya texts have been dated 200–100 BC. By the end of the classical period (900 AD) the recording of texts on architectural monuments had ceased. The individual script signs look remarkably complicated, but if considered closely they reveal themselves as compounds of simpler signs. Each sign seems compressed into the same rectangular, square or oval space. On stelae, signs are usually arranged vertically and have to be read in pairs (see p.54); in the case of horizontal inscriptions the direction runs usually from left to right.

The Mayas knew the meaning of zero, and their complicated mathematical system depended on the use of only three symbols: a stylized shell for nought, a dot for one and a bar for five. The position of a number symbol determined its value, with values increased by a factor of twenty from bottom to top in vertical columns. The first and lowest place has a value of one; the next, twenty; the next, four hundred; the next, eight thousand; and so on. For example —

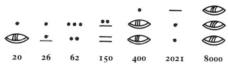

| 20 | 26 | 62 | 150 | 400 | 2021 | 8000 |

They did in fact use a binary code of astounding efficiency which allowed them to deal with periods of over five million years.

The written form of Maya glyphs differed considerably from the carved signs of the classical period, but how far this is the result of the difference in writing material (long strips of bark paper or deerskin folded accordion-wise — as opposed to stone), and how much represents genuine development, is difficult to assess. The only three surviving manuscripts, the Codex Dresden, the Codex Madrid (fig. 45) and the Codex Paris (named after the cities where they are now preserved), are thought to have been composed between 1300–1500 AD, though some scholars suggest slightly earlier dates. Illustrations standing below the passage to which they refer aid the identification of subjects. According to earlier sources Maya manuscripts covered subjects as diverse as history, prophecies, songs, traditional science and genealogy, but the three surviving manuscripts limit themselves mainly to divination in relation to astronomical events, ritual and ceremonies.

In 1320 AD the Aztecs, who according to their own tradition came from the north-west, a land called Aztlan (from *aztatl* + *–tlan*, a suffix for place names: i.e. 'heron-land'), consolidated their position in northern Mexico. Their advanced civilization, which two hundred years later astounded the Spanish conquistadors, was to a large extent the modification of an inheritance left behind by previous civilizations. Their most spectacular achievements were perhaps the lake city of Tenochtitlan (now Mexico City) and a highly effective administration, supported by a well-developed legal system and excellent methods of communication (trained runners and post houses every five to six miles) which treated the Palace as the centre of the Aztec world. In organization the army could match that of ancient Rome, but there was a fatal flaw which eventually contributed much to the destruction of the Aztec civilization: though highly organized, war was more a religious rite than an exercise aimed at gaining secular power, with the result that military success was hardly ever sufficiently consolidated by the incorporating of new territories and new people into one single Empire.

It is highly probable that the Aztecs received the idea of writing from the Mayas, but as far as appearance is concerned there is no recognizable likeness between the two scripts. Altogether, twenty Mexican manuscripts have survived, most of historical–mythological and calendrical–astrological content. Like Maya manuscripts, they consist of long sheets made of bark paper or deerskin, covered with a thin white coat of lime plaster, with writing on both sides. The individual signs are executed in a wide range of colours: black, white, red, yellow, blue, green, purple, brown, orange — each sign being encased in a black outline. The term *codex* which is generally used for Maya and Mexican manuscripts is a misnomer; the sheets could, opened up, serve as wall-hangings, but folded accordion-wise they formed a compact pile of pages where the beginning was placed next to the end. The text had to be read in a meandering, boustrophedon fashion, starting from the right-hand top and following vertical guide-lines in red (see Plate I). Aztec writing is highly pictographic and it served, up to a point, as a form of memory aid for the priests who knew how to write and read the manuscripts. Structurally, the script consisted of a mixture of logography (sometimes mixed with iconographic elements), ideography and rebus writing. The rebus writing — the phonetic element — was mainly used to reproduce names of places and persons. During most of the 16th century Spanish officials made use of this (phonetic) element for administrative purposes, just as missionaries tried to convey the Creed or the Lord's Prayer in Latin wording by use of the native script. This was not always an easy task, since there exists little correspondence between Latin and the sounds of the Aztec language. In most cases rather doubtful approximations had to suffice. Thus *Pater noster* was represented by *pa–te noc–te*, and this too in a somewhat tortuous manner —

*pa*mi–tl	·*te*–tl	*noc*–tli	*te*–tl
(flag)	(stone)	(fig thistle)	(stone)

Whether without the Spanish conquest, which put such a sudden end to the Aztec civilization, Aztec writing would have developed into a syllabic script — as has been suggested — is difficult to assess. As we have seen, this step was not taken in Mesopotamia, just as the Egyptians never moved towards a pure consonant script. As far as information storage and the ability to communicate information is concerned, Aztec writing was highly effective: two days after Cortez landed in Vera Cruz, Moctezuma received a written account of the arrival of the Spaniards, describing their ships, their horses (unknown in Mexico) and their weapons (GB, p.409).

Peru

The Inca Empire, stretching from Ecuador in the north to Chile in the south, which Pizarro encountered in 1531 AD, had reached its peak barely a hundred years earlier. Many of its most characteristic elements, such as the technique of building with interlocking stones, the advanced level of irrigation, weaving and metal work, or the meticulously controlled administration, were in fact a legacy of the Chimu or other earlier civilizations. The real contribution of the Incas was a strong expansionist urge, a natural flair for organization and the ability to enforce and submit to the strictest discipline. They had a large army of conscripts (with officers from the Inca's own household), an efficient way of enforcing their pattern of society on each newly-conquered province (if necessary with the aid of large-scale resettlements) and an almost foolproof system of taxation which required an awesome bureacracy (c. 1,331 officials per 10,000 head of population). Taxation was not however based on mindless exploitation (always counter-productive in the long run), but on a centrally planned increase in overall productivity. Great care was taken to ensure that everybody worked to the limit of his or her ability, but nobody was left unprovided for in times of emergency. As a whole the Inca empire can perhaps best be described as a totalitarian welfare state.

Such a society depends heavily on communication, and this the Incas had perfected. They had 3,250 miles of road running from north to south spanning 35° of altitude, posthouses every five miles (some of them fortified army magazines) and runners who could relay despatches at a rate of 150 miles a day. Above all, the Incas had the actual means of storing and transmitting information — the *quipu* (see fig. 6).

Quipus were kotted cords, some of them up to four kilograms in weight. Various means by which data were conveyed included the type and number of knots (from one to nine), the position of each knot (decimal place value), the colour and ply of each string and the position of a string along the main cord. It is generally believed that a special type of interpreter called a *quipu* master (*quipu–camayoc*) read and interpreted the strings, often in conjunction with abacus-like boards; verbal messages could also be sent with the runners who carried the *quipus*. Pedro Cieza de León, writing immediately after the Spanish conquest, gives an impressive eye-witness account of the way in which *quipus* were used:

'. . . in the capital of each province there were accountants whom they called *quipu–camayocs*, and by these knots they kept the account of the tribute payed by the natives of that district in silver, gold, clothing, flocks, down to wood and other insignificant things, and by these *quipus* at the end of the year, or ten or twenty years, they gave a report to one whose duty it was to check the accounts so exact that not even a pair of sandals was missing . . and I was much amazed thereby . . . the wars, cruelties, pillages and tyranny of the Spaniards had been such that if these Indians had not been accustomed to order and providence they would all have perished . . . and after the Spaniards had passed through, the chieftains came together with the keepers of the *quipus*, and if one had expended more than the others, those who had given less made up the difference, so that all were on an equal footing.'

46 Keros, *wooden drinking cups from Peru; the cup in the middle shows a band of geometrical decorations* (tocapu). *(British Museum; Department of Mankind; 1950 AM. 22-2)*

Besides recording numbers, *quipus* were also used as a memory aid in reciting narrative verses, genealogies and liturgical material. In addition, the knot and string arrangements may have been adapted to the phonetics of the Inca language. Nowadays *quipus* are still used in certain parts of Peru, but solely for recording of numerical data.

Sending runners to convey (written) messages was already a practice among the Moche people (200 BC–900 AD) whose life and customs can be partially reconstructed from scenes painted (or modelled) on pottery. An important category of Moche pottery decoration shows runners, often with animal, bird or insect heads (or sometimes bean-shaped heads) wearing military dress, and carrying small bags containing painted (or marked) beans (see fig. 2), obviously meant to transmit messages. Such decorated beans (see p.18) have also been found in archaeological excavations and the suggestion has been made (though not yet proven) that the parallel lines, dots and combination of dots and lines might constitute a system of writing comparable to that of the Mayas of Central America (GB/1, p.83). The beans may also have been used for the purpose of calculation (Spanish chronicles refer to piles of pebbles or grain), or together with counting boards like the ones used in later times by the *quipu–camayocs*.

It has been suggested that in addition to *quipus* the Incas had already developed other means of information storage. Wooden cups, or *keros*, (fig. 46) and certain textiles (fig. 47) are covered with geometrical designs, or *tocapus*, which may have had specific meaning. In 1970, at the International Congress of Americanists in Lima, the German scholar Thomas Barthel claimed that he had identified four hundred script signs and deciphered fifty of them (GB, p.412), with the help of notes made by Spanish missionaries. Since then nothing further had been heard about this discovery. It is in fact somewhat improbable that *tocapus* constituted a specific script where each individual design equalled one particular character. *Tocapus* may however have contained phonetic elements similar to those found in many forms of memory aids: Ashanti proverbs, Mide song-boards, Yoruba love-letters, or indeed the embryonic script signs found on some Olmec clothing.

47 *Post-conquest textile from Peru showing bands of geometrical designs in* tocapu *style. (British Museum; Museum of Mankind; 1980 M)*

Writing in the Far East

China

During the 4,000 years of its estimated history the Chinese script has undergone only comparatively minor remodelling. The actual nature of the script has remained more or less unaltered. It is still basically a word, or perhaps better, a concept, script with all the disadvantages and advantages such a system entails. The disadvantages are the large number of signs necessary — 50,000 altogether, though for more mundane and everyday use 2,000 to 4,000 may suffice. The advantages are that as a concept script Chinese does not depend on the spoken word; it can be read without regard to, or even knowledge of, the spoken language. This made it, throughout Chinese history, an ideal means of communication in an empire whose people spoke a large number of different dialects, yet were all ruled from the same centre. For administrators and scholars alike, the Chinese script was the least ambiguous (and therefore simplest) form of communication. It was also unnecessary for the written language to follow the development of the spoken language; indeed, modern Chinese do not need to know the ancient pronunciation of words to read the classical texts. On the other hand the many homonymous (monosyllabic) words of the Chinese language make it sometimes necessary to refer to a written character for clarification. For example the word *fu* can mean: to return, to send, kingdom, father, woman, skin — but a different written character is used for each meaning. (This is very different from Mesopotamian usage where one single cuneiform character can be used to form the syllabic component of a number of different words.)

The earliest Chinese inscriptions, found either on animal bones or tortoiseshell from the Shang period (*c.* 1766–1122 BC) or on bronze vessels from the Zhou period (*c.* 1134–250 BC) are already written in a highly developed and stylized form (fig. 48), which would imply a period of development prior to that date. In some, though not in all characters, the original picture-sign is still clearly recognizable. Chinese tradition itself offers various explanations for the origin of writing. Besides the usual accounts of legendary or semi-divine beings who acted as 'inventors' there are also written traditions which deserve perhaps more serious consideration. The *Dao de jing* of Laotze and also the supplement to the *Yi jing* (the ancient books on soothsaying) refer to knotted cords which in antiquity were used for information storage. The lexicographical work *Shuo wen* sees in the eight trigrams (representing sky, wind, moisture, water, fire, mountain, thunder and earth) a reproduction of these knotted cords in the form of lines; but some western scholars have been inclined to treat these trigrams (and hexagrams) as true script signs, used perhaps as some kind of local script (HJ, p.164). Other elements of origin may have been the 'staffs of office' — the insignia of rank and position which were usually worn as belt ornaments — and also tallies, tokens of royal command, and authorizations. The sign language, which because of the great diffusion of dialects has always played an important role, has been accorded similar rank. For example, a sign representing two hands turned away from each other can be read as *fei* (wrong); a sign representing two hands stretched out in greeting as *you* (friend, friendship); two hands raised above the head, perhaps in a gesture of obeisance, as *jun* (sovereign), and so forth.

Chinese tradition divides the script signs into six groups:
(1) Pictures of objects (*xiang xing*): about some 600 signs which still form the most basic element of the Chinese script.
(2) Symbolic pictures (*zhi shi*): representations of abstract words by signs borrowed from other words related to them in meaning (i.e. the half-moon for 'evening'), representations of gestures, of crafts by their tools etc., and metaphors. Not many Chinese characters fall into this category.
(3) Symbolic compounds (*hui yi*) which can be achieved by a two- or four-fold repetition of the same sign (for example, twice the character for 'child' – 'twins') or by an ideographic combination of the components which make up a particular concept (for example, sign for 'tree' plus sign for 'hand' – 'to collect').
(4) Signs that have arisen from 'deflections and inversions' or from a significant rotation of other signs (*zhuan zhu*). For example, 'child' written upside-down – 'childbirth' (relatively rare).
(5) Sound-indicating signs (*xie sheng*) — now the most important group. They were developed especially under the Han Dynasty (206 BC–221 AD) and consist of two elements: a determinative element indicating meaning and general concept, and a phonetic rebus which provides the sound for the whole sign (for example, to express 'shining', which already consists of the two signs 'sun' plus 'earth'; the sign for 'fire' is added).
(6) Borrowings (*jia jie*) show certain similarities to elements discussed under (5) and are often ambiguous (the character for *zu* – to 'suffice' is used for *zu* – 'foot' etc.).

48 Inscribed Chinese bronze vessel from the Western Zhou period; 1050–771 BC. (British Museum; Department of Oriental Antiquities; 1930-11-8-2 (11))

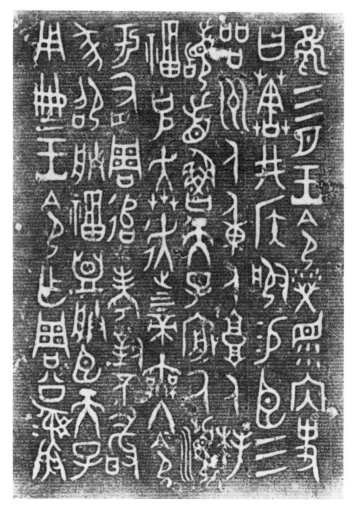

Although the internal structure of the Chinese script has remained unaltered the appearance of the individual script signs has changed considerably; the original pictorial element is still recognizable in a number of signs, however.

	Old form	Modern form
child	 �	子
tree	米	木
gate, door	 門	門
arrow	 食夫	矢
word, to speak	言	言
rain	 雨	雨
dog	犬	犬
large snake	乙	巴
hand	手	手
field	田	田

The reasons for these changes vary. For example, a change in writing material (from stone, bone, metal, to silk or paper) was often accompanied by a change in writing implements (from metal or bamboo stylus to brush). Or the change arose from purely calligraphic considerations which were enormously important and produced visually completely different forms of style.

A characteristic element of the Chinese script, noticeable from earliest times onwards, is the square arrangement of the individual elements in each character (see fig. 50). The script itself runs in vertical columns from the top of the right hand side downwards with the columns following each other from the right to the left. Graphically, Chinese characters can be reduced to nine strokes, but some of these strokes can have several variants so that there are characters with as many as seventeen different strokes.

Unlike other systems so far discussed which moved towards a reduction in the number of script signs, Chinese writing seems to have taken exactly the opposite course. The 2,500 characters of the Shang period increased to 9,000 by 100 AD, and about 18,000 by 500 AD and to 27,000 by 1000 AD. Comprehensive modern dictionaries number some 50,000 different characters, arranged around radicals or categories, 214 in number. Chinese characters consist usually of a radical and a complement made up of a certain number of strokes — though characters can also be formed by radicals alone or a combination of radicals. Generally the radical indicates the overall sphere of meaning (for example, radical 85 means 'water'); the complement supplies the phonetic element (radical 85 plus a complement consisting of five strokes becomes 'to anchor').

The way radicals act is similar, though by no means identical, to the way determinatives operate in Egyptian and cuneiform writing. Since the Chinese language is based on syntax (the order of words in a sentence) and not on what we would normally call grammar, it is possible, despite the large number of different signs with their complexity of strokes, to look up each character and to understand (up to a point) a Chinese text, without actually knowing the language. Once we appreciate this, we shall also realize how effectively the Chinese script served administrative, religious and political institutions throughout Chinese history. Far from dividing the country it helped to unite it. Admittedly there was, by necessity, a wide gap between those who could read and write and those who were illiterate, with literacy being accessible only to a relatively small portion of the total population. But this was a situation not in any way different from that of pre-industrial Europe.

China's cultural influence on the rest of the Far East can hardly be overestimated. Together with Buddhism, Chinese script, Chinese language and Chinese culture spread to the non-Chinese people of the south-western interior — to Korea, Vietnam and above all to Japan — similar to the way in which Christianity had at first introduced Latin and the alphabet to the countries of Europe and, after the 15th century, Christian-European culture had provided the inner drive for what was to become a political (and linguistic) domination of large parts of Africa, Asia and the Americas. The initial impact of the Chinese script was considerable; it was above all unopposed since none of the countries concerned possessed an indigenous form of writing. The fact that structurally the Chinese script was completely unsuited for many of these languages was not too great an obstacle, just as in Mesopotamia the Semitic Akkadians had accepted the cuneiform script originally designed for the agglutinative Sumerian language. However, after a period of acceptance, indigenous elements began to reassert themselves and local inventions, or better, local re-modellings based on a knowledge of the Chinese writing system, produced modifications which were simpler and on the whole more suitable for local information storage.

It is interesting to note that nearly all these 'inventions' moved towards syllabic script systems. Exactly the same thing happened when in the 19th century attempts were made to create indigenous forms of writing in Africa and among the Indians of North America by persons who knew the Roman (or Arabic) script. In the Far East an additional element was at the disposal of the script-creators: since the Buddhist scriptures propagated by the Chinese were translations of Sanskrit texts, elements of Sanskrit phonetics and of the Indian mode of writing — especially the order and the use of letter signs — were also passed on.

Korea

In 109 AD the Chinese (Han) Emperor Wu Di conquered most of Korea. As a result many Chinese emigrated to Korea, taking their advanced culture, their language, literature, script and religion with them. Although about 40 years later the Koreans succeeded in re-adjusting the political balance in their favour, Chinese culture continued to thrive on Korean soil. From the 1st century AD to the end of the 7th century Chinese was the 'offical script' (*kwan–mun*) and the only form of writing used in Korea. The unsuitability of Korean — a polysyllabic, agglutinative language — for the use of a concept script (and the fact that Korea was politically independent) encouraged experiments towards more acceptable alternatives. According to tradition th first serious attempt at creating a syllabic script based entirely on Chinese script signs was made in 690 AD by a scholar at the court of King Sinmum. Yet the difficulty of outwardly distinguishing the (thirty-six) syllabic signs from the Chinese ideograms, and the many new syllable signs which in the course of time were added to it, made the system both confusing and inadequate.

This inadequacy became painfuly apparent when, in 1403 AD, probably under Chinese influence, printing with movable metal type was introduced in Korea. Eventually, in 1446 AD, King Sejong of Korea promulgated, not without resistance from scholars and the ministers of his court who saw in it a threat to their privileged position, the 'script of the popular idiom' (*on–mun*), consisting basically of eleven vowel and seventeen consonant signs (fourteen basic consonants and ten single vowel signs according to some scholars), which were arranged in syllabic units. The king is often credited with having invented the new script himself, but such attributions are more often than not a mixture of courtesy and political shrewdness designed to give added authority to a new convention.

Three elements contributed to the creation of the Korean script: the existence of the Chinese model (the direction of writing remains the same), a knowledge of the Indian (Sanskrit? Tibetan?) order and use of letters brought to Korea through Buddhist/Chinese intermediaries, and finally, the invention of the external form of signs. These signs, simple and regular in shape, were designed on the basis of phonetic principles. The individual consonants are graphic representations of the way that the organs of speech are used in articulating them; while the vowels consist of different arrangements of one long line joined at right angles at the centre by one or two shorter lines. Syllables are formed on the basis of consonant plus vowel plus consonant.

The new script did not replace Chinese completely, but was used side by side with Chinese characters (fig. 49) as an aid to pronunciation, for grammatical words or to clarify ambiguities, in a way similar to the Japanese use of the syllabic *kana* signs. Indeed as in Japan the knowledge of Chinese, and the ability to write the Chinese script, were considered a sign of social elevation; popular literature, as for example historical novels written in the Korean script, was for consumption by women or people of low rank. Today the mixed script (interspersed with European loan words in Roman script) is still used in the south. In the north all literature is written in the Korean script.

Japan

Whether writing existed in Japan before the introduction of the Chinese script has been much discussed by both European and Japanese scholars. Local traditions cite a knot device, similar to the one used on the Ryukyu islands (HJ, p.163). Literary traditions such as the *Kogoshui* (807 AD) deny the existence of a pre-Chinese script, but the historical commentary *Shakunihongi* (c. 1200 AD) takes exactly the opposite view. In 1770 AD a Buddhist priest claimed to have discovered the original pre-Chinese script, the 'signs of the gods' (*shinji* or *kami mo moji*) which however, on close inspection, betray clear affinities with the Korean script.

According to archaeological evidence, Japan — still in the stone age in the 3rd century BC — first came into contact with the much more advanced Chinese civilization during the Han dynasty (206 BC–220 AD). From the beginning of the Christian era the Chinese script was known in Japan, though at first only to a very small circle of people. No direct sea trade seems to have existed between Japan and China in ancient times, and contacts were made via Korea. After the Chinese invasion of Korea in 109 AD Chinese immigrants reached some of the Japanese islands, together with elements of their superior culture such as the use of the horse, various tools, a knowledge of rice cultivation and the use of (inscribed) metal mirrors and swords. In 370 AD Japan invaded Korea and successfully held some of the newly acquired territory until 562 AD. In consequence the so far tentative contacts between Japan–Korea–China increased and became more stabilized, and in 285 AD — or, according to some scholars, in 405 AD (DC, p.16) — the Japanese Emperor Ojin is supposed to have brought two Korean scholars, well-versed in Chinese writing and Chinese literature, to his court to act as tutors to the Crown Prince. In the middle of the 6th century Buddhism became the official religion of Japan, with the result that a larger, though still strictly limited, section of society was now 'Chinese-educated'. From then on Japanese scholars went regularly to China for further studies, and in 645 AD a centralized

49 Hunmin chŏngŭm. *King Sejong's explanation of the Korean script; modern facsimile of a block-print. (British Library; Oriental Collections; 16509. a. 4)*

administration based largely on Confucian ideas was installed in Japan which lasted until the end of the Heian period. Chinese writing techniques too were adopted: the brush, ink, the ink-stone and, after 600 AD, the manufacture of paper.

With no writing system of their own, the wholesale adoption by the Japanese of Chinese writing and Chinese literature was a shrewd political move which accelerated the development of Japanese civilization. A similar move was made in the 19th century when, after a period of resistance, Japan accepted western industrialization almost *in toto*. In both cases the alien elements were quickly assimilated, and far from weakening the national character they in fact greatly strengthened it. How then was the Chinese concept or word script adapted to the polysyllabic, agglutinative Japanese language full of formal words? Again, basically with the aid of a syllabic system which supplemented the script, not by the use of newly invented signs (as in Korea), but by the addition of simplified Chinese characters used in a syllabic manner. It is true that as a concept script Chinese could simply be read in Japanese; for example, 'human being' (*hito* in Japanese and *jen* in Chinese) could be represented by the same (Chinese) character. But the Japanese syntax is vastly different from, in fact often exactly the opposite of, Chinese. This difficulty was overcome by indicating, through special notations, the order in which characters had to be read. But this alone did not solve the problem; to express the Japanese language fully and satisfactorily, proper phonetic elements had to be added to the Chinese script. The first step in this direction was to transfer the phonetic value of certain Chinese characters to represent the syllable of certain Japanese words — the already familiar rebus-like principle. This was a somewhat untidy solution (for example, the Japanese ending –*ru* had to be represented by the Chinese character for *liu*) which needed further refinement. The next step was the modification and simplification of these 'phonetic' characters to form a systematic

50 Kojiki. *Ancient history of Japan, completed in 712 AD, the first work of native Japanese literature. The copy was printed from woodblocks in 1803. The pronunciation is indicated by* kana *alongside the Chinese characters. (British Library; Oriental Collections; 16047. b. 10)*

syllabary (*kana*) with fixed phonetic values. Between the 8th and 10th centuries two such syllabaries evolved — or, according to tradition, were invented by two specifically named individuals. One of these systems, the *katakana*, is a square formal type of script formed from isolated parts of Chinese characters; the second, the *hiragana*, is a rounded flowing script derived from the cursive form of (whole) Chinese characters. The number of syllabic characters was eventually reduced to only forty-seven different (*kana*) script signs. Theoretically, Japanese could now be written entirely in *kana* syllables — and much poetry and prose literature of the Heian period (794–1192 AD) was indeed written in this way (but mainly by women authors). Chinese was too deeply entrenched as a prestigious form of communication and information storage to make its abolition a possibility. Borrowings from Chinese continued side by side with the use of *kana* and by the end of the Heian period a mixed Chinese/Japanese script (fig. 50) known as *kana-majiri* evolved and has remained in use until the present day.

Vietnam

Altogether three different forms of writing exist in Vietnam. Since the Vietnamese language is predominantly uninflected, monosyllabic and full of tonal accents, the introduction of the Chinese script in 186 AD by King Siyoung presented few difficulties — Chinese characters were simply read in Vietnamese. A second type of script, mainly known from inscriptions after the 14th century, used Chinese characters in a more modified way. The third script, still in use today, consists simply of the letters of the Roman alphabet extensively supplemented by diacritics. This script was first introduced by Portuguese missionaries, and has been used in dictionaries and grammars from the 16th and 17th centuries onwards.

Non-Chinese people of south-west China

The mountainous regions of south-west China have for long been an area of refuge for non-Chinese tribes, who, though nominally subjugated, preserved much of their cultural independence. Their languages, belonging mostly to the Tibeto-Burman group, differ greatly from Chinese, but the majority of their scripts, though in part the result of independent inventions, betray allegiance to, or at least a knowledge of, Chinese (in some cases also Indian) models. Some scripts are still used, or at least known, as for example the scripts of the Lolo, Miao or Yao; others have, despite considerable temporary and local importance, long vanished and are partly still undeciphered (the most prominent example in this category being the script of the Tangut). Many of these scripts combine the characteristics of a concept script with syllabic and/or ideographic elements. The outer appearance of the individual signs is either modelled on that of Chinese characters, or in some cases the script signs show considerable linear simplicity. None of these scripts was known to European scholars before the latter part of the last century.

An interesting, and in many ways unique, example is the Moso script (fig. 51) of the Nakhi people, a tribe speaking a Tibetan dialect who settled in north-western Yunnan. Moso manuscripts are written with a bamboo stylus on paper, and the script is almost completely ideographic, supported by only a relatively small number of phonetic (i.e. syllabic) signs. Only words absolutely necessary are written down, the rest being supplied by the hereditary Nakhi priests who each train their first-born son from childhood to memorize the stories and ritual texts, and to interpret the meaning of the written symbols. Thus the Moso script acts partly as a memory aid, in a way similar to the *kekinowin* of the North American Indians (see p.131). According to the genealogical records of the Nakhi rulers, the script was invented by Mou-pao A-tsung some time between 1200 and 1253 AD. But internal evidence and indeed the Nakhi name for the script (*ss dgyu* or *lv dgyu* – wood record, stone record) suggest a much earlier date. Moso script signs show no connection with Chinese characters, even in their earliest form, nor with any other kind of script so far discovered in the interior of southern China.

51 Magical invocations and prayers in the Moso script of the Nakhi people of south-western China; 19th century. (British Library; Oriental Collections; Or. 11508)

Semitic scripts

Semitic scripts are consonant scripts; they are neither alphabets nor syllabaries as has often been suggested, or at least implied. It is true that when adopted by non-Semitic people they developed into both: the alphabet in Europe and syllabic script forms in South Asia, with variants along the old trade routes which connected Central Asia and China with the West.

The characteristics of the Semitic script are the characteristics of the Semitic language: the meaning of a word is borne by the consonants (usually three), vowels play a secondary part and serve mainly to fashion grammatical forms. Thus k–t–b, depending on the interpolated vowels, can stand for 'book', 'to write', 'writer', 'written', 'wrote', 'to read books' etc. The absence of vowel signs was to some extent remitted, quite early on, by the use of consonant signs such as j and w for the representation of long vowels ī (ē) and ū (ō) and the sign for the glottal stop (*āleph*) for ā. Though this convention was retained it was rarely used consistently. Only at a much later date — the middle of the 1st millennium AD — was the possibility of indicating vowels by diacritical marks introduced for languages such as Arabic, Hebrew or Syriac, but this convention remained strictly optional.

The advantages of the Semitic scripts over those discussed in the previous chapters are twofold: writing can be done more quickly (demanding less skill), and less space is required for information storage. Whether the Semitic (or alphabetic) script is in itself an easier or simpler form of writing is less certain; after all, considerable powers of abstraction are needed to break down a language into its smallest possible components (phonemes) — in the case of early Semitic scripts not more than twenty-two different signs (representing consonantal phonemes). Indeed neither the Semitic consonant script nor the Roman alphabet has been a panacea for abolishing illiteracy. They provided the possibility but this possibility was not used before economic conditions arose (with the Industrial Revolution, colonial expansion and administration etc.) which created a definite need for literacy in a wider spectrum of society. In Europe and in the Western countries this did not happen before the 19th century. In Africa, Asia and Latin America this need is still largely absent and literacy is therefore as far removed from the majority of the people as it was in ancient Egypt, Mesopotamia, China, pre-Columbian America or medieval Europe.

The question of the origin of the Semitic script is one of the most debated subjects in the history of writing, and one that has occupied writers and scholars from antiquity to the present day. Was it an independent invention of the Semitic people, or an adapted borrowing from one of the prevailing scripts of antiquity — Egyptian, Cuneiform, Cretan, Cypriote, Hittite? All that seems reasonably certain is the fact that a consonantal script developed among Semitic people on the eastern shore of the Mediterranean some time between 1800–1300 BC. The use of single consonant signs however was, as we have seen, considerably older (see p.62).

The eastern shore of the Mediterranean was a highly cosmopolitan area, a meeting-place between Egypt, Babylon, the Aegean and the rest of western Asia, and as such subject to much political pressure. The international character of the coastal towns required a knowledge of several languages and made much demand on scribes, who had to be conversant with different systems of writing. This was especially true for scribes in the

52 Sandstone sphinx inscribed with the name of the goddess Ba'alat. From Serabit el Khadim, Sinai, 15th century BC. (British Museum; Department of Western Asiatic Antiquities; 41748)

employment of traders — for traders want to be understood, unlike politically dominant priests and administrators who can put the onus for understanding on others. Judging from archaeological evidence, some only discovered in the last few decades, several attempts at creating a simpler, basically consonant-orientated form of writing seem to have been made towards the middle of the 2nd millennium BC.

But though it is undoubtedly true that the change to a consistent and exclusive use of a phonetic script system occurred in this area at a certain time, it would not be correct to equate this development with the actual 'invention' of the phonetic principle as such. Nearly all systems so far discussed included and made use of phonetic elements; in most of them phonetic elements represented an integral, and in some the dominant, element. What must also be borne in mind is the fact that though the consonant script was a more economic way to express language, by being so it irreversibly interpolated the sound element between the thought, the storage of thought, and again, the retrieval of thought.

Among the many theories concerning the origin of the Semitic consonant script, the one claiming Egyptian connections has for long been the most popular — despite the fact that the factual (archaeological) evidence on which this theory rests is decidely slender.

In the winter of 1904–5 the British archaeologist Flinders Petrie found in the ancient malachite and copper mines of Sinai (worked for many centuries by Semitic slaves), and above all in and around the ruins of the temple of the Egyptian goddess Hathor, a number of short inscriptions which he dated *c.*1500 BC. He abstracted thirty-two different letter signs from these somewhat carelessly written hieroglyphs. In 1916 the British Egyptologist, Gardiner, after attempts at reading the script by inserting Egyptian values had failed, tried (inspired by possible connections with Phoenician script forms) to read the inscription in Semitic and succeeded, to begin with, in identifying a frequently recurring group of four signs, namely b–'–l–t, as *ba'alat* (fig. 52), which he interpreted as the Semitic name for the goddess Hathor. Based on this assumption he drew up a table for what was to become known as the Sinai script, which many scholars equated with proto-Semitic, the long sought forerunner of the old North Semitic script. The process by which those (badly drawn) hieroglyphs had become Semitic consonant signs was, according to Gardiner, as follows: the name of the object denoted by the Egyptian hieroglyph was translated into Semitic and the Semitic word provided, by the acrophonic principle, the new value for this sign (e.g. the Egyptian sign for 'house' (p–r) stands, when translated into Semitic, for *bet* and can thus be used for *b*, and so forth).

This seems a somewhat tortuous route; especially if one considers that the Egyptians already possessed a consonant script, namely the twenty-four single consonant signs which since early times had formed an integral part of the Egyptian system of writing. But such suggestions have generally been countered by the argument that anybody who knew the whole Egyptian (or cuneiform) system would also have been hampered by the sheer weight of tradition attached to it, and that it would have been easier for less informed persons (Semitic slaves working in the mines?) to take at random some Egyptian hieroglyphs and use them for their own language. Well, perhaps. Gardiner's theory was further enlarged by scholars such as A. Schmitt and others who not only declared the creation of the Semitic script an *Urerfindung* but felt that in the whole history of humankind the decisive step from idea script to sound script was made only once (probably amongst the Sumerians) and in all likelihood by just one person (AS, p.326). This however leads straight into the realm of First Causes and so uncomfortably close to theological thinking. Indeed many of the scholars working on the question of the origin of 'proper' writing — which they equated with the Semitic 'alphabet' — were persons deeply steeped in Biblical thinking, whether Christian or Jewish.

Whatever the exact origin of the Semitic script, there can be no doubt that it became one of the most powerful instruments for the dissemination of knowledge, stimulating the development and growth of new and highly efficient forms of writing in Europe and Asia, and becoming the vehicle for the spread of three major religious cultures, namely Christianity, Hinduism/Buddhism and Islam, while at the same time safeguarding, if not spreading, Judaism — which, after the rise of Christianity, became a strictly non-proselytizing religion.

North Semitic scripts

The Semitic scripts fall into two, considerably different, main branches: the North Semitic and the South Semitic cycle of scripts (with the latter being less important). The North Semitic scripts in turn split into various branches; the two most important ones, which became in one way or another responsible for the development of a large number of contemporary forms of writing, were the Phoenician and the Aramaic.

PHOENICIAN

The Phoenicians, whose recorded history begins *c*. 1600 BC, with the expansion of Egyptian power in western Asia, had at one point settled along the seashore of Syria/Lebanon. From then on essentially a seafaring nation, they were brilliant navigators who ventured far beyond the Pillars of Hercules (Gibraltar), the much feared boundary of the ancient Mediterranean world, reaching at least as far as Cornwall, and the west coast of Africa (and at the beginning of the 7th century BC they probably circumnavigated Africa). With an eye to possible trading monopolies they carefully guarded the secrets of their discoveries and sea-routes, and though much that was previously attributed to Phoenician influence must now be regarded as a legacy of the preceding Cretan trading empire, by the 12th century BC they were certainly a political reality in the Aegean. Phoenician city-states enjoyed the greatest amount of independent power in the period between the withdrawal of Egyptian rule from Syria and the western advance of the Assyrians.

The Phoenician language belongs to that sub-division of the Semitic language known as Canaanite, which includes Hebrew and the dialect of Moab. Although not a particularly literate people themselves, their main interest being trade, the Phoenicians became instrumental in the diffusion of the Semitic consonant-script throughout most parts of their trading empire (inscriptions have been found in Cyprus, North Africa, Malta, Sicily, Sardinia, Marseilles, Greece and Spain) and, indirectly at least, in the creation of the Greek alphabet — which was to become the basis of Western civilization.

The development of the Phoenician script (13th–3rd centuries BC) in all its colonial sub-divisions — Cypro-Phoenician (c. 10th–2nd centuries BC) and the Carthaginian or Punic script with its secondary branches (the last discovered Punic inscription dates from the 3rd century AD) — was, like that of the early Hebrew and early Aramaic scripts, purely external. The number of letters (twenty-two) and their phonetic value remained the same, and the direction of writing stayed horizontal, with the script running from right to left in nearly all recorded cases (fig. 53).

53 *Phoenician inscription on stone commemorating the dedication of gold plating by Melek-Yathon, king of Kition and Idalion (Cyprus) to the god Rešef-Milak. From Idalion, Cyprus, 391 BC. (British Museum; Department of Western Asiatic Antiquities; 125315)*

ARAMAIC

The original home of the Aramaic-speaking people is unknown; they apparently entered Syria and Mesopotamia from north-eastern Arabia in waves of immigration mainly between the 13th and 11th centuries BC. This was a period of great political and social instability, and the newcomers seem to have taken ample advantage of the situation. Soon they established a chain of small, but strategically well-placed, kingdoms along the international trading highways, with Damascus, Aleppo and Carchemish as some of the most important centres. Their political prominence was short-lived, and during the 8th century BC they again lost their independence to the Assyrians. Culturally and economically however they not only survived the decay of their city-states, but by the 7th century BC the Aramaic language, written in the Aramaic script, became the *lingua franca* of the empire. Under the Persian Archimaenides, Aramaic was one of the official languages, and the principal speech and script of traders between Egypt and India. Whereas the Phoenician script, despite its wide use among trading communities, had been a national script, the use of the Aramaic script was not politically motivated, and therefore was never

54 Part of a story written in cursive Aramaic on papyrus. From Elephantine, Egypt, 5th century BC. (British Library; Oriental Collections; Pap. CVI. A)

endowed with, or hampered by, nationalistic feelings: it was freely used by many different nations for purely practical purposes.

The outward appearance of the oldest Aramaic letter-signs differed little at first from those of the Phoenician script, but gradually special characteristics began to emerge: the tops of certain letters such as b, d, and r (originally closed) became open; a tendency to reduce the numbers of separate strokes in certain letters appeared; and finally angles became more rounded, and ligatures were introduced — in other words, the whole script became slightly more cursive (fig. 54). Until the 3rd–2nd century BC the Aramaic script preserved a fairly homogeneous form. After that it split into several branches which developed independently of each other, some of them gaining great prominence in their own right. These were the Hebrew square script, the Palmyra script, the Syriac script, the Nabataean and the Arabic script, and the Mandaic script. In Iran and in South and Central Asia the Aramaic script gave rise to a great many borrowings, which will be discussed later.

HEBREW

A third offshoot of the North Semitic script was Paleo-Hebrew, or, as it is sometimes referred to, Old Canaanite. This was a strictly national script more or less restricted to the people of Judea. By the 5th–4th century BC it was supplanted by one of the offshoots of the Aramaic script, namely the Square Hebrew. According to both Christian and Jewish tradition, the 5th-century reformer of Judaism, Ezra, was responsible for the adoption of this script for the writing of the Scriptures (HJ, p.305), thus giving it the official seal of approval and safeguarding its future prominence. Square Hebrew became the Hebrew script as such and after the 2nd century BC was the one most used by Jewish communities. Its outward appearance changed little, despite the fact that after the Babylonian exile an increasing number of Jews lived outside Palestine — an indication perhaps of connections between scribal schools inside and outside Palestine. Today it is still the vehicle for the religious and secular literature of all Jews, having gained a new status with the foundation of the state of Israel.

Square Hebrew letters are bold and well proportioned, though strictly speaking the invisible frame within which each letter is written (nearly all letters have a top bar or head, many have a base as well) is rectangular rather than square. The letters m, n, p, ts and one form of k have two forms, one when standing initially or medially, and another in a final position. Like all Semitic scripts Square Hebrew is a purely consonantal script — though, as we have already seen, some letters, generally referred to as *matres lectionis*, could be used for the representation of long vowels. In addition letters were used as numerical signs, the first nine representing units (1–9), the next nine representing the tens (10–90), and the last four the numbers 100, 200, 300 and 400.

When Biblical Hebrew became extinct as a spoken language, familiarity with its pronunciation decreased and the need for some form of vocalic distinction to safeguard the correct reading of the Hebrew Scriptures grew more urgent. According to the Talmud, 'the omission or addition of one letter might mean the destruction of the whole world' — a sentiment shared and repeated almost verbatim by the Indian Brahmins in relation to their sacred (orally transmitted) Vedic texts. It is not altogether clear when and how vocalization by means of punctuation marks, consisting of little dots or dashes placed above or below the consonants, was first introduced, but it was probably towards the 5th or 6th century AD, with the older Syriac vowel indiction system acting as model. Three main systems of vocalization are known; the Babylonian, the Palestinian and the Tiberian (fig. 55). The use of punctuation marks remained strictly optional, however; they are never used on synagogue scrolls, but appear regularly in the printing of the Bible.

55 Pentateuch, *accompanied by* Masorah Magna *and* Parva. *Square Hebrew with Tiberian type of vocalization. Early 10th century. (British Library; Oriental Collections; Or. 4445, f. 98r)*

56 A code by Jacob ben Asher; Rabbinical hand, 1475 AD. (British Library; Oriental Collections; Harl. 5716; f. 79r)

During the long centuries of the Diaspora, local styles developed — despite the continuous effort of scribes to remain faithful to the traditional form of letters, especially when copying the Torah scrolls. The two main types are Ashkenazi, used in north and eastern Germany, and Sephardic, used in Spain and in the Mediterranean world. The Hebrew script also had to adapt itself to the writing of other languages such as Arabic, Persian, Turkish, the language of Jews in China and India and to Judaeo-German and Judaeo-Spanish. In addition to the square script two other styles were used; the rabbinic (fig. 56), used mainly by medieval Jewish savants, and a cursive script, which became

57 Syriac manuscript containing the Recognitions of Clement of Rome *and other works;*
Estrangela hand; Edessa, 412 AD. *(British Library; Oriental Collections;*
Add. 12150, f. 171r)

responsible for the creation of many local variations in the Levant, Morocco, Spain and Italy.

SYRIAC

The Syriac script (fig. 57) played an important role in the history, development and dissemination of eastern Christianity. It shows, especially in its earliest forms, a close relationship with another offshoot of Aramaic, namely the cursive form of the Palmyra script — both having a tendency for their letters to be joined together. The order of the letters is the same as in Hebrew (a definite order of letters being one of the characteristics of all Semitic scripts), though there is some difference in the naming of the letters. As in Arabic, most letters are written differently according to whether they stand alone, at the beginning of a word, at the end of it, or joined on one or both sides to another letter.

Syriac was predominantly the language and script of Christian literature. Indeed all original documents written in Syriac deal exclusively with Christian subjects. Antioch and Edessa were important centres of early Christianity and remained so until the 7th century AD, when in the course of the Islamic conquest Syriac was replaced by Arabic. At Edessa the Christian faith was preached as early as the 2nd century, and from there it spread to Persia and the East. In the 3rd century the Scriptures were translated from the Greek, which meant that a great number of Greek words had to be transcribed into Syriac. The difficulties of transcribing words from a non-Semitic language, already written in an alphabetic script, into a Semitic consonant script was no doubt a contributory factor in the development of the three vocalization systems, namely:

(1) The Nestorian system, the earliest, which consisted of a combination of the consonants *w* and *y* and a dot placed above or below it, and of one or two dots placed above or below the consonant to be vocalized.

(2) The Jacobite system, created *c*, 700 AD, which consisted of small Greek letters placed below or above the line.

(3) The late Syriac system, consisting of a combination of diacritical vowel marks and small Greek letters.

Over the centuries, variations of the original Syriac scripts, mainly based on the above vocalization systems, came into being. The most important of these, and the only one in existence until *c*.500 AD, is the so-called Estrangela (from *satar angelo* – evangelical; DD, p. 221). In the middle of the 5th century the Syriac Church was divided by two great heresies hinging on the question of the true nature of Christ: the Nestorians (East Syrians), who held that in Christ's person a divine and a human nature existed side by side; and the Jacobites (West Syrians), who believed that Christ's person was undifferentiated, being simultaneously divine and human. As a result the Syriac language split into two dialects, developing two different styles of writing. The Jacobite variety became the one furthest removed from the original Estrangela, and remained in use until the 16th century. The Nestorian hand at first (until *c*.900 AD) differed little from Estrangela, but it was to gain far greater importance and influence later. In the 19th century it became the model for the New Syriac script, and was also used for printing by East-Syrian or neo-Aramaic Christian and Jewish communities living in the area around lake Urmia and near Mosul and Tabriz.

As the Nestorian Church grew in importance it became increasingly more involved in missionary activities. Since this proselytizing thrust coincided with the opening of the trade routes into Asia, Nestorian monks carried their teaching, their language and their script into the Kurdistan highlands, Central Asia and China (Marco Polo describes the trade routes from Baghdad to Peking as being lined by Nestorian chapels), to the Turki and Mongol tribes of Central Asia, to Turkistan and to the Sogdians. In the 7th century Nestorian monks reached the south-west of India, now the state of Kerala, and gave a new impetus to the Christian communities founded there some centuries earlier. To reproduce the native Malayalam language, eight more signs, borrowed from the syllabic Malayalam script, had to be added. Today a modified form of the Syriac script is still used for the liturgy of the local Saint Thomas Christians.

ARABIC

The Arabic script seems to have originated some time towards the end of the 4th, and during the 5th centuries AD from the script of the Nabataeans, originally Aramaic-speaking tribes living in the north, east and south of Sinai. Only a few examples of pre-Islamic writing have so far been discovered. The Arabs, though a language-conscious and poetically gifted people, had little use for writing. They were predominantly nomads without any strong central organization and, like most people of antiquity, they transmitted their literary compositions by word of mouth, each poet training a group of specially-chosen disciples for this purpose. In most of the cases so far discussed the stimulus for the advancement of writing had been an upsurge in productivity, commerce and administration. In the case of the Arabs the stimulus did not come from material advancement, but flowed directly from the creation of the Islamic faith in the first half of the 7th century. The text of the Koran, revealed to Muhammad by the one and only God, and reverently written down by the Prophet's followers (Islamic traditions claim that Muhammad, like the majority of his contemporaries, was illiterate), had to be recorded and taught without altering a single syllable. Thus a sudden change of attitude occurred in the second part of the 7th century, and writing assumed greater importance in the life of the people. This meant not only writing, but also calligraphy (see p.165), since the revelations of God had to be proclaimed not only accurately but also with proper reverence — which meant as beautifully and perfectly as was humanly possible. The prohibition against the representation of all living forms acted as an additional, if negative, incentive to this end by channelling much creative energy into the art of writing. This in due course gave rise to a number of well-defined and exceedingly pleasing styles.

The Arabic script consists of twenty-nine letter signs, made up of the original twenty-two Semitic consonant signs, plus seven more designed to represent the finer shades of pronunciation required by the Arabic language. Grammatically and graphically they are arranged differently from those of other Semitic scripts. Some Arab traditions name al-Khalil (d.786?) as the inventor of the vocalization system which gained prominence in the 8th century, though its roots almost certainly go back to an earlier pre-Islamic period (YHS, p. 13), perhaps again Syriac models. (Besides the vowel marks the Arabic script uses diacritical points to distinguish between otherwise identical letters.) The system of vocalization itself is relatively simple, consisting of vowel marks which are written above or below the consonant preceding the vowel, and a sign indicative of the absence of a vowel. To some extent vocalization was less important than in the case of other Semitic scripts, since Arabic remained a living language. On the other hand the sacred nature of the Koran made it necessary to treat the text with the utmost care, with the result that vocalization is an important feature of Koranic texts.

Already in the early Islamic period two distinct styles of writing existed: one bold and angular, the other more rounded and cursive. The first one, basically a monumental style, formal and geometrical in its features, was termed Kufic (fig. 58) after the Mesopotamian city of Kufah where it is said to have been developed. Kufic was used with great effect on stone and metal for carved and painted inscriptions on the walls of mosques. With the rise of Islam it also became a favoured style for the writing of the Koran. By the 12th century the use of Kufic began to decline. The other style, Naskhi (fig. 59), became the model for a number of different styles which developed at the courts of non-Arab rulers; it is also the parent of modern Arabic writing.

Of all the Semitic scripts, Arabic has gained the greatest prominence. Today it is the most widely-used form of writing after the Roman alphabet. Islam had united the Arabs, and by doing so it had unleashed tremendous expansionist energies, fanned by a burning

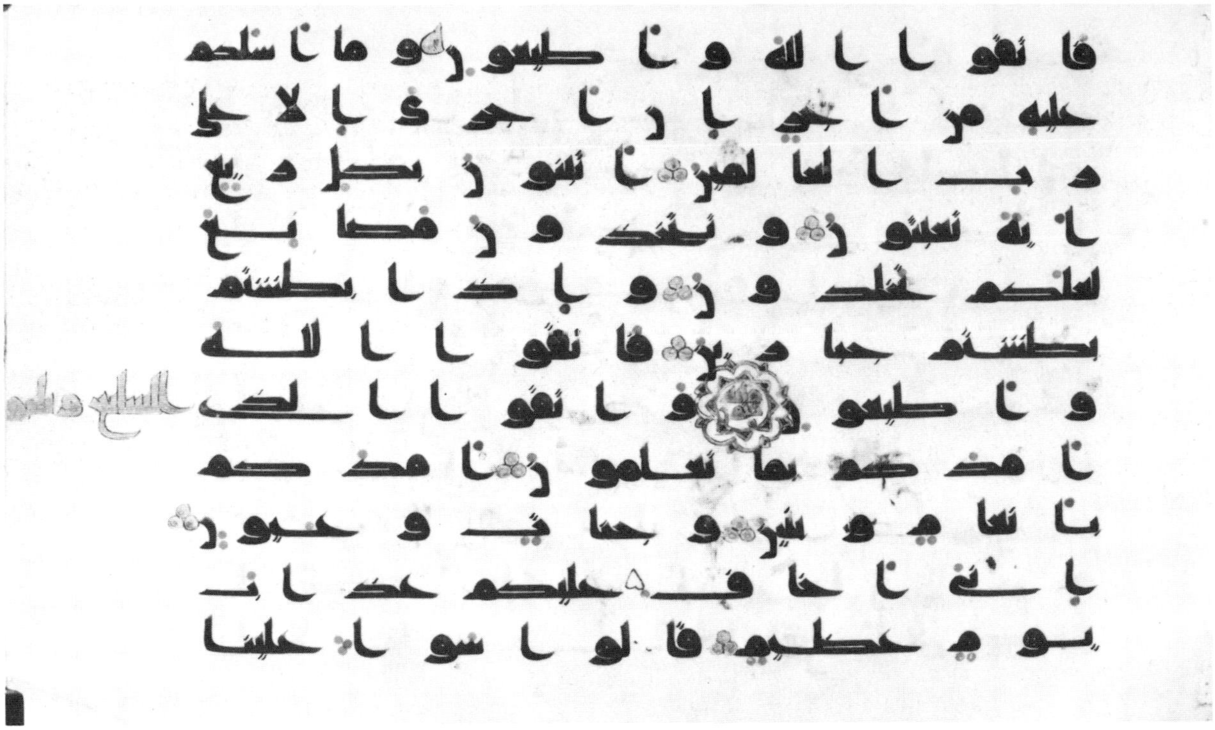

58

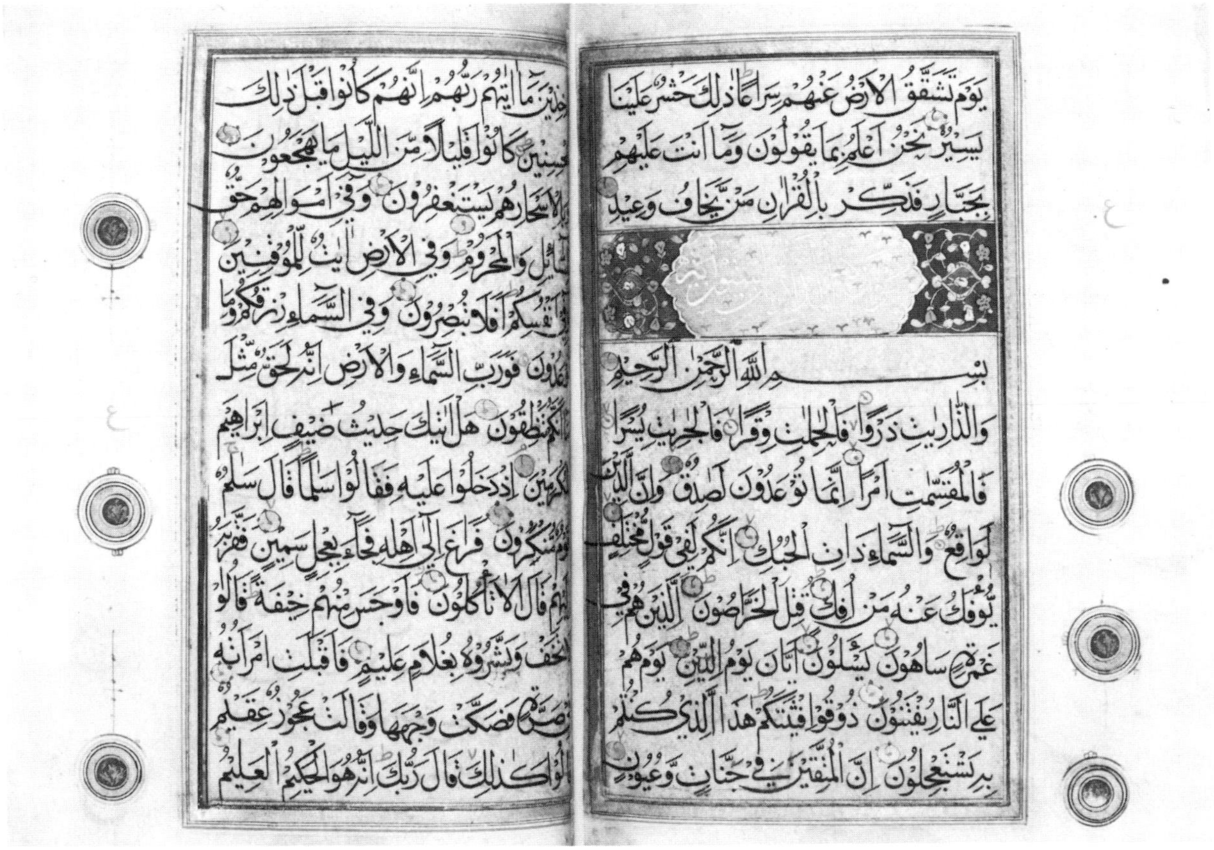

59

60 South Arabian inscription recording the construction of two aqueducts by Laḥay ʿAtat Šaṭran, Kabir of Fayśan, from Saba, South Arabia, 2nd century BC. (British Museum; Department of Western Asiatic Antiquities; 103021)

proselytizing zeal. Hardly more than a century after the death of Muhammad (632 AD) the new faith extended from Spain to India and China, and in consequence the Arabic script had to be adapted to several non-Semitic languages in Europe, Asia and Africa. The use of the Arabic script spread even further than the Arabic language, for since the Koran has to be studied in Arabic, every Muslim, whatever his nationality and daily speech, must, in theory at least, become conversant with the writing and reading of Arabic.

South Semitic scripts

The origin of the South Semitic scripts (which were discovered only during the 19th and 20th centuries in the course of adventurous and at times disastrous expeditions) is to some extent still being debated (DD, p. 277). Between the 8th century BC and the 6th century AD, southern Arabia was an important centre of civilization, an agriculturally well-tended region, with flourishing city-states, where goods from India and the East were trans-shipped to be carried overland to ports in the eastern Mediterranean.

South Semitic scripts can be divided into two sub-groups: the North Arabian scripts, used, according to inscriptions so far discovered, in north-west Arabia up to Syria, and the South Arabian scripts (fig. 60), which seem to have had their area of dissemination in the south of the Arabian peninsula and on the African side lying opposite.

◁ *58 Koran written in Kufic; probably from North Africa; 9th/10th century. (British Library; Oriental Collections; Or. 1397, f.13r)*

59 Koran copied in fine large Indian Naskhi verging on Thuluth; 1612 AD. (British Library; Oriental Collections; Or. 13203, ff. 367v/368r)

SABAEAN

A large number of inscriptions so far discovered are in the South Arabian Sabaean script, an elegant and imposing form of writing, decidedly monumental in character, with its letters carefully arranged and executed — often, especially after 300 BC, in hollow relief. A distinctive feature of the Sabaean script are the so-called 'monograms', that is the combination of several letters into a coherent group.

ETHIOPIC

Towards the end of the 1st millennium BC and about the beginning of the Christian era, South Arabian Semites, together with their language and some form of South Arabian script, migrated to Africa where they established a kingdom with Axum as its capital, in the neighbourhood of the old Meroïtic kingdom (see p.65). The indigenous language of Ethiopia (or Abyssinia, as it is often called) was non-Semitic, belonging to the Cushitic group of languages. The earliest evidence of a decidedly Ethiopian form of writing (on coins and inscriptions) comes from the 4th century AD, the time when the country was first introduced to Christianity by Greek-speaking Syrian missionaries. Inscriptions from this period are still strongly intermixed with South Arabic (script and language) and not yet vocalized. Among the Semitic scripts so far discussed, that of Ethiopia was to develop a number of unique characteristics, which included a visually different appearance, a new arrangement of the letters, another direction of writing (from left to right) and, most important, a systematic and obligatory form of vocalization (fig. 61). Whereas in Hebrew, Arabic and Syriac, systems were devised which indicated vowels by additional points above or below the consonants, in the case of the Ethiopic script the vowels were, and still are, indicated by the addition of small appendages to the basic consonant, either to the right or left, or at the top or bottom, or by shortening or lengthening one of the main strokes, or by other differentiations. The resulting script, which consists of twenty-seven consonant signs and seven vowel indications, bears great resemblance to the syllabic scripts of India; it has in fact itself become a syllabic script. In addition, in a manner similar to Indian conventions, all consonants are perceived with an inherent vowel, a short *a*, unless otherwise indicated.

This transformation of a consonant script into a syllabic one has given rise to a good deal of speculation. Causes put forward for it have included the inventiveness of one particular person, a general script reform, and/or the influence of foreign models — Greek, or (more plausible perhaps) Indian.

Semitic scripts in Iran and Central Asia

Semitic traders and Christian missionaries, as well as fugitive communities, took the knowledge of their particular form of writing along the old caravan routes across Central Asia and right into the border areas of China. Written records and accurate information storage had become an important tool of commerce and religious propagation. In consequence various scripts, some more and some less effecively, some long-lived and some quickly forgotten, replaced or improved, developed in Iran and Central Asia. Nearly all of them derived directly or indirectly from Aramaic (see p.91), the long-established common script and language of traders between Egypt and India, and the script which the newly-founded Christian communities in the Middle East had quickly adapted to their own needs.

After the 2nd century BC the Persians began to reduce the twenty-two Aramaic letter

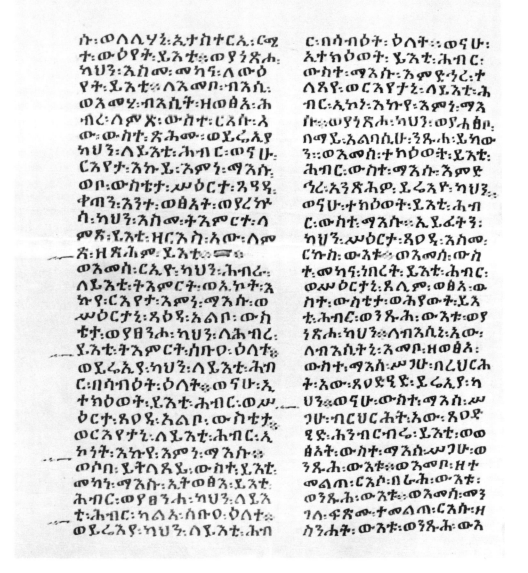

61 Octateuch; *Ethiopic, 15th century. (British Library; Oriental Collections; Or. 480, f.100v)*

signs to a mere fourteen, intermixing them with obsolete Aramaic words used like ideograms; for example, the Persian word *shah–an–shah* – 'king of kings', an important title of the Sassanian rulers, was represented by the Aramaic *mlk'n mlk*, but read *shah–an–shah* — an altogether rather unsatisfactory form of writing. More satisfactory was Avestan, the script used for recording the Zoroastrian scriptures, which employed fifty different letter signs and was somewhat better suited to the recording of an Indo-European language. Eventually the Persian religious leader Mani (*d.* 276 AD) improved the faulty and ambiguous Middle Persian script by introducing the Syriac consonant script, another offshoot of Aramaic, which he adapted successfully to Pahlavi. The cumbersome old ideograms were largely abandoned, and the new writing was used for Sogdian and eventually spread to the Turkish people of Central Asia.

62 Sogdian; fragment of a Manichaean or Zoroastrian text; 8th century AD (British Library; Oriental Collections; Or. 8212 (82))

SOGDIAN

The Sogdian script plays an important part in the history and development of Central Asian writing. Sogdian was an Iranian language, with a script, purely consonantal in structure, consisting of seventeen letters plus two more special signs. To begin with, every letter was written separately, but around the 7th century AD a more cursive and flowing hand developed, which linked the individual signs to each other by a continuous base-line (fig. 62). In all there existed three variations of the Sogdian script: (1) for Buddhist works and for everyday use, (2) for Manichaean works, and (3) for Christian texts.

UIGHUR

Until the beginning of the 20th century the existence of the Sogdian language and script had been largely unknown. What was known was Uighur, a script which had developed in the 8th century from a later form of Sogdian, and which survived into the second part of the 17th century (fig. 63). Indeed some offshoots of Uighur were still in use between 1940–45 when for political reasons the Russian Cyrillic alphabet, slightly modified, was introduced for writing the Mongolian language as well as all modern Turkish languages in those areas of Central Asia which had become part of the Soviet Union. To begin with, the Uighur script had been used by the Turkish Buddhists of Chinese Turkestan. It was not a

63 Sekiz Yükmek bögüzūk arviš. *An apocryphal Buddhist* sūtra. *Uighur, 8th century* AD.
(British Library; Oriental Collections; Or. 8212 (104))

particularly good instrument for writing Turkish, especially when the dots which helped to distinguish certain letters were omitted. The direction of the script was at first purely Semitic, from right to left, but later, under Chinese influence, it was written in vertical columns reading from left to right. When Islam reached Turkestan the Uighur script was replaced by Arabic, but was revived under quite remarkable circumstances some time later.

Until the 12th century the Mongols had never used any form of writing. Consisting of small groups of nomadic tribes, basically made up of extended family clans, they came together in times of need in loose and purely temporary alliances, in which amorphous structure they had never felt the need for any codified form of information storage. All this changed dramatically when Chingiz Khan (*d.* 1227) welded the often feuding groups into a formidable fighting machine and within a relatively short time established an empire, or at least a sphere of influence, which eventually stretched from Hungary to China. An empire of this size and magnitude, consisting of so many different nations, many of them culturally superior to the Mongols, needed organization, some form of administration and, if not a common language, then at least a common script. According to traditional records it was the great Khan himself who in 1206 AD decided that all officers and dignitaries as well as the members of the ruling Mongol families had to learn to read and write, choosing Uighur for this purpose. Thus Uighur became the script of the Mongol chancellery, just as the Uighur

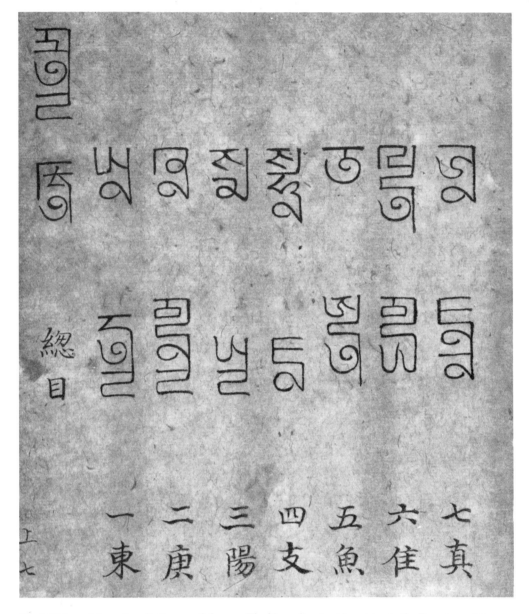

64 *A Chinese-Mongolian dictionary of rhymes. The Mongolian part is written in the Passepa script; 14th century. (British Library; Oriental Collections; Or. 6972)*

language served as the language of diplomacy in the whole of Central Asia. It was not an ideal solution and soon attempts were made to replace the Uighur language by Mongolian, written in a script better suited to its linguistic peculiarities. In 1272 the so-called Passepa script (fig. 64), an adaptation of the Tibetan seal script, was introduced by order of the Mongol ruler Kublai Khan, only to be replaced in 1310 by the so-called Kalika script, the forerunner of modern Mongolian (fig. 65). Kalika is yet another adaptation of the Uighur script, with the addition of special distinguishing marks and five signs taken from Tibetan.

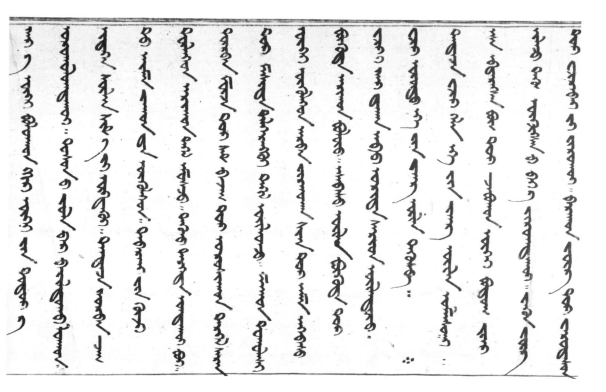

65 *Fragment of the Mongolian version of the* Kanjur; *18th century. (British Library; Oriental Collections; Add. 27568 B)*

The order of the letters followed the Indian model, the vowel indications are similar to those of Uighur, and the script is written in vertical columns from left to right.

Two further scripts evolved from the Mongolian, both more accurate in the representation of vowels, both surviving in one way or another until the 1940s: the script of the Kalmucks and the Manchu script.

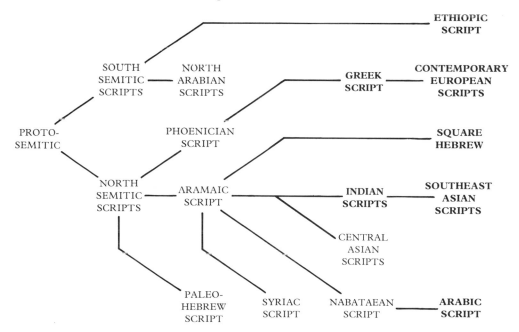

Indian and Southeast Asian scripts

Indian scripts

A knowledge of writing seems to have been brought to India by Semitic traders, perhaps in the 7th or 6th century BC, or even earlier. To begin with, the new art did not make much impression on the cultural life of the people. Hinduism, with its emphasis on stratification and exclusiveness in all aspects of life, not only relied but insisted — more strongly than any other ancient civilization — on the oral transmission of its essentially religious literature. It was not until the Buddha and Mahavira (the founder of Jainism) had considerably disrupted the established order by propagating two heterodox movements which rejected caste, ritual and occupational exclusiveness in favour of a more egalitarian society, that a change in attitude made itself felt. Indeed the first literary evidence indicative of a more widespread use of writing, that is, one not exclusively related to trade and commerce, comes from Buddhist sources of the 5th century BC.

The earliest epigraphical records of a decidedly Indian script form are the often cited rock edicts of the Mauryan Emperor Ashoka (272–231 BC). Written in the language of the people, they served a double purpose: to proclaim the secular achievements of the Emperor who, after a series of ferocious wars and conquests, had created a more or less unified India (an achievement not repeated until 1947); and to announce his spiritual victory over such temporary ambitions, brought about by his conversion to Buddhism. The edicts are written in two different but already fully developed scripts: Kharoshthi and Brahmi.

KHAROSHTHI

Kharoshthi (fig. 66), short-lived and less important than Brahmi, never spread beyond a well-defined geographical area. It appeared in the north-west of India and in Central Asia on coins, wooden tablets, rough pieces of leather, some gems and on a few rock inscriptions between the 3rd century BC and the 3rd century AD; in Central Asia it survived sporadically until the 7th century AD. It was basically a commercial and clerical script, cursive in character, written from right to left, in most cases with obvious speed and not always too much attention to orthographical detail. In origin it seems to have been decidedly Semitic. Aramaic (fig. 54) had for long been the script and speech of international trade. Under Darius I, the Persians conquered the Indus region and used Aramaic, together with Greek, as the language of administration. The diplomatic intercourse between the Persian and Indian chancelleries led in all likelihood to the use of the Aramaic script for Indian languages (north-western Prakrit), and modifications according to the (phonetic) principles of the Brahmi script might have fostered the development of Kharoshthi.

BRAHMI

Only a few of Ashoka's inscriptions are written in Kharoshthi; the rest, displayed throughout his vast empire, are in Brahmi (fig. 67) — a script which was to play an important role in the development of writing in South and Southeast Asia. Directly or

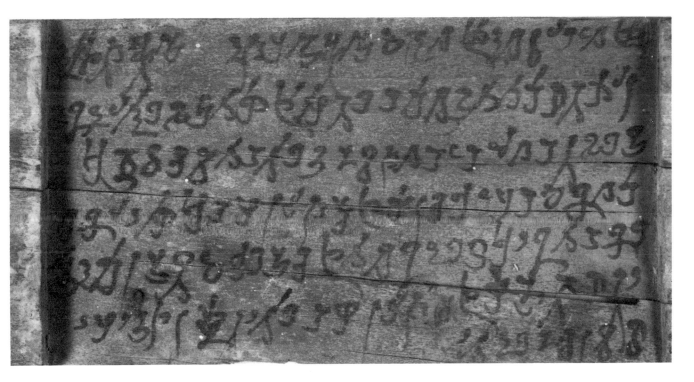

66 *North-western Prakrit written in the Kharoshthi character; from Central Asia, 3rd century* AD. *(British Library; Oriental Collections; N.xv. 357 (1675))*

67 *Fragment from an Ashokan pillar, inscribed in Brahmi characters; 3rd century* BC. *(British Museum; Department of Oriental Antiquities; 1880-21)*

indirectly, no less than about 200 different scripts can claim descent from Brahmi. Nearly all contemporary Indian scripts, with the exception of those imported by Islam, are in one way or another modelled on Brahmi — even those of the South which serve languages belonging to an altogether different family.

As far as the origin of Brahmi is concerned, conflicting theories have been put forward: the Greek alphabet, a mixture of Greek and Aramaic, the cuneiform script, a South Semitic prototype, a Dravidian (South Indian) form of writing, even Tantric symbols, have been suggested. Nowadays some Indian scholars tend to look for connections between Brahmi and the Indus script (see p.67), but such theories are based more on sentiment than scientific proof. The most widely accepted theory is still the one which derives Brahmi from a (North) Semitic source. We have no records of the early stages of Brahmi. To begin with, most writing was without doubt done on perishable materials, since engraving stone needs considerable skill and the availability of codified models, but by the 3rd century BC Brahmi had become perfectly adapted to the sounds of the Indian languages. This could hardly have been achieved by merchants, mostly concerned with speedy communication, but only by those well-versed in the science of phonetics. The correct pronunciation of the sacred Vedic hymns has always been an essential part of the ceremonial aspect of Hindu religion, and an exact, orally transmitted, knowledge of phonetics existed long before the Sanskrit grammarians codified the language in the 5th century BC and long before it was committed to writing. By the time of Ashoka, Brahmi, though not yet fully perfected, was already a most rational and scientific script, and one which provided Indian languages with an exact reflex of their pronunciation (something, for example, which can no longer be said about the alphabet and the English language).

What then are Indian scripts? They have been variously described as alphabetical, consonantal, or as an imperfect attempt to convert a consonant script into an alphabet. None of these descriptions can really be justified. Indian scripts are from their recorded beginnings clearly syllabic. They consist, with the exception of Tamil, of about forty-eight to fifty-four basic signs, which allow for a sophisticated level of manipulation. The particular features that distinguish all indigenous Indian scripts and also those derived from them are:

(1) All consonants are perceived as syllabic, that is, containing an inherent short *a*, the vowel which occurs most frequently in Indian languages.

(2) Vowel signs are written in their full form only if used on their own or in an initial position; in conjunction with a consonant they are abbreviated to auxiliary signs before, after, below or above the consonant sign.

(3) Consonants which have no vowel after them are if possible amalgamated, usually by writing one above the other, by forming ligatures or by having a special sign added to them, such as a stroke below or a dot above, indicative of the absence of any vowel. (This principle was already fully developed in Brahmi.)

(4) The arrangement of letters is strictly phonetic: the vowel signs, short and long, are listed first, followed by the diphthongs as understood in India. The consonants are arranged in seven groups indicative of the way in which they are pronounced, beginning with sounds produced at the lowest level of the larynx, and moving forward to those produced by the tongue, the lips etc. in the following order — (i) gutturals: ka, kha, ga, gha, ṅa; (ii) palatals: ca, cha, ja, jha, ña; (iii) cerebrals: ṭa, ṭha, ḍa, ḍha, ṇa; (iv) dentals: ta, tha, da, dha, na; (v) labials: pa, pha, ba, bha, ma; (vi) semi-vowels: ya, the various ra and la sounds and va; (vii) sibilants: sa, śa, ṣa and the aspirate ha. In languages

which have additional sounds, those are, as a rule, lodged in the system in a position appropriate to their phonetic value.

(5) The direction of all Indian scripts runs from left to right, with the exception of some of the earliest Brahmi inscriptions which were written from right to left or even boustrophedon.

Indian culture has always been plural in all its aspects. Even in the 3rd century BC the Brahmi script had not been completely homogeneous. After the 3rd and 4th centuries AD an increasingly large number of scripts began to become differentiated, forming localized groups which were not always easily definable and were often overlapping. Most of them are associated with the names of ruling dynasties, simply because whatever evidence exists comes mostly in the form of royal inscriptions on stone or metal. Surviving manuscripts, that is, records written on perishable materials, are (in India itself) rarely older than 500 years, thus post-dating the most important stylistic developments. Usually the climate has been blamed for this absence of material; but India is not the only country with climatic conditions adverse to the preservation of manuscripts. Though the climate did undoubtedly play an important part, equally important was the casual attitude to the written word which characterizes Hinduism. The text itself has always been considered immensely important, but the written record of it was merely one form of storage, and not the most revered one. Written records could be, and were, regularly copied, though often less faithfully than they were memorized, in order to safeguard the survival of the text. It was not until Muslim influence began to be felt, after the 12th century, that the 'book' in whatever form was eventually treated with the kind of respect originally reserved for the memorized text.

Linguistically and ethnically, the population of India can be divided into two main groups: the Indo-European speaking people of the north — descendants (though much intermixed) of the original Indo-Aryans, a pastoral people who moved into the north-west of India *c.* 1500 BC — and the Dravidians in the south. There are other minor groups, but those do not concern us in this context. In many ways the Dravidians (a term introduced by Robert Caldwell in the last century) are, as far as any definite classification of their linguistic and ethnic affinities or their original homeland is concerned, as elusive as the Sumerians of Mesopotamia (who, incidentally, also used an agglutinative language). But the modern scripts of the south, as well as those of Sri Lanka — which was colonized by both Indo-Aryans and Dravidians as the present population distribution testifies — ultimately go back to the Brahmi of the Ashoka inscriptions. At present India recognizes about fourteen official languages, written in nineteen different scripts (fig. 68).

ग्यारह बजे वहां पहुंचा था और पौने तीन बजे अवकाश पा यह सन्देश लाया हूं कि कमला अपनी भाभी माया के साथ आयेगी। उसकी मां तो रजनी भाभी के घर पर थी। उसके भाई बिहारी-

HINDI

ਉਲੂ ਵਲ ਵੇਖਿਆ ਈ ਨਾ ਜਾਏ। ਉਸ ਨਾਲ ਅੱਖਾ ਈ ਨਾ ਮਿਲਾਈਆਂ ਜਾਣ। ਪਿੱਛੇ-ਤਾ'ਨ ਤੁਰਦੇ ਤੁਰਦੇ ਸੀੜੀਆਂ ਤੋਂ ਕਾਗਜ ਚੁੱਕੇ ਜਾਣ... । ਜੇ ਉਲੂ ਉੱਡ ਕੇ ਖਾਏਗਾ ਵੀ ਜਾਂ ਦੰਦੀਆਂ ਵੱਢੇਗਾ ਤਾਂ ਵੀ ਮੂੰਹ ਤਾਂ ਬਚ ਈ ਜਾਏਗਾ। ਲੱਕ

GURMUKHI

68 Contemporary South Asian scripts.

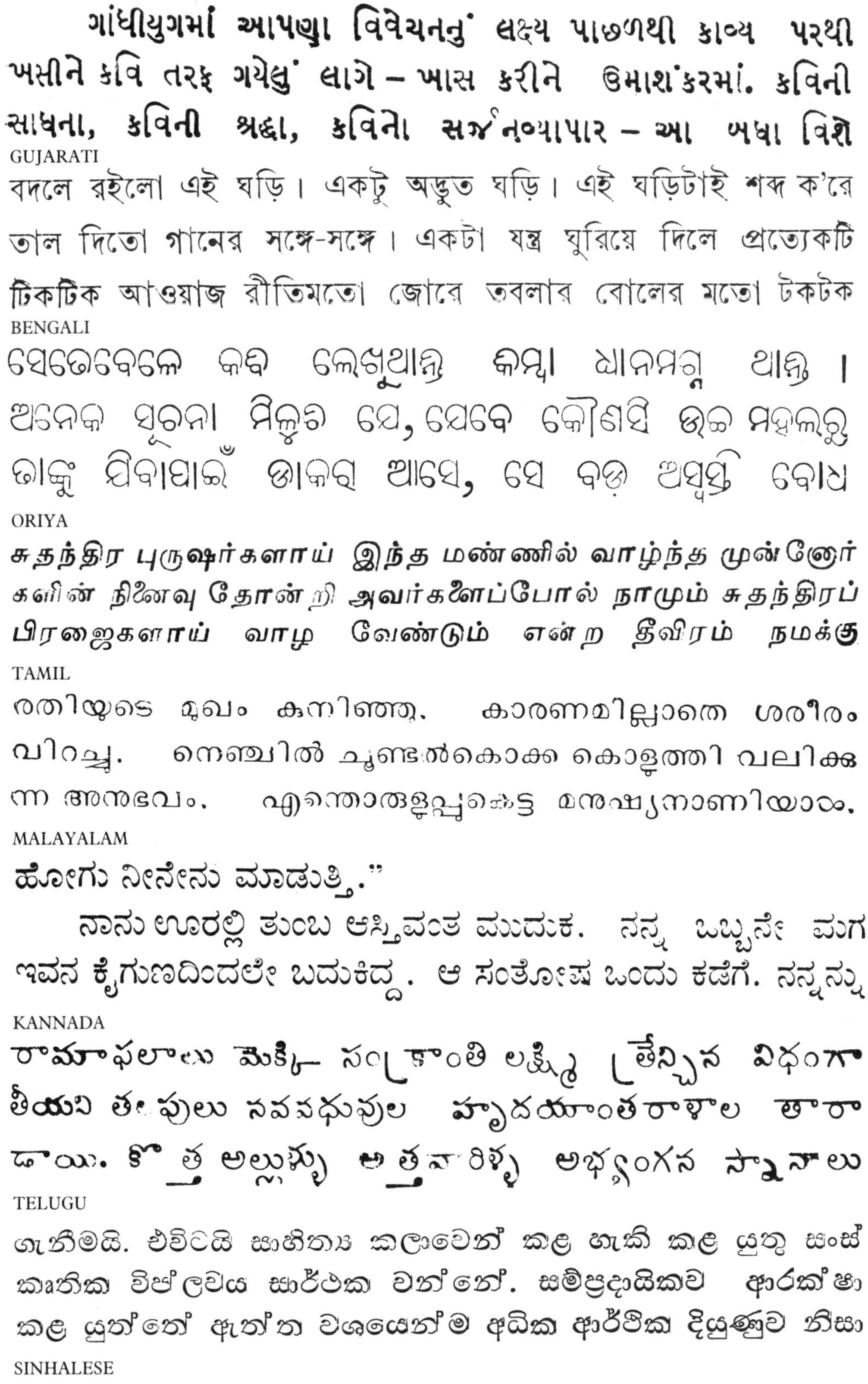

ગાંધીયુગમાં આપણા વિવેચનનું લક્ષ્ય પાછળથી કાવ્ય પરથી ખસીને કવિ તરફ ગયેલું લાગે – ખાસ કરીને ઉમાશંકરમાં. કવિની સાધના, કવિની શ્રદ્ધા, કવિનો સર્જનવ્યાપાર – આ બધા વિશે

GUJARATI

বদলে রইলো এই ঘড়ি। একটু অদ্ভুত ঘড়ি। এই ঘড়িটাই শব্দ ক'রে তাল দিতো গানের সঙ্গে-সঙ্গে। একটা যন্ত্র ঘুরিয়ে দিলে প্রত্যেকটি টিকটিক আওয়াজ রীতিমতো জোরে তবলার বোলের মতো টকটক

BENGALI

ସେତେବେଳେ କବ ଲେଖୁଥାନ୍ତି କମ୍ପା ଧାନମଗ୍ନ ଥାନ୍ତି। ଅନେକ ସୂଚନା ମିଳୁର ସେ, ଯେବେ କୌଣସି ଉଚ ମହଲର ଢାଙ୍କୁ ଯିବାପାଇଁ ଡାକରା ଆସେ, ସେ ବଡ଼ ଅସ୍ୱସ୍ତି ବୋଧ

ORIYA

சுதந்திர புருஷர்களாய் இந்த மண்ணில் வாழ்ந்த முன்னோர் களின் நினைவு தோன்றி அவர்களைப்போல் நாமும் சுதந்திரப் பிரஜைகளாய் வாழ வேண்டும் என்ற தீவிரம் நமக்கு

TAMIL

രതിയുടെ മുഖം കനിഞ്ഞു. കാരണമില്ലാതെ ശരീരം വിറച്ചു. നെഞ്ചില് ചൂണ്ടക്കൊക്ക കൊളുത്തി വലിക്ക ന്ന അനുഭവം. എന്തൊരുള്ളപ്പുകെട്ട മനുഷ്യനാണിയാം.

MALAYALAM

ಹೋಗು ನೀನೇನು ಮಾಡುತ್ತಿ."

ನಾನು ಊರಲ್ಲಿ ತಂಬ ಅಸ್ತಿವಂತ ಮುದುಕ. ನನ್ನ ಒಬ್ಬನೇ ಮಗ ಇವನ ಕೈಗುಣದಿಂದಲೇ ಬದುಕಿದ್ದ. ಆ ಸಂತೋಷ ಒಂದು ಕಡೆಗೆ. ನನ್ನನ್ನು

KANNADA

రామాఫలాలు మెక్కు సంక్రాంతి లక్ష్మి త్రేన్చిన విధంగా తీయవ తేపులు నవవధువుల హృదయాంతరాళాల తారా డాయా. కొత్త అల్లుళ్ళు అత్తవారిళ్ళు అభ్యంగన స్నానాలు

TELUGU

ඇනිමයි. එවිටඑ සඟිතය කලාවෙන් කල හැකි කල යුතු සංස් කෘතික විප්ලවය සාර්ථක වන්නේ. සම්ප්‍රදායිකව ආරක්ෂා කල යුත්තේ ඇත්ත වශයෙන්ම අධික ආර්ථික දියුණුව නිසා

SINHALESE

68 Contemporary South Asian scripts.

Language is an important and contentious issue in India; indeed the various states are based, at least in theory, on linguistic areas. The attempt by India's first Prime Minister to make Hindi, written in the Devanagari script, the official language of the whole sub-continent has never become a reality and as time goes by the chances of its doing so are becoming even less.

69 Saddharma puṇḍarīka sūtra. *Fragment of a manuscript from Gilgit (Kashmir) written in Central Asian upright Gupta; on birch bark, 7th–8th century AD. (British Library; Oriental Collections; Or. 11878 A)*

Most contemporary North Indian scripts can be traced back to the so-called Gupta script (fig. 69) which developed in the 4th century AD. The characteristic long top line of modern Devanagari, the most widespread script in India, seems to have developed from the top wedges caused originally by the stone cutter's tools when carving the Kutila (or Siddhamatrika) script, a later and highly important branch of Gupta.

TAMIL

In South India variants of Brahmi began to evolve from the 2nd century AD onwards. The ancestors of the Telugu-Kannada group become recognizable in certain local forms from around the 10th century. Modern Malayalam owes much to Grantha (see fig. 16) — the script used for the writing of Sanskrit in the Tamil country — and appears in inscriptions of between the 5th and 8th centuries. This leaves Tamil, the script of the most important Dravidian language, which does not fit as neatly as do other Indian scripts into the mould determined by Brahmi. Instead of the thirty-six or more basic syllabic consonants, Tamil has no more than eighteen. The same signs are used for voiced, unvoiced and aspirated forms. In addition Tamil has no sibilants (sa, śa and ṣa), no signs for two of the palatals (ja and jha) and no aspirate (ha). It also lacks ligatures, which in other modern scripts help to identify consonants used without the inherent short *a*. In other words, the principle of economy which we have already encountered in the case of the Cypriote and other Mediterranean syllabic scripts (see p.70) is taken to considerable lengths; and the ancient Tamil grammarians took pains to counterbalance this deficiency by carefully framing rules not only for correct pronunciation, but (especially) for euphony. Unlike other Indian scripts, Tamil is singularly unsuited to the writing of Sanskrit, the classical and liturgical language of Hindu India, and Grantha was used for this purpose.

Epigraphically the Tamil script becomes identifiable from the 8th century onwards — but this unfortunately means little, since writing on perishable materials in nearly all instances pre-dates, often considerably, the writing on stone or metal. From around the same period come records of another variant of the Tamil script, namely Vatteluttu (see fig. 16), a script which seems to have been widely used in the old Pandya kingdom. Various theories have been put forward concerning the origin of Vatteluttu and its connections with both the Tamil and the Brahmi scripts. Vatteluttu is a distinctly cursive script, slanting slightly to the left, in all appearance more suited to speed (and the stylus or pen, on palm leaf or some other perishable material) than to monumental use. It seems fairly certain that Vatteluttu is older than Tamil, but for quite some time the two seem to have existed side by side — rather like Brahmi and Kharoshthi in the 3rd century BC — one perhaps serving commercial and administrative needs, the other reserved for Imperial use. That both Brahmi-Grantha and Vatteluttu are responsible for the shaping of modern Tamil is borne out by a variety of facts: for example, the retained paucity of signs, four signs obviously taken from Vatteluttu for which there were no equivalents in Grantha, and the Brahmi-inspired order of signs. Taking speculation a step further, one could, without too much difficulty, visualize the possibility of Vatteluttu going back to some earlier and quite independent connections between southern India and the West, connections largely based on relations with Semitic, perhaps Phoenician traders. That such trading connections existed is borne out by a good deal of historical and literary evidence.

In the 15th century Vatteluttu disappeared from the Tamil country. In Kerala, the south-western part of the sub-continent, it stayed in use for another 200 years. Then a modified form of it, called Koleluttu, took its place. Among the Mappilas, descendants of early Arab traders, the knowledge of Koleluttu lingered on until it was superseded, only very recently, by a modified and exceedingly cumbersome form of the Arabic script.

Indian scripts in the Himalayan countries, Central Asia and the Far East

In the 3rd century BC Buddhism became the state religion of India. From then on, for well over a millennium, it maintained a dominant position on the sub-continent. Like other creeds created by the revolutionary vision of a small group centred around a single individual (for example, Christianity, Islam and Communism), Buddhism depended from the very beginning on its ability to increase its ranks quickly with a growing number of new converts. Propaganda was essential for its growth and survival, for which the multiplication of basic texts by writing (and later by printing) was more effective (and more controllable) than oral transmission. Together with traders and colonists, monks and missionaries have indeed always played an important part in the dissemination of writing.

In India the 1st millennium AD was a period of great cultural expansion into Central and Southeast Asia. The export of manuscripts to Buddhist centres in Chinese Turkestan brought the Gupta script to Central Asia, where it became instrumental in the development of a variety of scripts which served not only Sanskrit but also Iranian and Tocharian dialects; descendants of Gupta writing remained in use in Central Asia until after the 10th century. Buddhism and Buddhist manuscripts took the Siddhamatrika script as far as China, where, under the name of Siddham, it introduced the knowledge of Indian syllabic writing and a phonetic letter arrangement. In the wake of Buddhism this knowledge spread from China to Korea and Japan and became a contributory factor in some major script reforms (see pp.83–84).

Tibetan civilization as we know it today, and the origin of the Tibetan script, are closely associated with Song-tsen-gam-po, who ruled the country between 620 and 649 AD. Song-tsen-gam-po succeeded in unifying the various tribes, and by doing so, he created a kingdom which spread its influence to China and India. Apart from his political achievements, he introduced paper and ink from China, writing from India, and is

70 Folio from the first volume of the Tibetan Buddhist canon (Kanjur); formal Tibetan script with headmarks; 18th century. (British Library; Oriental Collections; Or. 6724)

71 The history of the Sakya tradition of Tibetan Buddhism; in cursive 'headless' Tibetan script; 15th century. (British Library; Oriental Collections; Or. 11375 f.1)

generally credited with laying the cornerstones of Tibetan orthography. This latter was in itself no mean task. Tibetan belongs to a group of languages entirely unlike the Indian ones, and possesses some quite different sounds. The formation of six new signs and various other modifications were necessary to adapt the original script, though still somewhat inadequately, to those needs. According to tradition, the Indian script model was brought back to Tibet, in 632 AD by a minister of the court whom the king had sent to India to study Buddhism and the Sanksrit language. But some scholars have suggested that the Indian system of writing may well have been introduced by way of Buddhist monasteries in Chinese Turkestan or Kashmir. Almost from the beginning two distinctly different styles seem to have existed side by side. One was the *dbu-can* (head-possessing) variety, a beautifully accentuated script, rather top-heavy like Siddhamatrika or modern Devanagari, which was used mainly for handwritten religious texts (fig. 70), for blockprints and eventually also for printing with movable type. The other was a more cursive form called *dbu-med* (headless) (fig. 71) which served for correspondence and administrative records. *Dbu-can* produced some highly stylized 'seal-scripts', from which the Mongols chose the so-called Passepa script for the writing of their own language (see p.104). In the course of time variations of the Tibetan scripts developed in the neighbouring Himalayan countries.

   Incidentally, if Chinese records from the Shang period are reliable, knotted cords and tallies were used in Tibet before the introduction of Indian script models.

Writing in Southeast Asia

The area referred to as Southeast Asia consists of the mainland countries of Burma, Thailand (Siam), Kampuchea (Cambodia), Laos, Vietnam and the southern archipelago stretching from Malaysia and Indonesia to the islands of Java, Bali, Sumatra, Borneo, Celebes and the Philippines. Geographically, linguistically and anthropologically it is one of the most diverse areas in the world. Culturally however there exists a certain degree of hegemony — a hegemony not, as a look at the map might suggest, orientated towards the geographically dominant neighbour China, but towards the Indian sub-continent. The main artery, the vital line of communication which acted as common denominator, and along which, during the 1st millennium AD, elements of cultural consistency were introduced into various parts of Southeast Asia, was the sea; a knowledge of navigation and the monsoon winds, and trade, were the spurs to movement. Along this route came Indian traders, colonists, military adventurers, Hindu priests, Buddhist monks and missionaries, bringing their language (Sanskrit), their script (a South Indian Grantha variation of Brahmi) and their religion (Hinduism/Buddhism) with them. Over the centuries these elements were assimilated by the local population: Sanskrit, the ritual language of the Hindu priests, lost its position, often after a period of co-existence, to the local vernaculars, and eventually Buddhism proved more congenial to Southeast Asian thinking than Hinduism. The original kingdoms no longer exist but two elements have survived which have essentially influenced the character of Southeast Asia: the Buddhist religion, reinforced by the import of Pali manuscripts from Sri Lanka in the 11th and 12th centuries; and the various scripts, which, despite their visual diversity, derive from a common Indian source.

As we have seen, phonetically Indian scripts seem to have been carefully designed to fit Indian languages, Indo-European as well as Dravidian. In the case of the Tibetan language difficulties arose and adaptations had to be made. In Southeast Asia the Indian system of writing had to accommodate the linguistic peculiarities of four further and entirely different language groups: Sino-Tibetan, Thai, Malayo-Polynesian and Austro-Asiatic. This called for a good deal of modification and compromise. But such compromise was in most cases limited to the usage and the number of the syllabic consonant and vowel signs, which were either enlarged, diminished or interchanged; sometimes diacritic marks were added for the representation of the tonal range. The basic internal structure of the Indian script, the arrangement and construction of the syllabic units, the way in which vowels were represented (either initial or auxiliary), and the phonetic arrangements of characters, remained largely the same, as did the direction of writing. Visually the contemporary scripts of Southeast Asia look very different from each other, and from the various styles that evolved during the course of their development; but the same can be said about the modern scripts of the Indian sub-continent.

The development of Southeast Asian scripts is closely connected with the history of Southeast Asia, with the frequent shifts in the pattern of power, population movements and interactions between political and ethnic groups. Broadly speaking, the majority of modern mainland scripts such as Burmese (fig. 72), Cambodian, or Thai (fig. 73) can be traced back directly or indirectly to scripts introduced by Hindu colonists who created the

72 Kammavācā. *A set of disciplinary formulae for the regulation of Buddhist monastic life; written on gilded and lacquered palm leaves in Burmese square characters; 18th century. (British Library; Oriental Collections; Or. 4949)*

73 *Astrological text written in Thai; 19th century. (British Library; Oriental Collections; Or. 4830)*

72

73

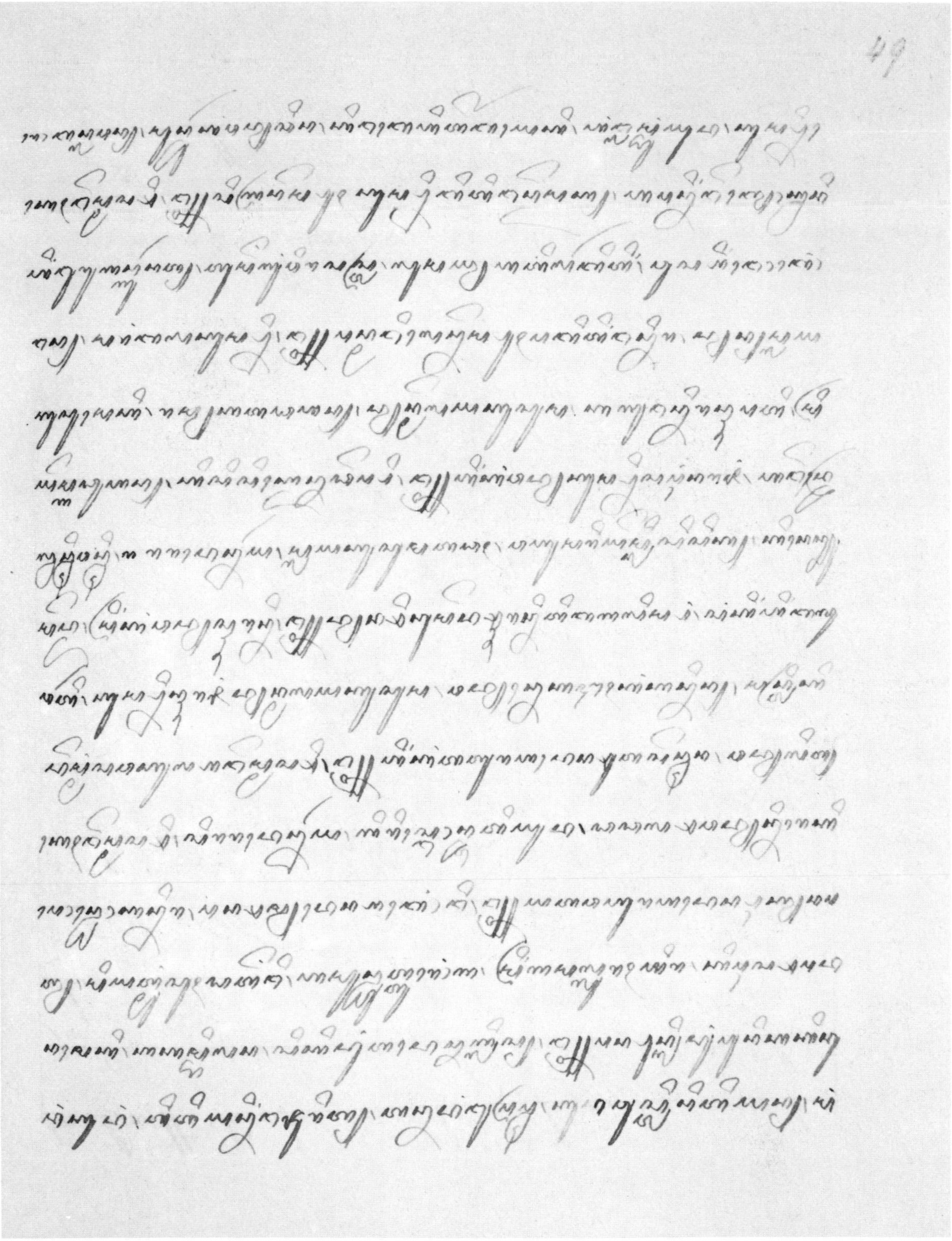

first independent Hindu kingdoms in Fu-nam and Champa (now southern Vietnam) early in the 1st millennium AD. In the case of Burmese, the import of manuscripts written in Pali introduced (as has already been pointed out) additional elements. In fact, at one time, Southeast Asian scripts were (wrongly) labelled as the Pali branch of Indian scripts.

Most of the scripts used at one time or another on the various islands of Southeast Asia are linked to India, indirectly, via the so-called Kavi script which prevailed in Java between the 9th and 15th centuries. It is now generally thought that Kavi is not, as has sometimes been suggested, a new invention, or introduction (directly from India), but a later development of a script used for Sanskrit inscriptions during the middle of the first Christian millennium. This script differed only slightly from the South Indian (Pallava?)–Grantha and showed similarities to the Cambodian script of the time. Kavi was directly responsible for the growth of modern Javanese (fig. 74), and it also stimulated the development of the greatly simplified scripts of the Bataks, Redjangs and Lampongs of Sumatra. In all three scripts the number of signs is greatly reduced; to twenty-three in the case of the Lampong, and to only nineteen in the Batak (see figs. 20, 22) and Redjang (fig. 75) scripts. Apart from the left to right direction, Batak is also written in vertical columns beginning at the lower left hand side.

It seems fairly certain that the two scripts of Celebes, namely Buginese and Macassarese, were equally derived from Kavi, perhaps through the intermediary of Batak. Kavi may also have been responsible (directly or indirectly) for the creation of the ancient and by now extinct Philippine scripts (DD, pp.432–441) which first became known in 1521 when the Spanish 'discovered' the Philippine Islands. In the early years of Spanish domination, Catholic priests used them for the printing of religious books, as for example a translation (into Iloko) of Cardinal Roberto Bellarmino's *Dottrina Christiana breve* which was published in Manila in 1631.

◁ 74 Babad Pa-Cinan. *A history of the Chinese war in Java, written in Javanese script; 19th century.* (British Library; Oriental Collections; Add. 12301)

75 *A Redjang manuscript from South Sumatra, inscribed in strips of bamboo. The language is Malay and the writing the local Redjang script known as* Ka-ga-nga; *19th century. (British Library; Oriental Collections; Or. 12986)*

The Greek cycle and the European situation

For nearly 3,000 years the alphabet has been the primary form of information storage in Europe and in all the regions where European civilization extended its influence. It is a purely phonetic system of writing, though not, as we have seen, the only one: syllabic and consonantal scripts were, and are still, used to the same effect. How then do these systems differ from each other?

In a syllabic script the basic unit represented by a graphic symbol is the syllable. Such a syllable may consist of consonant, plus vowel, plus consonant (e.g. *kam*), or consonant plus vowel (e.g. *ka*), or vowel plus consonant (e.g. *am*), or, in certain cases a vowel on its own may have syllabic value. Graphically a syllable may be represented either by an individual sign or a sign created by the combination of a consonant and an abbreviated vowel sign. The latter usually presupposes the existence of full vowel signs for the representation of vowels whenever they appear initially or on their own. One might say that such syllabic scripts exhibit certain alphabetic tendencies, but it is important to note that those tendencies are never enlarged or developed; not perhaps, as some scholars claim, because syllabic scripts are *Sackgassen* (blind alleys) from which it is impossible to progress any further, but because syllabic scripts are an excellent vehicle for the representation of a large number of languages. In the case of consonantal scripts, words are represented by their consonants only; and this in turn presupposes that they are used for languages where the meaning of the words is carried by consonants and where vowels are of only secondary importance. Vowel indication may eventually develop, but remains strictly auxiliary and optional.

In alphabetic scripts the exact opposite holds true. Vowels and consonants have equal status and, at least in theory, each phoneme (smallest sound unit) is represented by one single sign. In practice this is no longer quite true, as in most modern languages two (*sh*) or three (*sch*) signs are at times needed to express some consonantal sounds, and diacritics are used to represent modified vowel and consonantal sounds (ä, ø, ç etc.); but such alterations are mostly peripheral. From the point of information storage, the alphabet can be adapted more effectively and more easily to languages of different sound and grammatical structures than can consonantal and syllabic scripts; being more flexible it can be manipulated with greater ease.

As to the question whether there does in fact exist a fundamental difference between the alphabetic, syllabic and consonantal scripts, scholarly opinion is divided. Some scholars designate all three systems alphabetic, others hold the view that consonantal scripts are really syllabic, and so forth.

The Greek alphabet

Greek tradition and modern scholarship alike consider the Greek alphabet a successful mutation of the Phoenician consonant script (see fig. 53). The earliest inscriptions of an alphabetic nature so far discovered come from the 8th century BC. It can be assumed that

76 *An early Greek inscription; omens derived from the flight of birds. From Ephesus, 6th century* BC. *(British Museum; Department of Western Asiatic Antiquities; 67-11-12, 441)*

the Greek came into contact with the Phoenician form of writing in one or several of the many Phoenician trading posts, either in Asia Minor, in Syria, or perhaps on one of the Greek islands. The time when the transmission took place may have been around 1000 BC, earlier or later according to various scholars.

The Phoenician consonant script was neither the first nor the only script that the Greeks tried to borrow and use for their language. Two attempts had previously been made to use a syllabic form of writing — the Cypriote script (see p.70) and the Cretan Linear B (see p.69). Neither script had proved particularly suitable and their use was short-lived and localized. In its original form the Phoenician script was if anything even less suitable, since Greek, as an Indo-European language, places equal importance on vowels and consonants. But this time the Greeks went beyond a mere borrowing. Inspired perhaps by the model of the Cypriote script which possessed separate signs for syllabically-used vowels, they established a convention by which some Phoenician consonant signs, for which the Greek language had no corresponding sounds, were used to represent vowels (a, e, i, o). In the course of time further modifications were made (such as the use of supplementary signs for ph, kh, ks, ps, etc.) but none was quite as important and as far-reaching as the stabilization of vowel representation and its continued systematic use. To begin with, a number of local variations of the alphabet arose to fit the various dialects spoken in different parts of Greece, but in about 403 BC the Athenians passed a law that made the use of the Ionian alphabet compulsory in official documents. Eventually the Ionian alphabet superseded the other local variations, and after this the Greek alphabet underwent no further radical alterations.

At first the Greek alphabet was written in the Semitic right-to-left direction, but eventually, in the 5th century BC, after a number of attempts to write in a boustrophedon fashion, the current left-to-right direction became firmly established. This change was accompanied by a reversal of all non-symmetric letter signs; in other words, letters such as B, K, N, Δ, and Σ acquired their present form in this process. The term 'alphabet', taken from the names of the first two letters, *alpha* and *beta*, is documented from the 3rd century BC onwards. *Alpha* and *beta*, as indeed the names of nearly all Greek letters, are variations of the original Semitic names (*aleph, beth* etc.). The order of the letters too remained basically unchanged.

Over the centuries various styles of writing developed, some influenced to no small extent by the material used for writing. The early monumental style (fig. 76), also referred to as stone majuscule or capital script, was a beautiful epigraphic form with simple straight

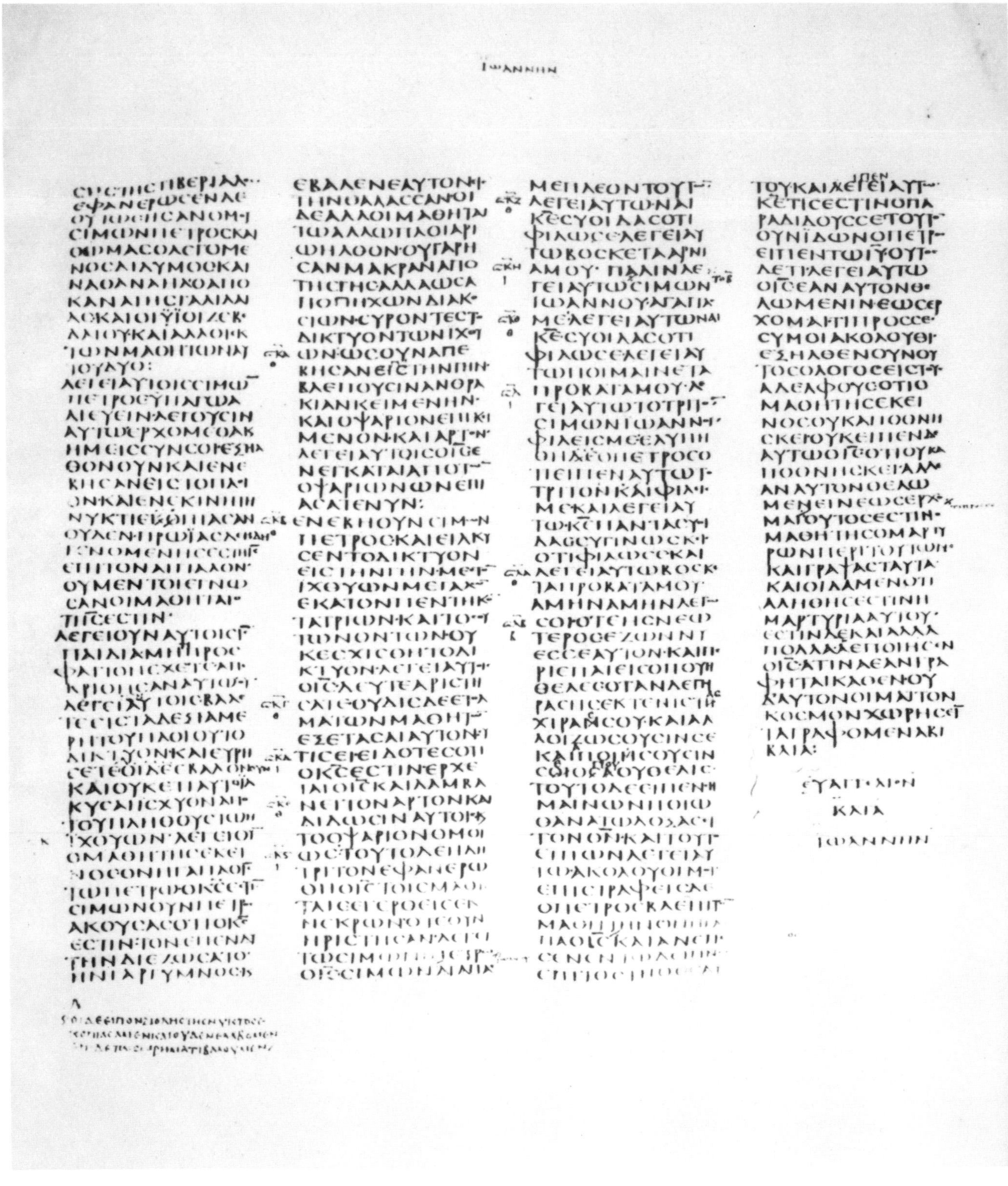
ΙΩΑΝΝΗΝ
ΕΥΑΓΓΕΛΙΟΝ
ΚΑΤΑ
ΙΩΑΝΝΗΝ

78 Pantocrator Lectionary *with text in the shape of a cross; Greek minuscule; 11th century.* *(British Library; Department of Manuscripts; Add. 39603, f. 1b)*

◁ 77 Codex Sinaiticus. *The Bible written in Greek (uncials), middle of the 4th century* AD. *(British Library; Department of Manuscripts; Add. 43725, f. 260)*

lines well-suited for chiselling in stone or, more rarely, in metal. More rounded signs were preferred for writing with brush or reed pen on Egyptian papyrus, hide or, later, parchment. These rounded characters were moulded into a proper style in the so-called uncial script (fig. 77), which remained, until the 9th century AD, the prevailing book script. Eventually this style was in turn replaced by various more cursive forms, in particular the minuscule script (fig. 78), the true parchment script of the Middle Ages.

79 A miscellany of historical and geographical works; in Armenian, written in the notrgir, *or cursive hand; 1616* AD. *(British Library; Oriental Collections; Or. 5459, f. 202v)*

Coptic, Armenian and Georgian

In the first millennium BC a number of alphabets — such as Phrygian, Lycian, Lydian, Carian — were used (mainly by non-Hellenic peoples) in Asia Minor, but none of them gained lasting importance. In Egypt the situation was different. Alexander's conquest and the foundation of Alexandria as a centre of Greek learning had caused the introduction of the Greek language and the Greek alphabet. Attempts were made during the first three centuries of the Christian era to adapt the Greek alphabet to the writing of the Egyptian language, but it was not before the 4th century, when Christian, Manichaean and Gnostic missionaries began to work among the Egyptian-speaking element of the population, that translations of the Scriptures were made, and the then contemporary form of the Egyptian language, Coptic (from *qobṭ-gyptios* – Egyptian), became a literary speech.

Coptic was written in a modified Greek alphabet consisting of thirty-two vowel and consonant signs, of which twenty-five were taken from the uncial Greek script and seven from the demotic script of Egypt (see fig. 39). The Islamic conquest in 641 AD introduced Arabic to Egypt but the Coptic script (see fig. 26) remained in use until the 9th century.

80 A Georgian book of prayers written in the ecclesiastical hand; 1621 AD. (British Library; Oriental Collections; Sloane 1338, f. 50)

The Christian communities continued to use Coptic until the 13th century (longer in some places) as their written and spoken language, and later as the liturgical language of the Coptic Church. The Coptic alphabet was borrowed, and further modified (for example, three signs were added from the cursive Meroïtic script) by the Nubian Church, for the writing of liturgical books in the vernacular.

At the beginning of the 5th century, sometime between 404 and 406 AD, St Mesrob, with the active encouragement of Catholicos Sahak, created a system of writing for the Armenian people. This new script, which consisted of some thirty-six letters, was largely based on the Greek alphabet. At first mainly capital letters were used, but in the 13th century a more cursive form called *notrgir* (fig. 79) developed.

Tradition ascribes the creation of the Georgian alphabet to the same St Mesrob — who is also supposed to have devised an alphabet for the Albanians of the Caucasus (DML, p.266). The main Georgian styles of writing are *mkhedruli* (lay hand), still used at present, and the old ecclesiastical script which employed thirty-eight letter signs (fig. 80).

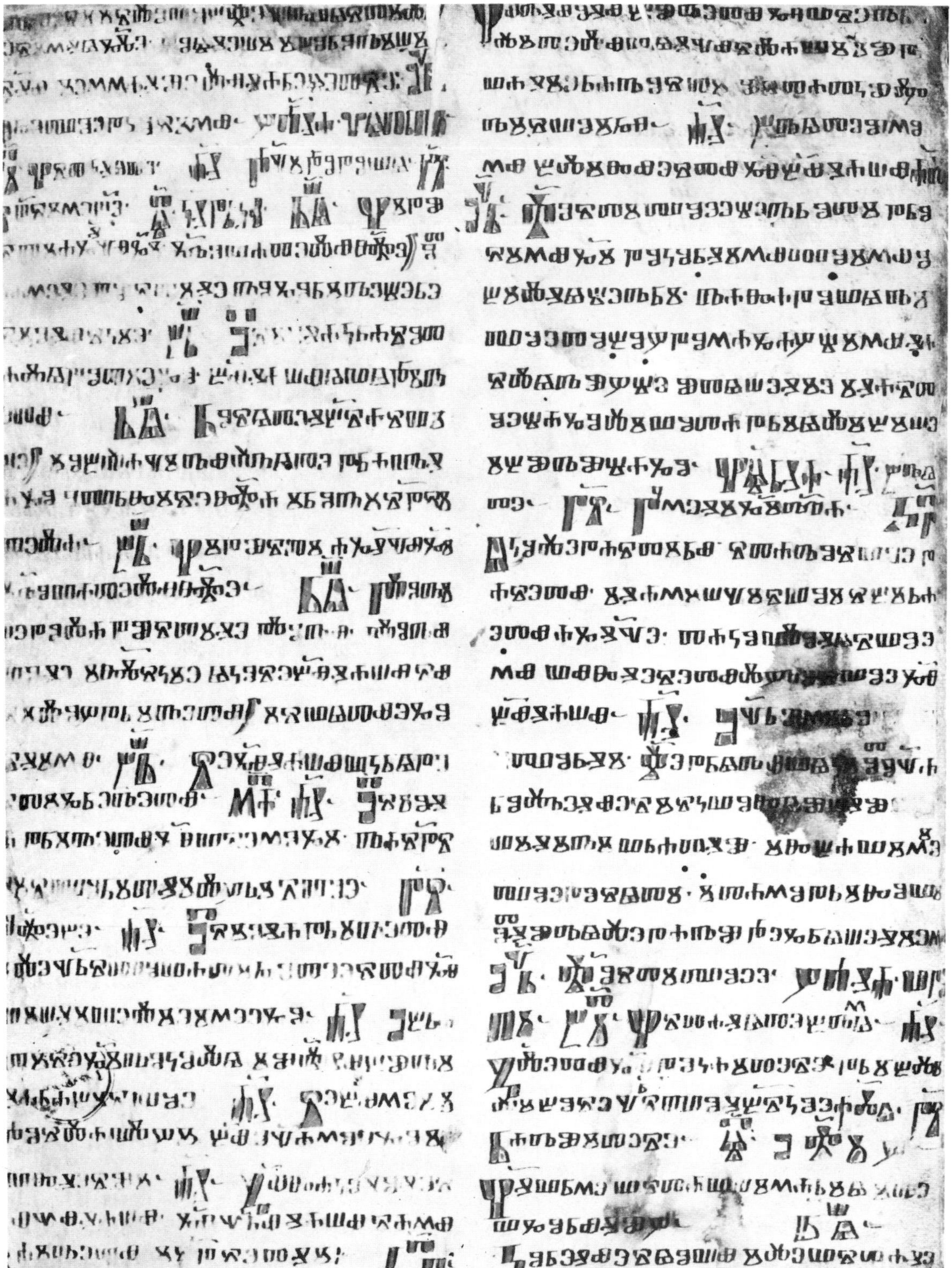

81 Fragment of a Glagolitic (Croatian) Breviary; first half of the 13th century. (British Museum; Department of Manuscripts; Add. 31951, f.1)

82 The Four Gospels; written in Cyrillic script between 1355–1356 for Tsar Ivan Alexandre of Bulgaria. (British Library; Department of Manuscripts; Add 39627, f.11v)

The Slavonic scripts

The origin of the two most important Slavonic alphabets, Glagolitic and Cyrillic, is to some extent connected with the rivalry between Constantinople and Rome, which had its origin in the division of the Roman Empire by Diocletian in the 3rd century AD. In the 9th century, after the establishment of a Slav principality in Moravia, King Rastislaw of Moravia, in an attempt to free himself from the influence of the Roman Church, asked the Byzantine Emperor Constantine for teachers who would instruct his people in the true Christian faith in their own tongue. As a result the two brothers, Constantine (or, as he was later called, Cyril — *d.* 869) and Methodius (*d.* 885) were entrusted with the Slav mission, and, against considerable opposition from the Roman Church, which recognized only Hebrew, Greek and Latin for the translation of the Bible, Canon Law and other ecclesiastical books, they had translations made in the Slav language. According to the *Vita Cyrilli*, Cyril, after whom the Cyrillic alphabet is named, is traditionally credited with the invention of a script. Whether this script was Glagolitic (fig. 81) or Cyrillic (fig. 82) has for long been a matter of controversy, but the question has now more or less been decided in favour of Glagolitic. The two alphabets differ considerably in appearance, but as far as the phonetic value of the letters is concerned Glagolitic and Cyrillic (with forty and forty-three letters respectively) are very nearly identical; Cyrillic may contain borrowings from Glagolitic. The majority of letters are thought to have been derived from the Greek scripts of that period — although other elements seem to have been active. Of the two alphabets Cyrillic is without doubt the more important one. In due course, after a number of reforms and modifications, it became the national script of the Slavonic people. The Russians, Ukranians, Bulgarians and Serbs accepted it, together with the Greek Orthodox religion. With the growing importance of Russia, Cyrillic became the 'Russian alphabet', and by replacing all other scripts in the European as well as the Asian part of the Soviet Union, it became the vehicle of information storage for more than sixty different languages.

83 Bronze jug with Etruscan inscription, c.400–200 BC; probably from Bolsena. (British Museum; Department of Greek and Roman Antiquities; 1873. 8-20.197)

The Roman alphabet

At some time in the 8th century BC Greek settlers seem to have taken their alphabet to Italy, where it was adopted, after some more or less minor alterations and a great many local variations, by the Etruscans. Like the Sumerians and the people of the Indus Valley civilization, the Etruscans retain an air of mystery. So far nearly 10,000 inscriptions have been discovered, most of them (though not all) admittedly rather brief, and, being to a large extent funerary in kind, predictable. The Etruscan script is perfectly legible to us; the close connections between the Etruscans and the origins and early history of Rome are fully documented; yet we are still unable to reconstruct or even fully classify the Etruscan language. The early Etruscan alphabet (fig. 83) consisted of twenty-six letters, and like the early Greek script it was written from right to left. In some inscriptions the words are separated by dots in a manner reminiscent of a syllabic form of writing.

From among the various offshoots of the Etruscan alphabet which flourished for short periods in different parts of Italy (HJ, pp.507–520) the Roman (or Latin) alphabet, documented from the 7th or 6th century BC onwards, evolved as the most important one. It gradually supplanted all other Italian scripts and became in due course the script of the western half of the Roman empire. Through the agencies of the Roman Catholic Church and (later) Western colonial expansion, it spread its influence beyond Europe to America, Asia and Africa.

The oldest Roman alphabet contained only twenty-one letters (aspirated sounds such as th, kh or ph do not occur in Latin) and at first a right to left or boustrophedon direction of writing was employed. Some inscriptions for public use on stone and metal showed word separation by points placed at mid-height. Externally the difference between Greek and Roman letters was slight, manifested mainly in a tendency, in the case of Roman letter signs, to replace (wherever possible) angular lines by curves (e.g. D for Δ, S for Σ). The semitic-based Greek letter names were discarded in favour of the familiar *abecedarium*, which we still use. Subsequent developments were limited to an increase in the number of letters (twenty-six in our contemporary alphabet), alterations in the shape and sound quality of certain letters, and the development of distinct calligraphic and national styles.

Runes

Since the 17th century, when Scandinavian scholars first began to take note of Runic inscriptions (GB, p.190), several theories concerning their origin have been advanced. Some believe Runes to be an independent invention by a single individual, others relate them to the Greek, the Roman or a mixture of the Greek and Roman alphabets. There are yet other theories which look upon Runes as a primordial Germanic script, derived (acrophonically) from prehistoric pictograms, but influenced and modified by the Roman uncial script. According to what is still the majority view, the Runes arose from a North Italian, Etruscan-based alphabet probably sometime in the 1st century BC. They were however never a literary script, existing records being mainly found on memorial stones, or on objects such as weapons, rings, and clasps, and not only their name (Old Saxon *rūna*, Old Irish *rūn* – secret; Middle High German *rūne* – secret, whispering) but their actual documented use indicates connections with cult and secret forms of writing.

A characteristic of Runes (fig. 84) is their angularity, there being practically no curved lines. This is usually attributed to the fact that wood (in all likelihood wooden sticks) or bones are supposed to have been the original writing material. The order of the letters and their names differ from the Greek and the Roman alphabet, but just as those alphabets are named after the first placed letters, so the Runic script is referred to as *futhark* after the initial letters (F U T H A R K) of its alphabet.

Two main groups may be distinguished. One is the old Germanic Runic alphabet, consisting of twenty-four letters arranged in three groups of eight *aettir* (families), which was used between 200–750 AD. Between 450 and 600 AD the Anglo-Saxons brought this script to England, where the number of letters was increased, first to twenty-eight and later to thirty-three. In the 7th century Irish and Roman missionaries went to considerable pains to suppress this script — no doubt because of its association with heathen practices — and replace it by the Roman alphabet.

The second main group is the later Nordic Runic alphabet which, at the time of the Viking expansion between 800 and 1050 AD, spread over various parts of Europe down to the Black Sea. Whereas in England the letters had been increased to cover phonetic

84 A side view of the Franks Casket; carved in whalebone with Runic inscription, c. 700 AD.
(British Museum; Department of Medieval and Later Antiquities; 67.1-20.1)

demands, in the Scandinavian countries the exact opposite happened and eventually only sixteen script signs remained, providing a rather inadequate coverage for the whole range of sounds employed by the spoken language. In the 10th century an attempt was made to remedy this shortcoming by the use of dotted Runes, which made it possible to distinguish between k and g, p and b, d and t, e and i, and so forth (HJ, pp.550–579). After the 13th century the use of the Runic script diminished.

Ogham

The Ogham script seems to have been restricted to the Celtic-speaking people of the British Isles. The 360 inscriptions so far discovered in southern Ireland, Wales and Scotland and the Isle of Man date from between the 4th and 7th centuries, and are mostly found on tombs or memorial stones; but the script was also used for letters and messages, which were written on wooden staves, shields or similar items.

The origin of the Ogham script and the principle upon which the letters were arranged are still uncertain. Legend names Ogma mac Elathan as the inventor, while modern scholarship has tried to link Oghams with Germanic Runes and, more tentatively, with a knowledge of the Greek and/or Roman alphabet. The Oghams are, like Runes, divided into 'families': four groups, each containing five letters. The alphabet consists of twenty letters, which are represented by straight or diagonal strokes varying in number from one to five, drawn or cut below, above or right through a horizontal or vertical line (fig. 85), or along the edges of the object on which the letters are incised. Vowels are represented by one to five notches (or strokes) on the central line. Visually an Ogham inscription bears close resemblance to a tally or to the representation of a knotted cord.

It is generally agreed that the Oghams were a cryptic script. The Gaelic word *ogham* refers also to a particular form of cryptic speech in which the names of letters could, in certain syllables, replace the letters. One theory suggest that the Oghams were originally a finger-alphabet (hence the basic unit of five) invented by the Druids as a private code for signalling, and that this code was only much later translated into a written form. Though the Ogham script disappeared from use in the 7th century, it was known and much discussed during the Middle Ages; nor was the Church entirely indifferent to it, for with the firm establishment of Christianity in the British Isles many inscriptions were either erased or at least neutralized by having the sign of the cross placed next to them.

85 Ogham inscription from north-east Scotland, near Brandsbutt Inverurie. The serpent and Z rod and the crescent and V rod are Pictish and of enigmatic meaning. The vertical Ogham lettering is incomplete and reads irataddoarens *. . . , which cannot be translated; c. 8th century* AD. *(Photographed by the author)*

Invented scripts

The question has often been asked: is writing — and in this context writing is usually equated with phonetic writing — the outcome of an evolutionary process, with scripts evolving independently from each other in various places and periods whenever socio-economic conditions created similar needs? Or, is writing the result of a series of (mostly secondary) inventions, each one made by a particular individual in one particular place, all of them going back to one single *Ur – invention?* Those who believe in the monogenesis of writing usually credit the Sumerians with making the first — and only — decisive step from pictography to phonetic writing. But not all phonetic scripts can be traced back to ancient Mesopotamia. Even if we were to accept that the Egyptian hieroglyphs, the ancient Mediterranean scripts and, indirectly all consonantal, syllabic and alphabetic scripts go back to one common root, this would still leave the Chinese and the pre-Columbian American scripts outside the framework thus prescribed. Furthermore, rudimentary phonetic elements can manifest themselves quite convincingly (see p.21) within the limits of simple memory aids.

In the preceding pages we have repeatedly come across references to invented scripts. In civilizations where writing was held in high esteem, and practised by a priestly or otherwise privileged class, this invention was usually attributed to divine or semi-divine beings, or else to that group of persons referred to as culture-heroes. Thus in ancient Egypt the ibis-headed god Toth (see Plate V) was considered the inventor of writing and the official scribe of the gods. The Assyrians saw Nabu as the god of wisdom and writing. In ancient Mexico the Mayas regarded one of their most important deities, Itsamna, the son of the Creator god, not only as the inventor of writing but also the inventor of 'books'. The Ogham script has been called an invention of the Druids, an important priestly class among the ancient Celts. And according to at least one tradition the family of the Prophet Muhammad is supposed to have invented the Arabic script. This is to give but a few examples.

The desire to give additional authority and sanctity to writing is equally prevalent among tribal communities. The Abnaki Indians of North America, for example, believed that the Oonagamessok, a special group of deities, presided over the making of petroglyphs, and explained the gradual disappearance of these rock engravings by asserting that the Oonagamessok were angered by the lack of attention accorded to them since the coming of the white man (GM, p.32).

Moving from legend and mythology into the realms of recorded history, we repeatedly find the names of kings, rulers, statesmen, writers, reformers, Buddhist monks and Christian saints associated with the invention of certain scripts. Both Cyrus the Great (558–529 BC) and Darius (521–486 BC) have been credited with the invention of the Old Persian cuneiform script; King Sejong of Korea was named as the inventor of the Korean script, in 1446 AD. The Tangut script is supposed to have been created by a Tangut prince in 1036 AD. In the same way St Mesrob (4th/5th century) is thought to have created both the Armenian and the Georgian scripts; St Cyril (9th century) the Cyrillic and the Glagolitic alphabet, and Bishop Wulfilas (again 4th century) to have invented the West Gothic script (from a knowledge of the Roman and Greek alphabets) for his translation of the Bible into the West Gothic tongue. Classical Greek tradition attributes the introduction of the Greek alphabet to the Phoenician King Cadmus, who brought the sixteen 'Cadmean' letters from his homeland to Boeotia. During the time of the Trojan war, Palamedes is supposed to have added four more letters to this alphabet, and finally the lyric poet Simonides of Ceos (556–468 BC) a further four.

The list could easily be extended, and indeed the most prominent traditions have already been mentioned in the preceding pages. Some of them are well documented; others may have arisen primarily out of a desire to give added authority to a new convention. In many cases fact and legend will no doubt be closely intermingled.

A fascinating chapter in the history of writing tells of the way in which a number of phonetic scripts evolved during the 19th century, quite suddenly, among primitive societies in Africa, America and certain parts of Asia — sometimes under the influence of western missionaries, sometimes as a result of contact with, or at least a knowledge (often quite rudimentary) of the Roman alphabet, or more rarely, the Arabic consonant script.

The majority of these scripts show considerable similarity in their development. In nearly every case the inventor is known by name, and the date of the invention is recorded. Most of these scripts began with pictographic signs for objects, ideas and actions. These early pictures were often not very different from those habitually used by tribal communities for communication and information storage (see *Idea transmission*, pp.18–29). In almost every instance the direction of development followed similar lines: an idea script moved towards a word (picture) script and on to the introduction of phonetic elements, mostly on the basis of the rebus principle, to culminate finally in a syllabic script. The only script that was from the beginning alphabetic, with twenty-two consonants and five vowel signs, was invented by the son of the Somali Sultan, Yusuf Ali, who knew Arabic as well as Italian. The progress towards a syllabic structure was usually accompanied by a reduction in the number of signs and a simplification of their shape. The process of evolution was in most cases complete within two generations, and in spite of (at times considerable) local success, all scripts were soon replaced by the Roman alphabet.

In Africa the most important of these invented scripts were the Bamum, the Vai and the Mende. The Bamum script was invented by King Njoya in collaboration with some of his dignitaries between 1903 and 1918. The Vai script first became known in Europe in 1849 through publication by an American engineer. It is supposed to have been invented by Momoru Doalu Bukere between 1829 and 1839 — though subsequent research suggests that his contribution was perhaps limited to the phoneticization of a much older picture script. Finally, the Mende script of Sierra Leone, known since 1935, was invented by Kisimi Kamala, a Muslim tailor, who is said to have accomplished his task in three and a half months.

In North America the most successful examples include the Cree script, invented by the English Methodist missionary John Evans, who lived in the Hudson Bay area between 1840 and 1846; the Cherokee script (fig. 86) invented by the Cherokee Indian, Sikwayi, between 1820 and 1824; and the much-discussed Alaska script (AS, pp.15–122) invented, with a group of assistants, by the Eskimo Neck (Uyako) who lived between 1860 and 1924. A modified version of the Cree syllabary is still in use among the Eskimos on Baffin Island. There was another Arctic script, invented by the Chukchi shepherd Tenevil in 1920, but this script did not progress beyond the word picture level.

At the end of the last century Christian missionaries working in south-western China among the non-Chinese Miao, and ignorant of their indigenous script, tried at first to preach the Gospel in spoken and written Chinese, a task which soon proved too arduous. As a result Samuel Pollard and other members of the Bible Christian Mission set about

Cherokee Alphabet.

D *a*	R *e*	T *i*	Ꭷ *o*	Ꭳ *u*	i *v*
S *ga* Ꭴ *ka*	Ꭼ *ge*	Ꮍ *gi*	A *go*	J *yu*	E *gv*
Ꮣ *ha*	Ꭾ *he*	Ꭿ *hi*	Ꮂ *ho*	Ꭻ *hu*	Ꮀ *hv*
W *la*	Ꮄ *le*	Ꮅ *li*	Ꮆ *lo*	M *lu*	Ꮑ *lv*
Ꮆ *ma*	Ꮇ *me*	H *mi*	� *mo*	Ꮎ *mu*	
Ꮕ *na* Ꮏ *hna* Ꮐ *nah*	Ʌ *ne*	Ꮒ *ni*	Z *no*	Ꮖ *nu*	Ꮕ *nv*
Ꮤ *qua*	Ꮗ *que*	Ꮙ *qui*	Ꮝ *quo*	Ꮙ *quu*	Ꮛ *quv*
Ꭴ *sa* Ꮝ *s*	Ꮞ *se*	Ꮟ *si*	Ꮠ *so*	Ꮡ *su*	R *sv*
Ꮭ *da* Ꮤ *ta*	S *de* Ꮦ *te*	Ꮧ *di* Ꮨ *ti*	Ʌ *do*	S *du*	Ꮩ *dv*
Ꮝ *dla* Ꮅ *tla*	L *tle*	C *tli*	Ꮳ *tlo*	Ꮴ *tlu*	P *tlv*
Ꮳ *tsa*	V *tse*	Ᏼ *tsi*	K *tso*	Ꮵ *tsu*	Ꮶ *tsv*
Ꮹ *wa*	Ꮃ *we*	Ꮻ *wi*	Ꮼ *wo*	Ꮽ *wu*	6 *wv*
Ꮿ *ya*	Ᏸ *ye*	Ᏹ *yi*	Ᏺ *yo*	G *yu*	B *yv*

Sounds represented by Vowels.

a, as *a* in <u>father</u>, or short as a in <u>rival</u>.
e, as *a* in <u>hate</u>, or short as *e* in <u>met</u>
i, as *i* in <u>pique</u>, or short as *i* in <u>pit</u>

o, as *aw* in <u>law</u>, or short as o in <u>not</u>.
u, as *oo* in <u>fool</u>, or short as u in <u>pull</u>.
v, as *u* in <u>but</u>, nasalized.

Consonant Sounds

g nearly as in English, but approaching to *k.* — *d* nearly as in English but approaching to *t.* — *h.k.l.m.n.q.s.t.w.y.* as in English. Syllables beginning with *g.* except Ꮝ have sometimes the power of *k.Ꭰ.Ꮝ.Ꮝ.* are sometimes sounded to, tu, ts; and Syllables written with *tl* except Ꮭ sometimes vary to *dl.*

inventing a syllabic script for the Miao language, a task successfully achieved by 1904. The new script consisted of simple geometric signs (fig. 87) and was, according to the missionaries, an immediate success — so much so in fact that Pollard's system was adopted for other non-Chinese dialects. Subsequenly similar syllabic scripts consisting of Roman capital letters, differently positioned and given different phonetic values, were devised by the American Baptist Mission in 1915, and the British and Foreign Bible Society in 1930.

Fragments of some ideographic scripts using purely pictorial signs have been found written on pieces of old Dutch paper or pieces of woven material during the last century in some parts of Peru, around Lake Titicaca, and in Central America in Panama. The first two of these show clear connections with Christian ideas, but the third seems to have been used mainly for magic and ritual purposes, and some scholars have speculated on possible connections with the pre-Columbian scripts of Mexico (DD, p.154).

This does not, by any means, constitute a full account of the scripts which developed in the course of the 19th century. Others exist, less well documented, and yet others may well have been completely forgotten. Much research has still to be done in this field. In nearly all cases the invention itself seems to have been stimulated by the existence of foreign models and by a knowledge of the possibility of creating a phonetic form of writing. However, none of the societies concerned had reached a stage of development where such a form of information storage was essential to its survival and they were often already under pressure to accept the alphabet. The inventions were in most cases determined by a desire to imitate, to show ability equal to that of foreign and dominant groups, and in consequence nearly all the new scripts remained experiments without lasting importance.

III Decipherment

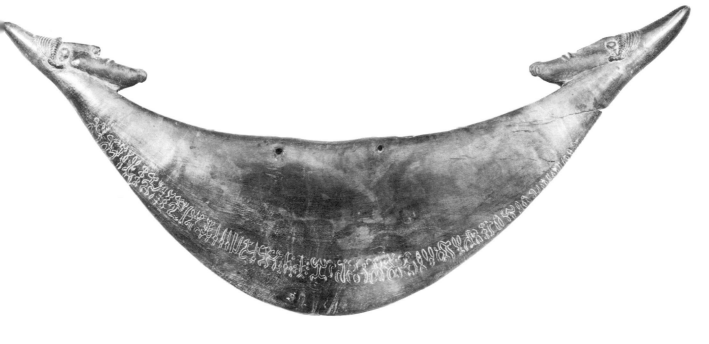

The scholars and their work

The 19th century witnessed a tremendous extension in the knowledge of human history and human achievements. The credit for this goes, to no small extent, to the dedicated and often greatly undervalued work of a large number of scholars who painstakingly pursued the decipherment of hitherto unknown scripts, discovering languages that had long been forgotten, bringing into focus civilizations which up to then had featured mostly in legends and semi-historical tales. Among the many discoveries made in this field the two most spectacular were, without doubt, the decipherment of the Egyptian hieroglyphs and that of the cuneiform script of Mesopotamia. Together they added another 3,000 years of recorded history to our knowledge of the past.

The Egyptian hieroglyphs

Once the Greek alphabet had begun to establish itself in the Nile Valley (see p.122) the art of reading the ancient script of Egypt was soon forgotten. Greek and Roman writers seem to have made little attempt to understand the true nature of the hieroglyphs, and from then on, right through the Middle Ages until well into the modern period, they were regarded as enigmatic symbols full of ancient and fundamental wisdom, but not a script. A change in attitude occurred towards the end of the 18th century when scholars such as the German Arabist, Carsten Niebuhr, began, tentatively at first, to reject the concept of symbolism, realizing for the first time that hieroglyphs were characters used to write an ancient language, and that hieratic and demotic (see p.63) were cursive forms of the same script. At the same time an incident occurred which dramatically increased the possibility of a full decipherment, namely the discovery of the Rosetta stone (fig. 88) in the village of Rashid (better known to Europeans under the name of Rosetta) in the Western Delta of the Nile by an officer of the Napoleonic army in 1799. The Rosetta stone, a slab of black basalt (now in the British Museum), contains inscriptions written in two languages (Egyptian and Greek) and three scripts. The Egyptian version is written in hieroglyphs and in demotic (at first wrongly identified as Syriac); the Greek version is given in capital letters of the Greek alphabet. The text is a copy of a decree passed by a council of priests at the first anniversary of the coronation of Ptolemy V in 196 BC. (The Ptolemies were descendants of a general in Alexander's army, and most of their official documents seem to have been bilingual.)

Right from the beginning, the Rosetta stone attracted a good deal of attention; the inscriptions were copied and the Greek text was translated, first into French and later into English. In 1802, after the defeat of the Napoleonic army, the stone was brought to England, and attempts at a decipherment began in earnest. The early and promising success of the French orientalist, Silvestre de Sacy, and the Swedish diplomat, J. D. Åkerblad, who identified in the demotic version the equivalents of some proper names (and a few words) which occurred in the Greek section, did not lead any further. Since those particular names (and words) were written phonetically (or, as de Sacy and Åkerblad thought, alphabetically) they presumed that demotic itself was an alphabetic script.

88 *The Rosetta stone. (British Museum; Department of Egyptian Antiquities)*

89 A page from Thomas Young's diary. (British Library; Department of Manuscripts; Add. 27281 (v.1), f.41)

The first real breakthrough came when the English physician, Thomas Young, realized that the demotic script consisted of both phonetic (which he still perceived as being alphabetic) and non-phonetic signs, and even more vital, that the hieroglyphic and the demotic scripts were interrelated. Young then turned his attention to the hieroglyphic part of the inscription, and presuming rightly that the elongated oblongs or cartouches which enclosed certain groups of signs contained royal names, he identified the correct phonetic value of six hieroglyphic signs, and read another three at least approximately correctly. Between 1814 and 1818 Young devoted a good deal of effort to the Rosetta stone, and to copies of other inscriptions he had been able to obtain from Egypt. In all he eventually succeeded in equating, either correctly or nearly correctly, over eighty demotic words with their hieroglyphic counterparts, and, with the help of Greek words, translated most of them. Young's notebooks from this period are now in the British Library (fig. 89). Young communicated the results of his investigation to the French scholar Jean François Champollion, and also published them in an article in the *Supplement to the Encyclopaedia Britannica* in 1819. Yet Champollion, who since early youth had been obsessed by the idea of deciphering the hieroglyphs, and who had meticulously prepared himself for this task by studying Coptic and collecting all available copies of hieroglyphic, hieratic and demotic texts, clung for another two years to the belief that the hieroglyphs were symbols without phonetic value. The turning point came in 1822. Champollion had counted the signs in the hieroglyphic portion of the Rosetta stone, and discovered that they outnumbered the Greek words three to one. This meant that instead of one hieroglyph equalling one word, several hieroglyphs were obviously needed to construct a single word. Around the same time Champollion received copies of another bilingual inscription taken from an obelisk (now at Kingston Lacy, Dorset) which had been excavated by W. J. Bankes in 1815. By comparing the Greek names, which he knew how to read, with their equivalent in demotic, hieratic and hieroglyphic, he correctly identified the names of Ptolemy and Cleopatra.

In September 1822 Champollion wrote his now famous *Lettre à M. Dacier relative à l'alphabet des hiéroglyphes phonétiques* to the Paris Academy. In it he corrected and greatly enlarged the list of phonetic hieroglyphs drawn up by Young, and correctly deciphered the hieroglyphic forms of the names and titles of most of the Roman emperors of Egypt. Between then and his early death in 1832 he drew up a classified list of hieroglyphs, identified the names of many Egyptian kings, formulated a system of grammar and successfully read and translated a large number of texts.

The decipherment of proper names, though undoubtedly the initial key, would not have led to an understanding of the Egyptian language without the assistance of Coptic (see p.122). The Coptic vocabulary consists of Egyptian words supplemented by a considerable number of Greek loan words. Champollion had drawn extensively on his knowledge of Coptic by translating words in the Greek version into Coptic; then, comparing them with the appropriate group of hieroglyphic signs (or vice versa), he ascertained their correct meaning and, up to a point, their pronunciation. Coptic, until the 13th century the language of the Christian population of Egypt, and still used in Coptic churches, is indeed the main guide to the actual pronunciation of the ancient Egyptian language, since the (phonetic) part of the Egyptian script supplies only consonants (see p.62). Though much work had still to be done (by such scholars as Lepsius, Birch, Hincks, Gardiner, Rougé, Chabas, Maspéro, Brugsch etc.), Champollion had without doubt provided the foundation of all further research. He had found the key to a script which had been lost and forgotten for almost 1,400 years, and by so doing initiated modern Egyptology. It is equally certain that Young had understood the basic principles two years earlier. Champollion knew this, but he never acknowledged it in print.

The cuneiform script

Until about 150 years ago the script and the languages of ancient Mesopotamia were almost completely unknown. Indeed less than 600 years after Darius (521–486 BC) had carved his inscriptions on the rockface of Behistun (the inscriptions which were to play such an important role in the decipherment of the cuneiform script), the script and the three languages he had used to ensure that his victories would be remembered by future generations had passed from use. In fact until quite recently the existence of the Sumerians (see p.65), who had originally created this form of writing, was not only forgotten but largely denied.

The reasons for this almost total disappearance (even from memory) of what had been one of the most important and influential civilizations of all time are many. There is first of all the history of Mesopotamia itself (see p.65). After some 3,000 years of changes in the pattern of power, with invasions accompanied by periodical devastations of the city-states, the economy — vulnerably inter-linked with irrigation — finally collapsed, and the cities, the people and the civilization they had created, vanished. There is also the question of basic raw material. In Egypt it had been stone. Consequently, even after the art of writing in the Egyptian language had passed from memory, innumerable hieroglyphic inscriptions remained clearly visible on the walls of temples, inside funeral chambers, on obelisks and pyramids. Their meaning may have become incomprehensible but they themselves could not be forgotten. In Mesopotamia the basic raw material had been clay, a much less spectacular and, at least to some extent, less stable material. Thus in the course of centuries the once-splendid cities vanished under ever-growing mounds of rubble, until eventually even their location was forgotten. And then, most of what was known about Mesopotamia, and especially about Babylon, came from a hostile source, namely the Bible.

The second half of the 18th century witnessed a great upsurge in travel and exploration. The literary output of men such as Voltaire, and the effect of the French and American revolutions were stimulating a spirit of (religiously) unbiased curiosity. Very many of the travellers who came to the Middle East — diplomats, soldiers and political agents — possessed intellectual brilliance coupled with remarkable physical courage. Often at their own expense, nearly always at the expense of their health, they excavated the various mounds which lay between the two great rivers, Euphrates and Tigris. At first the multitude of inscribed bricks, the remains of once-famous libraries, aroused little interest. The 'excavators' and their public back home were captivated by more spectacular discoveries: monumental winged lions, man-headed bulls and the large battle friezes, now to be seen in places such as the Louvre or the British Museum. Unlike the Egyptian hieroglyphs, the cuneiform script is physically undistinguished, and to begin with doubts were expressed as to whether the wedge-shaped signs were indeed writing or just some form of ornamentation. There was in addition the sheer volume of inscribed bricks. In 1771 the Abbé de Beauchamp wrote that there were 'too many of them for any of them to have any particular value'. Even after the cuneiform script as such had been recognized there was simply no known language to which this script could be related, and early speculations varied between Hebrew, Greek, Latin, Chinese, Egyptian and the Ogham script of the British Isles.

From among the many scholars who contributed to the decipherment of the cuneiform script (and the re-discovery of the languages that this script had served) the greatest name is that of Sir Henry Rawlinson, the copier and translator of the inscription of Darius on the rock of Behistun. The Behistun inscription consists of ten columns of cuneiform text written in Old Persian, Elamite and Babylonian, and it is placed 150 metres above ground level on the surface of an almost sheer rock which rises to a height of 1,200 metres. It is difficult to reach the inscriptions from either above or below, since the platform that the Persian workmen must have used has since been cut away, except for a short ledge half a metre wide below one of the inscriptions. Only an exceptionally experienced and daring mountain climber can hope to reach the inscription; to copy it needs almost suicidal dedication. In the event Rawlinson used ladders of varying length, precariously balanced on the narrow ledge, and by steadying his body and the ladder against the rock with his left arm and holding his notebook in the palm of his left hand he was able to copy the text with his right hand. According to his own account 'the interest of the occupation entirely did away with any sense of danger'.

Between 1800 and 1857 a large number of scholars, and some gifted amateurs, worked diligently on the decipherment of the cuneiform script and the reconstruction of the languages of ancient Mesopotamia. Early on, when the Babylonian language was still largely unknown, Joseph Hager published a small book on the 'newly discovered Babylonian inscriptions' in which he made certain already basically correct observations, namely: (1) that the 'nail-headed' signs were real characters, and not ornaments, as previous scholars had supposed; (2) that these characters had been used not only in Persia but also in Babylon, whose civilization was anterior to that of Persia; and (3) that they were read horizontally from left to right.

Two intriguing figures in the long story of decipherment (and there are too many to name them all) were the German schoolmaster Georg Grotefend and the Irish parson Edward Hincks, neither of whom received quite the recognition that their work warranted. Grotefend for example had used copies of two different Old Persian inscriptions, and by treating the problem in terms of cryptology and mathematics (instead of linguistics), he had arrived at a more or less correct reading of the names of Darius and some other Persian kings. But when in 1802 (the year the Rosetta stone was brought to London) Grotefend presented a paper to the Göttingen Academy, it was rejected — on the grounds that he was not an orientalist.

By 1850 the three inscriptions which Rawlinson had copied in Behistun had been more or less translated. Though most of the credit goes to Rawlinson (who had by then renounced his diplomatic career to devote himself exclusively to the task at hand) other scholars, as for example Norris, Westergaard, Sayce and Oppert, and most of all the retiring Hincks who hardly ever left his country parsonage, had made essential contributions. The decipherment of the last — the Babylonian — inscription caused a good deal of controversy, despite convincing arguments put forward by Rawlinson and Hincks. In the end this was resolved, in rather dramatic fashion, by the mathematician William Henry Fox Talbot who sent his translation of the Tiglathpileser cylinder (see fig. 24) to the President of the Royal Asiatic Society with the request that Rawlinson and Hincks should likewise submit their translations in sealed envelopes. The Society agreed and invited the orientalist Jules Oppert to join in the contest. The four sealed packets were opened on 29 May 1857 by two examiners who concluded that the resemblance of the passages in the different translations was 'so great as to render it unreasonable to suppose the interpretation could be arbitrary or based on uncertain grounds'.

Other scripts

Many other ancient scripts were successfully deciphered in the course of the 19th century; James Prinsep, for example, deciphered the Brahmi script (see p.106) in the years between 1834 and 1839. Several scholars worked (like Hincks) on not just one, but on several different scripts more or less simultaneously. But no other decipherments had quite the same dramatic appeal as that of the Egyptian hieroglyphs and the cuneiform script, and none brought about quite the same public interest and acclaim. In both cases the great achievement lay in the combination of contributory factors. Both scripts were not only unknown, but constructed on principles entirely different from those hitherto known and used. Western scholars were familiar with the alphabet, with consonantal and syllabic scripts; at the most, with the mixture of concept and sound writing (e.g. Chinese). They knew about the possibilities of pictography but they had not previously encountered the same intricate mixture of phonetic and pictographic elements. They had no guidelines about the direction of writing or on how the text could be divided into sentences and words. In addition those scripts were used for languages entirely unknown as far as vocabulary, grammar, syntax and structures were concerned. Nothing was known about their pronunciation or the ideas they represented, and the type of information they were meant to store. Both scripts were keys to new worlds, new civilizations, new areas of perception. In fact only one other decipherment has aroused any similar amount of interest: the decipherment of Cretan Linear B (see fig. 41) by the architect and amateur archaeologist, Michael Ventris, in 1953 (see p.69).

Undeciphered scripts

A good number of scripts are still only partly deciphered. The reading of the hieroglyphic signs of the Meroïtic scripts (see p.65), for example, is more or less assured, but the interpretation of the inscriptions presents difficulties since their language seems to bear no relation to any known language. The decipherment of proto-Elamitic inscriptions which date from the first half of the 3rd millennium BC has likewise remained very much in its early stages. In the same way, while the cuneiform script of the Hittites was deciphered by the Czech Assyriologist Hrozný in 1915/16, the picture script presents a large number of uncertainties. Sayce made some rather fanciful attempts at a decipherment as early as 1880, and several scholars, including Hrozný himself, have in the meantime tried their skill, but a true understanding is still a good way off. There have been speculations about the possible (phonetic) script value of the *quipus* used by the Incas of Peru, as well as that of signs displayed on some of their textiles and drinking vessels (see p.79) but, despite some claims to the contrary, no proper reading has been made. The same holds true for the signs painted on beans used by the Moche people (see p.78). Claims have been made for the decipherment of the Tangut script of north-west China (see p.87) but they have not yet been fully substantiated; and the same can be said about the script of the Moso, Lolo, and of Old Hungarian (HJ, p.427).

While these and similar problems are likely to interest just a small group of specialists, there are three scripts which continue to attract a good deal of attention, speculation and, in part, controversy. They are the still undeciphered scripts of ancient Crete, pre-Columbian Central America and prehistoric India.

Scripts of ancient Crete

Ever since Sir Arthur Evans discovered and excavated the palace of Knossos at the beginning of this century, the ancient civilization of Crete has greatly stimulated the imagination of scholars and laymen. It is perhaps not without interest to note that Evans himself had originally become interested in Crete after examining a number of inscriptions (discovered in the 1880s) which were written mainly on stone, in what was obviously a non-Greek script. So far only one of the three Cretan scripts, Linear B, which was used not for the (still unknown) Minoan language, but for a contemporary form of Greek, has been deciphered. The earliest script, a distinctly pictorial (though not necessarily pictographic) form of writing, described at times as a series of ideograms representing a standard shorthand for objects listed on tablets, is still undeciphered. The same applies to Linear A, the script assumed to have evolved from those early picture signs. Both the number of signs (about 77–85) and the evidence of the (later) Linear B script point towards a syllabic script, but without a knowledge of the Minoan language and/or some substantial bilingual text, the possibilities of a decipherment are restricted.

The decipherment of Linear B, the latest Cretan script, only became possible after Michael Ventris recognized that it must have been used for writing the Greek language.

90 The Phaistos disc. (Photograph by courtesy of the British Museum; Department of Greek and Roman Antiquities)

This brilliant deduction was to no small extent influenced by the fact that tablets inscribed with short texts in Linear B have been found not only at Knossos but also on the Greek mainland, in places such as Pylos, Messina and Mycenae.

In 1908 the so-called Phaistos disc (fig. 90), one of the most puzzling objects ever discovered, was found in an outbuilding of the Minoan palace at Hagia Triada. The disc, 160 millimetres in diameter, and preliminarily dated 17th century BC because of some tablets of that date found next to it, is inscribed on both sides. 'Inscribed' is perhaps not the right word: a text, arranged in bands spiralling either to or from the centre, has been impressed with forty-five different wooden or metal punches into the originally soft clay. There are altogether 241 signs arranged in groups (words?) divided by vertical lines. Nothing similar has ever been found in Crete — or indeed anywhere else. The method of impressing the signs by means of specially prepared matrices (practically a form of printing with movable type) has apparently never been repeated, and it seems strange that such matrices should have been cut solely for the purpose of producing one single inscription or imprint. The signs themselves are clearly recognizable pictures of human beings, parts of the human body, objects, houses and plants. They bear no resemblance to the ancient pictorial script of Crete or indeed to any other hieroglyphic form of writing. Because of the number of different signs used in the text (forty-five), it has generally been assumed that the script was syllabic in character, but without any knowledge of the language, or the possibility of a comparison with other texts (which may well contain additional signs), this assumption does not really lead much further.

Decipherment of an unknown script is generally considered possible if either the script or the language is known, or if there is available some supplementary information in the form of bilingual inscriptions such as the one found on the Rosetta stone. This theory seems to be borne out in the case of the Cretan scripts: the decipherment of Linear B became possible after the language of the text had been recognized as Greek. Linear A, the script on the Phaistos disc, and the early hieroglyphic script have (despite all efforts) remained undeciphered, since nothing is known about the language for which they were used, and no substantial bilingual texts have so far come to light.

There are however exceptions to the theory. For example, despite the relative ease with which we can read the Etruscan inscriptions (our own Roman alphabet having largely been derived from an earlier Etruscan one), even despite internal evidence (the repetitious nature of funeral inscriptions and the ability to decipher names — which provided a vital breakthrough in the case of Egyptian, Old Persian and indeed a large number of other languages), it has not been possible to reconstruct or even adequately classify the Etruscan language. In other words, we can read the inscriptions but we cannot really understand them, nor can we use the information gained to build up a comprehensive picture of the language itself.

The Maya glyphs

Equally at odds with the above theory is the failure to decipher, completely, the writing of the Mayas of Central America — despite the fact that the language expressed by the glyphs is still (subject to some time-shifts) spoken today, and that efforts at decipherment have been made ever since the 16th century when the script was first discovered.

The first attempt at a decipherment of the Maya glyphs was made by Diego de Landa, a Franciscan who reached Yucatan in 1549. Landa, who eventually became Bishop of Yucatan, showed (for the 16th century) a rare interest in native culture. He collected a vast amount of information on Maya religion, history, customs, everyday life, the Mayan calendar, which he recorded, together with drawings of the day-signs and copies of inscriptions found at ceremonial centres, in a lengthy manuscript entitled *Relación de las cosas de Yukatán*. This manuscript, which also contained his decipherment of the Maya script, disappeared but was later found again and a (perhaps abbreviated) version was published just over a century ago.

On the surface Landa should have been ideally suited for the task, but a number of unavoidable prejudices (Landa perceived the Maya script as alphabetic), shortcomings (he seems to have been somewhat tone deaf) and misunderstandings (his informants apparently thought he was asking for the equivalent of the Spanish name of the letters, not their sound values) led him astray. Thus for A (pronounced 'ah') his informant drew the head of a turtle, *ac* in the Maya language; for B (pronounced 'bay') a foot, the Maya symbol for travel and roads; for C (pronounced 'sek') a truncated form of the month sign *zek*; for X (pronounced 'xay') the head of a vomiting man, since *xe* means 'to vomit', and so forth.

Over the years the Maya system of writing has attracted a good many would-be decipherers. In 1933 and 1952 the linguist Whorf and a Russian, Yuri Knorozov, respectively, tried to read the glyphs phonetically, giving them a predominantly syllabic value (that is, consonant plus vowel or vowel plus consonant); but both failed. J. E. S. Thompson, who has done much valuable work in identifying and interpreting glyphs, doubts whether a full and unchallenged decipherment will ever be possible. The reasons he cites are fairly convincing: the varying ways in which so many glyphs could be used, the way the reading of the texts depended on the interpreting priests, and last but not least the failure of the early Spanish word collectors to include religious terms in their dictionaries (JEST, p.63). Altogether the Maya system seems to consist of about 350 main signs, 370 affixes and about 100 portrait glyphs, mainly of deities; but those glyphic elements are combined to form far more numerous compounds. In addition, the Mayas ingeniously utilized ideograms, pictograms, synonyms and, above all, the system of rebus writing.

The Indus script

Until 1921/22, when the remains of urban settlements were first discovered in the Indus region, nothing was known about the civilization that flourished in the north-west of the Indian sub-continent some four to five millennia ago. Even Indian literature, noted for its antiquity, contained no valid reference to it. Now, sixty years later, after extensive excavations, much research, speculation and some controversy, we know a good deal about the material (and by inference the socio-religious) aspect of the Indus Valley, or Harappan, civilization (see p.67) but still lack conclusive evidence about the ethnic affinities of the population, the language they spoke, and, despite much effort and several claims to the contrary, we still cannot read the script.

Put briefly, the Indus script seems to consist of some 400 different signs — though it is doubtful that all of them were in regular use. It is generally assumed that the direction of writing was right to left: the majority of inscriptions start at the right-hand side with empty spaces, if any, at the left end of the line. Most of the inscriptions are on seals. There are no long texts (the average inscription numbers five to seven signs, the longest about twenty) and there are no bi-lingual ones. The majority of signs are pictorial, much in the manner of other contemporary scripts (Sumerian, Egyptian, Cretan) but there seems to have been no development towards more cursive forms (as in Egypt) or towards greater abstraction (as in the case of the cuneiform script). Whether there did exist lengthy texts on palm leaf or, as has been suggested, wax, cannot be ascertained; just as on the basis of existing evidence we do not really know whether the script served mainly administrative and commercial needs, or whether (or how far) it had a place in religion and ritual. Nor can we do more than speculate about the nature and extent of phonetic elements.

Ever since the Indus script was first discovered, it has attracted a great deal of attention. Scholars have linked it variously with the Minoan or Sumerian script, the Hittite script (and language), Sanskrit, proto-Dravidian (the common ancestor of the contemporary languages of South India), or, because of similarities in the appearance of certain signs, with a form of writing found on Easter Island (fig. 91) in the Pacific Ocean. Over the last thirty years or so the Indus script has assumed political connotations, and scholars (especially those from the sub-continent itself) are inclined to favour either Sanskrit (highly improbable) or Dravidian (possible though difficult to prove) connections depending on their own affiliations. Each year books or articles appear proclaiming decipherment, but none of the theories so far advanced has been totally convincing. Nearly all founder on the time factor — the long hiatus between the extinction of the Indus Valley civilization (*c.* 1600 BC) and the first evidence of an apparently Semitic-inspired Indian script (3rd century BC). In the same way, some 2,000 years would separate the unknown language of the Indus people from the first recorded evidence of a Dravidian tongue. Thus speculations — such as those put forward by the so-called Finnish Team in the 1960s — which identify, for example, the picture of a man carrying a yoke with the plural suffix (-*kaḷ* in modern Dravidian languages from -*kaḷai* – bamboo pole, *kaḷḷai* – collection, bundle) look seductively convincing, but are based on the linguistically untenable assumption that the language itself remained practically unchanged for over three millennia. Connections with Sanskrit are equally far-fetched. Sanskrit did not yet exist at the time when the Indus Valley civilization flourished, nor were the Indo-Aryans (who later used Sanskrit) anywhere near the area in question. So far as the Easter Island script is concerned, three millennia and a vast geographical distance separate the two civilizations. It is true that the similarity of some of the signs is indeed startling, but graphic similarities alone are never conclusive. Most pictorial/pictographic scripts contain signs which look alike; the possibilities of representing a man, a fish, a star, the sun, the eye, a tree, and so forth are distinctly limited. It is in fact just as likely that the language of the Indus people disappeared together with their civilization, as happened in the case of the Minoan, the Sumerian and indeed several other languages and scripts.

91 He kohau rongorongo, *a 'speaking wood' or 'news board' from Easter Island. According to local tradition king Hotu Matua (*c.1100–1200* AD) *brought this script with him by ship; despite recent claims to the contrary it is still basically undeciphered. (British Museum; Museum of Mankind; 9295)*

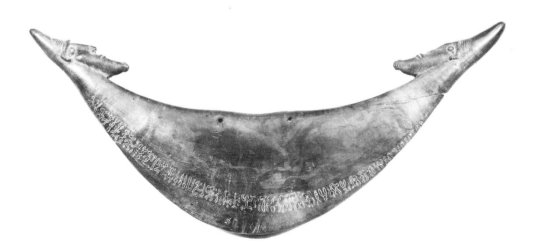

IV Social attitudes to writing and literacy

The position of the scribe in society

Ancient Egypt and Mesopotamia saw the heyday of the scribal profession, for the contribution of the scribe was essential to the economic and political survival of society. In addition the system of writing was complex, warranting a high level of skill only to be acquired through lengthy studies. Enjoying a high social status, the profession was able to attract recruits from the wealthy and privileged classes, which added further prestige. It was also to some extent a hereditary profession; both societies preferred a son to follow in the footsteps of his father. In Mesopotamia all parents were in theory encouraged to see that their children knew how to read and write, but in practice only a few were in a position to do so. Descriptions of Sumerian scribal schools dating from the first quarter of the 2nd millennium BC speak of the sons of governors, senior civil servants, scribes, and priests as pupils, and, occasionally, of a poor boy or orphan who had been adopted by a wealthy man.

Egyptian scribes led privileged lives and considered themselves superior to other men. They seem to have been exempt from taxation and, equally important in a country where at least in theory everybody could be called upon to perform manual labour, they were not expected to work outside their profession. ('Put writing in your heart that you protect yourself from hard labour of any kind', writes an Egyptian from the period of the New Kingdom.) The divine model of the royal scribe was Toth (see Plate V), the ibis-headed scribe of the gods — and, according to myth, the inventor of writing. Either as priests or civil servants, scribes wielded considerable power and influence, and even high officials had themselves depicted as scribes in their votive or funerary statuary. Wall-paintings, illustrations on papyrus or statues show the scribe either standing (see Toth), half kneeling or, more often than not, in a squatting position, the partly unrolled papyrus ready for writing placed on top of his tightly-stretched kilt (see fig. 34), with the scribal palette (fig. 92), his badge of office, either at hand or hanging over his shoulder.

Proficiency in the art of writing was not easily acquired. Pupils spent a good number of years in strictly disciplined scribal schools, at first only copying texts and styles of writing, before being finally allowed to develop their own style. In addition they were often made to learn accountancy, assessment of taxes, mathematics, the composition of letters and other auxiliary accomplishments. Trade, economics, data relating to the agricultural year, co-ordination and control of the labour force digging the all-important irrigation canals, the organization of essential festivals and events — in fact the whole and vital interaction between the Palace, the Temple and the people — depended on the efficiency of a vast army of scribes. Mesopotamian scribes accompanied military expeditions, writing dispatches and accounts, acting as quarter-masters for the issuing of rations and equipment, recording booty and counting the slain enemies. Bas-reliefs often depict a pair of scribes (see fig. 35), one bearded, inscribing a clay tablet or ivory board with a coating of wax, the other clean-shaven, writing or perhaps drawing (the scenes on the bas-reliefs have the detailed accuracy of a visual eye-witness account) on what may either be a papyrus or a leather scroll.

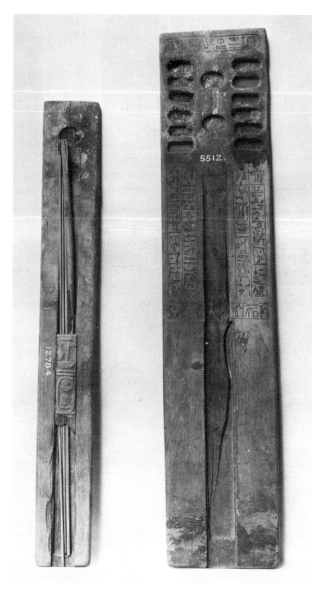

92 Wooden scribal palettes from Egypt; 18th Dynasty, c. 1570 BC. (British Museum; Department of Egyptian Antiquities; 15512 and 12784)

Since privilege feeds on exclusivenes and the preservation of the *status quo*, scribes were a highly conservative force in both Egypt and Mesopotamia. It was after all not in their interest to simplify the system of writing and make the profession accessible to a wider spectrum of society, or worse, create a situation where society no longer depended on professional scribes. In Egypt three different styles of writing (hieroglyphic, hieratic and demotic) developed in the course of three millennia (see p.60), but the script itself remained basically unchanged, maintaining the same complex interplay of phonetic and ideographic elements, despite the fact that the concept of phonetic writing, even the use of (only twenty-four) single consonant signs, was clearly understood from an early date onwards. In the same way, as long as the socio-economic system did not change, the cuneiform script of Mesopotamia became, if anything, more complex after it had been taken over by the Semitic-speaking Akkadians.

Among the Aztecs of Mexico the knowledge of writing was largely in the hands of the priests (and those trained by them) who were responsible for keeping written records of all essential festivals and occasions—such as the much feared end of each calendric cycle which, if proper rituals were not observed, could mean the end of the known world. They also recorded historical events (ensuring the identity of the group), genealogy (essential for placing each individual in correct chronological order within society), tribute paid to the king and the Temple (one of the mainstays of the economy), legal trials, and other information vital to the continuation of society. Since the highly-developed picture script with its sprinkling of phonetic elements used for the *codices* was unintelligible without the special knowledge that the priests alone possessed, their position and power was, if anything, even more assured than that of the Egyptian and Mesopotamian scribes.

Aztec writing acted to some extent as a form of memory aid. Memory aids, or mnemonic devices, represent an important transitional stage between oral and literary traditions (see p.25). Even the Brahmins of India, hostile to writing, had (mental) memory aids to safeguard the correct recitation of the sacred hymns. In tribal societies memory aids are mostly in the hands of priests who have the necessary, often orally transmitted, knowledge to interpret them for the benefit of the rest of society. Thus the priest becomes the interpreter between the deities and the people, between profane and sacred knowledge, and it is very often left to his discretion how much of this knowledge he reveals to whom. Many memory aids can be read in different ways on different occasions in front of a different audience.

It would however be wrong to think that the existence of scribe-priests or even scribe-civil servants automatically meant a high level of privilege and material advantage for each member of the scribal profession. Once the unity between Palace and Temple disintegrates, and the economy moves in the direction of non-stratified individual enterprise, the situation changes and the position of the scribe often deteriorates. In other words, instead of depending on the scribe, society begins to use him. If in addition a complex system of writing, mixing elements of sound and idea transmission, is replaced by a simpler (democratically usable) phonetic script which, at least in theory, is well within the intellectual grasp of the majority of people, the professional scribe can become a mere secretary, a servant or even a slave.

Scribes in the service of religious communities did not always fare much better. Among the Israelites the position of the scribe was at first largely influenced by Akkadian and Egyptian models. Scribes learned their profession in family-like guilds (fig. 93) and, according to their competence, were attached to government and Temple offices where they enjoyed considerable influence. The highest post was that of the royal scribe, who fulfilled an advisory capacity and in addition seems to have been in charge of financial matters. There were also independent scribes who either served the public (to draw up documents, write letters etc.) or who were employed by persons of means very much in the capacity of personal secretaries. In Judaism scribes became professional experts for writing the Torah scroll. Theoretically every Jew was supposed to write a Torah scroll for himself, but the high level of technical skill necessary for such a task made it more practical to commission a professional scribe instead. Professional scribes were indeed indispensable to the Jewish community; in fact, the Talmud advises scholars not to dwell in a town where there are no scribes. Yet during the Talmudic period, scribes were very poorly paid on the

93 Pentateuch *with the five* Megilloth, *1395 AD. The illustration shows a teacher, with a whip, and a pupil pointing to Hillel's maxim written in his book 'whatever is hateful unto you, do not unto thy fellowman'. (British Library; Oriental Collections; Add. 19776, f.72v)*

ובהמה ובשדיה אחזתו לא ימכר ולא יגאל כל חרם קדשים הוא ליהוה בל חרם אשר
יחרם מן האדם לא יפדה מות יומת וכל מעשר הארץ מזרע הארץ מפרי העץ ליהוה
הוא קדש ליהוה ואם גאל יגאל איש ממעשרו חמישתו יסף עליו וכל מעשר בקר
וצאן כל אשר יעבר תחת השבט העשירי יהיה קדש ליהוה לא יבקר בין טוב לרע ולא
ימירנו ואם המר ימירנו והיה הוא ותמורתו יהיה קדש לא יגאל אלה המצות אשר
צוה יהוה את משה אל בני ישראל בהר סיני

חזק

סימן סכום פסוקי דספרא בטה

grounds that should they become rich they would desert their vocation! Strict rules laid down in a special compendium for scribes (*Tikkun Soferim*) governed the writing of the Torah scroll. The scribe was not allowed to write from memory but had to copy the text from a written model; before beginning his work he had to take a ritual bath and specially prepare himself so that he would be able to write the name of God in a state of perfect devotion and ritual purity. Scribes also acted as recording clerks and court secretaries, with the understanding that the party which derived greater benefit from a case would pay the scribe (perhaps not always an altogether satisfactory arrangement!). Religion and commerce were essential to the Jewish community; neither could function without an extensive use of writing. But writing itself was no longer a secret lore only to be acquired after years of study. Theoretically it was within the reach of a wide section of society, who in turn could afford to leave the task to a professional scribe if necessary. In other words, the power was no longer in the hands of the specialist but in the hands of those who could afford to commission the specialist.

Islam greatly respected the scribe (fig. 94), especially the scribe who was also a skilled calligrapher and who devoted himself to the writing of the Koran. The first words the archangel Gabriel spoke to the Prophet in the cave of Hira near Mecca were 'Recite! In the name of the Lord who created all things. He has taught us the use of the pen. He has taught us that which we know not.' (Koran, XCVI, 1–5).

94 An illustration from a Turkish manuscript showing members of the scribal room; a scribe (holding book), an artist (holding drawing) and the instruments necessary for writing such as pen, ink, scissors, brush, pen-case and hour glass; 1681 AD. (British Library; Oriental Collections; Or. 7043, f.7v)

Before the coming of Islam the Arabs had mostly been illiterate nomads who relied for the preservation of their literature on oral tradition. At first the Koran was similarly transmitted, but when after 633 AD a large number of Huffaz (men who memorize and recite the Koran) were killed in the battles which followed the Prophet's death, the alarmed Muslim community turned to writing as a more reliable medium of information storage. Writing and Islam became a powerful combination, facilitating the unification of the Arab tribes, the conquest of a large part of the known world and the perpetuation of the new faith. In this context the scribe, especially the calligrapher, was never a mere servant or artisan, but a man in harmony with the will and purpose of God. The names of famous calligraphers have been carefully preserved for posterity; often they were persons of high social standing — princes, scholars, statesmen, even Caliphs.

Hinduism on the other hand has never shown much respect either for writing or for the scribal profession. Since the central Jewish, Christian and Islamic texts are directly related to the word of God, the (publicly verifiable) accuracy of the written word was, quite early on, considered preferable to oral tradition, just as the multiplication of those texts aided the task of conversion. Buddhism (basically a secular creed like Communism) found itself in a similar position. It is true that up to a point Judaism is highly exclusive, insisting like Hinduism on the accident of birth, but within Jewish society all Jews are entitled to the same level of information. Exactly the opposite is true of Hinduism. There the sacred texts were originally the carefully-guarded property of certain Brahmanical sub-groups whose power and status depended on their ability to maintain this monopoly. Once a point had been reached when the texts with their innumerable commentaries and sub-commentaries had to be written down (the sheer volume of information outstripped human memory), temples and other religious institutions did of course use scribes and copyists, but whereas in Islam and Christianity it was meritorious to write the text of the Koran or the Bible, in Hinduism the merit went mostly to the person who commissioned the work. Scribes were equally necessary for the administration of the Hindu kingdoms, but since the rendering of personal service to anybody outside the family group is likely to lower one's status, scribes as a class were largely prevented from realizing a high level of social prestige. Ritual purity is one of the central themes of Hinduism; even the Brahmins who perform the essential rituals, either for the dead or in the temple, are of lower status than other Brahmins, since the execution of those rituals makes them subject to pollution through contact with unclean elements or persons. The Khayasthas, nowadays mostly business people or bureaucrats, are generally considered a scribal caste. On feast days they worship pens and pencils — something often copied by modern students. The caste status of the Khayasthas, who exist in various local sub-divisions, is widely disputed. They themselves will either claim to be Brahmins, tracing their descent from Chitragupta, the record keeper of Yama, the god of the dead, or in certain areas they will claim affiliations with the Kshatriya caste. The actual Kshatriyas (the second highest caste) have long become extinct, but descent from them is frequently claimed by groups anxious to establish their credentials at the upper end of the social scale. Most authorities look upon the Khayasthas as Shudras (the lowest caste), at best 'clean Shudras'. In North India popular consensus often argues that the Khayasthas had originally been Brahmins, but had lost their caste by serving as scribes for the Muslim administration.

In Mycenaean Greece, split into a number of small but heavily-administered districts, the scribal class which served the great warrior leaders based its position (like the script they used) largely on Cretan models. After 1300 BC the disruption of international trade by sea raiders and pirates, with the resultant loss of the most vital export markets, initiated a slow but irreversible disintegration of the commercial empire. By the end of the millennium most of Greece had been overrun by Dorian invaders who knew nothing of, and indeed had no use for, large palace bureaucracies. The old scribal tradition and the socio-economic pattern of society, which had for so long placed the scribe in the essential position of interpreter and coordinator, became obsolete.

Greek democracy was a new experiment in human history. After the Dark Ages came a sudden acceleration of cultural, political and intellectual interest. The re-introduction of writing after a period of illiteracy, with the adoption of the Phoenician consonant script, soon to be transformed into the alphabet, was one of the by-products of a revitalized sea trade. Diringer has called the alphabet a 'democratic' script, as opposed to the 'theocratic' script of ancient Egypt. But the reason why this particular form of writing was adopted at precisely this point and why, unlike the two previous attempts at writing the Greek language — Cretan Linear B and the Cypriote script (see pp.69/70) — this particular adoption proved successful, lay in the fact that Greek society was reaching a stage where it was in need of a 'democratic' form of writing. Under the Athenian democracy citizens were actively involved in the affairs of state. The machinery of government depended not on scribal coordinators but on the contribution of all free men. Private citizens participated in legislation and day-to-day administration, performing duties that would today be undertaken by permanent civil servants, and in ancient societies by professional scribes. Records of their reports were made public in the form of inscriptions. Inscriptions played an important role in ancient Greece; they often served the purpose of today's printed documents or newspaper announcements, disseminating and recording information which enabled citizens to participate in government. In Athens temporary notices, such as drafts of proposed legislation or lists of men required for military service, were written on boards and displayed in the civic centre. The spread of democracy relied on the spread of literacy. Even to ostracize (banish) an undesirable person from Athens for ten years was only possible if 6,000 men each wrote his name, simultaneously, on individual pieces of *ostraca* (potsherd). Writing, far from being a (semi-) secret art practised by a specially trained élite, was an essential element of Greek democracy. The Greek word for 'element' was in fact the same as that for 'letter of the alphabet', and Plato compares the first basic principles of his philosophy with the child's first contact with the alphabet.

Though writing and literacy were considered important in Imperial Rome, the position of the scribe was often ambivalent. Indeed in many cases he would be a slave (or at best a freedman), and — as one discovers if one examines the forms of recorded names — often a slave of Greek origin.

This however does not mean that the free citizens of Rome were indifferent to writing and literacy. Many of them, especially those belonging to the great and wealthy families, were well versed in Latin and Greek, and quite early on a number of formal and informal styles arose to accommodate the differing needs of business, administration and ceremony. The Latin language and the Roman alphabet were brought by Roman legionaries and imperial officials to Western Europe (which had no writing system of its own) and to the rest of the vast Empire (much of it already under Hellenistic influence). The Empire itself, which at times reached from Britain to the Euphrates, depended for its survival on the effective use of written communication; but though writing was absolutely essential in the Roman world, scribes were never accorded the status they had enjoyed in Egypt and Mesopotamia. The Roman Empire was based on conquest and secular ambition, not on the (usually hypocritical) desire to extend the domain of some divine agency. The scribe worked for Caesar, not for the Temple.

In 311 AD Christianity became the official religion of the Roman Empire. Whereas Roman religion had depended on outward ceremonial, Christianity possessed in the Bible (and the subsequent corpus of commentaries), the revealed word of God, and the desire to propagate it created an almost instant need for competent (and ideologically reliable) copyists. In the 5th century the Roman Empire disintegrated under an onslaught of tribal insurrections which swept throughout most of Western Europe; and in 410 AD Rome itself was sacked by the Goths. In consequence the organized and civilized way of life that had prevailed for so long came to an abrupt end and the need for common literacy decreased. It may well have become extinct altogether without the Christian Church — which took over the mantle of Rome, creating a new empire which once again united the interests of the Temple and the Palace.

During the 7th and 8th centuries Christianity began to spread along the old (Roman) lines of communication, taking with it the Bible, the vellum *codex*, the quill pen and the current forms of writing which soon expanded into a number of new and important stylistic variations (see p.167). In this new context the scribe was once more of the utmost importance. All the large monasteries in Ireland, Britain and on the Continent had their special *scriptoria* where dedicated and gifted monks worked as scribes (see fig. 36), illuminators and bookbinders. Their status within the monastic community could be high: St Columba (521–597), the founder of Iona, was much praised for his activities as a scribe, and Eadfrith, who wrote the famous Lindisfarne Gospels (see Plate VI), became Bishop of Lindisfarne, in 698 AD. Much of the work, especially the copying of illuminated texts, was team-work — for practical reasons and as a guard against pride and vanity. The hours were long (every daylight hour was a working one); the work itself was arduous, especially during the winter months when, sometimes, the completion of a text had to be postponed until the onset of the warmer weather.

As soon as the political situation became again more stabilized in Western Europe, government and administration once more developed a need for the clerical skills, which to begin with were inevitably provided by the Church in the shape of the *clericus* or clerk. As in ancient Mesopotamia (Ashurbanipal had been the first Babylonian king to master the 'clerical skills') the ruling classes were often illiterate. Charlemagne (*d.* 814), whose name will always be associated with one of the finest medieval scripts, the Carolingian minuscule (see p.172) and who tried hard to master the art of writing, even taking his writing tablets to bed with him, did not progress much beyond the ability to write his name; other noble personages contented themselves with the use of three crosses in place of a signature. There were of course noteworthy exceptions: Henry I of England (1068–1135) was known as Beauclerc for his proficiency in the art of writing and, later, Maximilian I of Austria (1459–1519) not only took great interest in fine printing, but was himself an accomplished calligrapher.

As the Middle Ages progressed, economic and political life grew increasingly more complex, creating the need for a wider spread of literacy. Clerks ceased to be clerics, and administration and commerce alike made use of accomplished and trained laymen. In fact from the 12th century onward, the Church monopoly of scholarship and learning began to decline and the gradual secularization of society led to the foundation of independent universities and schools. The monastic *scriptoria* ceased to be the main centres of book production, and the book market increased, catering for the needs of students, scholars, and the newly wealthy merchant classes. In the towns, professional scribes set up workshops and formed themselves into guilds to protect their interests. Side by side with the traditional book hands used in the *scriptorium*, less formal and more cursive styles gained prominence.

The introduction of printing into 15th-century Europe brought reading and writing to a wider and more diverse audience. It also made the medieval copyist more or less obsolete.

95 *A writing master at work surrounded by the various instruments of his craft.* Libellus valde doctus *by Urban Wyss, 1549. (Victoria and Albert Museum; 86. D. 95)*

96 A tutor to penmanship: or the writing master *by John Ayres, 1698. John Ayres was one of the best known English writing masters; he was a great protagonist of the round hand, which was to become the dominant script in England in the next century. (Victoria and Albert Museum; 86.K.17)*

97 The universal penman *by George Bickham, 1743. Would-be clerks in commercial firms needed a good round business hand, an accomplishment that could only be acquired through tuition and practice. (Victoria and Albert Museum; 86.T.107)*

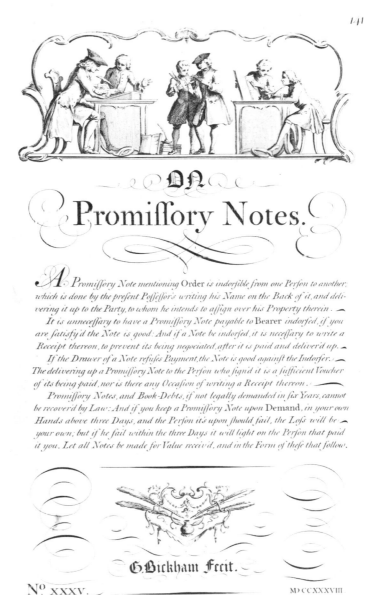

His place was soon taken by the writing master (fig. 95) whose position in society was somewhat ambiguous: higher than that of a craftsman, not quite as high as that of a scholar. Writing masters taught their craft in schools, to private pupils, and also published their copies (fig. 96) to gain fame, recognition of their individual styles and no doubt also to increase their commercial viability. Some developed exceedingly pleasing styles, others advocated excessive ornamentation; fashion began to play a part (JIW, pp.144/182) but in the end the scribe as writing master met with the same fate as the scribe as copyist. The accelerating demands of commerce, trade and colonial administration led, especially in 18th-century England, to an ever-increasing need for clerks (fig. 97) who were able to write

98 Drake's Treasure. *When Sir Francis Drake returned to England in 1580 from his voyage round the world, Elizabeth I suggested to the Spanish Ambassador that his conduct be investigated and if misconduct could be proved he should be punished and the treasure returned; but six months later she knighted him on the deck of his ship. This warrant to the master of the Jewel House and the Mint is dated 26 April 1584, just three years after the ceremony. Good example of contemporary 'Secretary hand', with signature of Elizabeth I. (British Library; Department of Manuscripts, Harl. 6986, f.37)*

a clear, fluent business hand, unlike the often rather difficult-to-read 'secretary hands' up till then used for most public and private documents (fig. 98). Writing became a practical subject, and developments in calligraphy all but ceased. With the spread of primary education in Western Europe and America, universal literacy became the ultimate aim and writing ceased to be a rare accomplishment. The scribe was no longer a specialist, since, at least in theory, everybody was expected to be his or her own scribe — if he or she did not use the telephone or the typewriter. During the 19th century and for most of the 20th century, the ability to read and write assumed an almost moral dimension as missionaries and educators at home and overseas propagated the idea of universal literacy as the ultimate panacea for all ills.

Women and writing

Whilst in the rest of the world the 10th century was generally a rather bleak and precarious period, in Japan the Heian period had just reached its halfway mark, producing a highly advanced and totally original form of culture. Translation of literary works from this period such as Murasaki's *Tale of Genji* and Sei Shonagon's *Pillow Book* allow us glimpses of a courtly society where a small number of men and women led lives of almost unbelievable sophistication and artistic refinement. In those circles the art of writing occupied a very special place. Arthur Waley goes so far as to say that the true religion of the Heian people was the cult of calligraphy, and though this is perhaps an exaggeration, it is certainly true that the way a man or woman handled the brush was considered a far better guide to his or her breeding, sensitivity and character than what they actually wrote (or said). A fine calligraphic hand came close to being a moral virtue, and being, in the opinion of the people, a mirror of a person's soul, it also played an essential part in the complex games of courtship which occupied so much of the leisure hours of people of Heian. Often it was the sight of a lady's (or gentleman's) handwriting which first gave rise to romantic speculation and to a desire to meet the writer in person. Calligraphy was a powerful aphrodisiac and during the initial stages of a love affair both partners awaited the first written communication from the other with a good deal of trepidation — since an indifferent handwriting nearly always meant the end of the affair. At one point in the *Tale of Genji* Prince Genji receives a letter from a lady he had known in Akashi. His favourite companion, Murasaki, is consumed with anxiety, not about the contents of the letter, but about the lady's handwriting. When she finally manages to catch a glimpse of it she at once realizes 'that there was great depth and feeling in the penmanship. Indeed it had style that might give pause to the most distinguished ladies of the Court', accepting sadly that it was 'small wonder that Genji felt about the girl the way he did'. Years later Genji takes the thirteen-year-old Princess Nyosan as his official wife and again Murasaki waits anxiously for her first glimpse of the girls' handwriting, knowing that her own future might depend on it. Genji, lying next to Murasaki, is equally filled with anticipation. But this time the handwriting turns out to be unformed and childish, and both Genji and Murasaki are embarrassed that somebody of the princess's rank could have reached this age without developing a more polished style. Tactfully Murasaki 'pretended not to have noticed and made no comment. Genji also kept silent. If the letter had come from somebody else he would certainly have whispered something about the writing, but he felt sorry for the girl and simply said, "Well now, you see that you have nothing to worry about".'

This may give the impression that in 10th-century Japan aestheticism outweighed political and economic considerations so far as the attitude of society to writing and to those who wrote was concerned, and that at least in this sphere men and women enjoyed equal status. But appearance can be highly deceptive. The level of capriciousness and sophistication that prevailed in court circles was the prerogative of a very small and already highly privileged group. The ordinary business of writing associated with administration, religion and learning was left to men — to scholars, priests and officials who, despite a growing independence from Chinese role models (in 894 AD the Japanese government had decided to stop sending official embassies to China), continued to use the Chinese language and the Chinese script; in fact the Chinese language and the Chinese script remained the exclusive and highly prestigious medium for any serious writing among men. Women were largely restricted to the use of Japanese and the (phonetic) *kana* script (see p.86) and it was to no small extent this restriction which resulted in the remarkable growth of indigenous Japanese literature during the Heian period.

99 *St Ann teaching her daughter the Virgin Mary to read from a book. (British Library; Department of Manuscripts; Add 24686, f.2(b))*

100 *Japanese print by Utamaro (1753–1806) from the* Twelve hours of the Gay Quarters. *The hour of the dog; a courtesan writes a love-letter to a client, attended by an apprentice. The ink-box, with its stone for rubbing down the ink stick into the water, is on the floor. (British Library; Department of Oriental Antiquities; 1906-1230-341 (b27))*

This brings us to the question of women and writing. Was the position of the Heian ladies unique? The answer must be a cautious 'Yes' and 'No'.

Whenever the ability to write was associated with power and influence, women were, as a rule, excluded. There were no professional female scribes in Egypt or Mesopotamia. In Judaism and Islam the position of women was generally too low to allow them to tamper with the writing of the name of God, though this did not necessarily condemn them wholesale to illiteracy. Hinduism did. Whereas there had been female scholars, poets and even teachers during the Vedic period, once Manu and the other Brahmanical lawgivers (500 BC–400 AD) had codified the ritually unclean status of women and deprived them, among many other things, of the right to study the Vedas, learning soon became a qualification for women of ill-fame. Only Ganikas, a certain class of public women consisting of dancing girls, married women hired out by their husbands for a fee, the wives of artists and bards, dissatisfied wives and all women with meretricious yearnings(!) were taught how to read. Indeed until very recently the belief prevailed (and is still not far from the surface in rural areas) that disaster would befall the family if a woman so much as held a book or pen in her hand. Christianity on the other hand encouraged literacy among women, though not always without ulterior motives. St Ann, the patron saint of mothers, is usually portrayed teaching the Virgin Mary, her daughter, how to read from a book (fig. 99). During the Middle Ages, women of noble estate were often better versed in Latin

and other school learning than boys, whose education centred around hunting, warfare and the courtly arts. The Church was anxious to encourage this trend, hoping that a better education might make girls more suited for the religious life should their parents decide to dedicate them — appropriately endowed with wordly possessions of course — to a nunnery. Convents, especially those based on the Benedictine Rule, were often great feminist institutions where able women, freed from the drudgery of repeated childbirth and the constant supervision of men, could carve out a career for themselves as administrators, scholars or scribes. Sometimes nuns and monks worked jointly on the copying of illuminated texts. In an astronomical treatise made in Alsace in about 1154 the illuminator painted on the dedication page a portrait of himself and of the scribe, who in this case was Guta, the canoness of the nearby sister house (DJ, p.70). The admiration the Heian ladies received for their proficiency in handling the brush was largely related to their erotic charms. They wrote as women, not as scribes or scholars. They also wrote, as we have seen, exclusively in Japanese and in the *kana* script. To write in Chinese, using Chinese characters, was considered highly unseemly, and ladies who had somehow acquired such knowledge, like Murasaki who came from a family of scholars, discreetly abstained from emphasizing this fact. But though the Heian ladies had no direct political influence they were of great importance to their families. The advantageous marriage of a daughter, if possible to an emperor, an imperial prince or a member of a distinguished family such as the Fujiwaras, greatly increased the political influence of her own family. Daughters were in many ways more useful than sons. A son, even from the most renowned family, could never hope to become an emperor, but a daughter married to an imperial prince might give birth to a future emperor. To make such a marriage possible the girl had to be well-versed in the prescribed accomplishments (music, the composition of poetry, the preparation of incense etc.), and an indifferent calligraphic hand would have quickly disqualified her, despite all other charms.

Thus the art of writing remained a mere accomplishment, designed to make women more attractive to those who ultimately controlled society — namely men. In just the same way, 700 years later, the great courtesans of the 'Floating World' were expected to be adept in music, poetry, calligraphy (fig. 100) and conversation. Patriarchal societies have usually been skilful at introducing a strict division between women meant to breed (respectable wives), who were kept as ignorant as possible, and women meant to entertain (hetaerae, courtesans, dancers, actresses), who were allowed a varying modicum of skills and education. Only occasionally, as in the Heian period, did the two roles combine; and, to their everlasting credit, the Heian ladies made full use of this opportunity.

Writing and aesthetics

Calligraphy

What exactly is calligraphy? The term derives from the Greek words *graphein* (to write) and *kallos* (beautiful), but fine writing and the development of distinct styles is not in itself calligraphy. To create, or better, to achieve, true calligraphy several elements have to combine: the attitude of society to writing, the importance of the texts, definite (often mathematically based) rules about the correct interaction between lines and space and their relationship to each other, mastery and understanding of the script, the writing material and the tools used for writing. Calligraphy is more than craftsmanship; it demands individuality, but individuality expressed within strictly prescribed boundaries. Calligraphy is to a large extent an expression of harmony, harmony as perceived by one particular civilization. The calligrapher is in harmony with his script, his tools, the text and his own cultural heritage. Only three civilizations have produced true calligraphy: the Arabs (and those who used the Arabic script), the Chinese (and those who used the Chinese script), and Western civilization, based on the Roman alphabet, Roman laws and the Christian Church.

ARABIC CALLIGRAPHY

Islam and the Koran played a central part in the development of Arabic calligraphy. At the time of the Prophet's death in 632 AD the Arabs were still basically an unlettered people. The only script in existence was rather rudimentary and distinctly lacking in elegance, and few chose to master it. Some hundred years later, by the time the Abbasid Caliphate was established in Baghdad, the Arabic script had not only been effectively reformed, but the art of calligraphy was beginning to establish itself in the Arab world. Several elements contributed to this development. There was first of all the sacred nature of the Koran itself. Since the text was a direct revelation from God, it had to be rendered not only perfectly correctly (hence the script reform), but in a manner that did visual justice to its illustrious origin. In addition Islam forbids the representation of the living form, and whereas in China painting and calligraphy became closely interrelated, among the Arabs who followed the new faith the painter had to turn himself more often than not into a scribe in order to express his vision of the world. In Islam perfect calligraphy is a manifestation of spirituality, of an inward perfection which comes from being in harmony with the will and purpose of God. There have always been strong connections between mysticism and calligraphy, and calligraphers and Sufis alike trace back their spiritual lineage to the same person, the Prophet's cousin Ali ibn Abi Talib.

Early calligraphic styles are mainly associated with the names of certain towns, such as Mecca, Medina, Basrah and Kufah (see p. 97). From among them Kufic (see fig. 58), a bold angular script with horizontally stretched lines, gained the widest acceptance as the most suitable script for the writing of the Koran. By the 9th century two derivations from Kufic appeared; one was Western Kufic (fig. 101) from which all the later scripts of north-west Africa and Andalusia (Spain) claim descent, the other Eastern or 'bent' Kufic (fig. 102).

101 Koran. The chapter headings are in Western Kufic, the rest in Maghribi; written in Morocco in 1568 AD. (British Library; Oriental Collections; Or. 1405, f.371v).

By the 10th century more than twenty different cursive styles were in common use, many of them lacking in elegance and discipline, all of them in danger of degenerating into an endless multiplicity of styles. It was time for a reform, and the reform came in the person of Ibn Muqlah (*d.* 940), an accomplished calligrapher from Baghdad who, by the later part of his life, had served as Vizir to three Abbasid Caliphs. Ibn Muqlah set himself the task of radically redesigning the cursive script so as to make it a vehicle suitable for the writing of the Koran. He laid down a comprehensive system of calligraphic rules based on the rhombic dot, the 'standard' *alif* and the 'standard' circle.

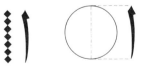

The rhombic dot is formed by pressing the pen diagonally on paper so that the length of the dot's equal sides are the same as the width of the pen. The 'standard' *alif* is a straight vertical stroke measuring a specific number of rhombic dots (five or seven according to the style) placed vertex to vertex. The 'standard' circle has a diameter equal to the length of the 'standard' *alif*. The 'standard' *alif* and the 'standard' circle also supply the basic geometric forms for fashioning the individual characters (YHS, p.18).

After Ibn Muqlah several other famous calligraphers added their contribution to the perfection of Arabic calligraphy, but without altering the basic principles of his system.

102 Koran. Late eastern Kufic; 13th–14th century. (British Library; Oriental Collections; Or. 6573, ff.210v/211r)

Ibn Muqlah is in fact supposed to have already applied his rules successfully to the *sittah*, the six major cursive scripts of classical tradition: Thuluth, Naskhi (see fig. 59), Muhaqqaq, Rayhani, Riqa and Tawqi.

WESTERN CALLIGRAPHY

Regularity, organization and (at times individualistically interpreted) disciplines are the hallmarks of Western calligraphy. These qualities were already apparent in the capital or monumental script of Imperial Rome. The basic forms of this script are the square, the circle and the half-square. The square in addition provides the 'perfect number', namely ten; the width of the main line of each letter is supposed to measure one-tenth of its height. All letters (of an inscription) are of equal height, as if written between two invisible horizontal lines. The finishing line (serif) at the top and/or foot, a by-product of the way letters are cut into stone with a chisel, accentuates the impression of overall harmony:

This script had no ligatures or abbreviations and was, like the early Greek script, ideally suited for inscriptions on stone and metal; written with a (square) pen, it was also used in

ETSICUBIQVISFEROACRABIDOFURORECAPTETUR·SIFORTEFUERIT·PSALMVIITITA
DIXERIMCARMINIBVSINCANTATVS·CONTINUOOMNISRABIESFEROCITATIS
ABSCEDIT·PSALMVSTRANQVILLITASANIMARVMEST·SIGNIFERPACIS
PERTURBATIONESVELFLUCTVSCOGITATIONVMCOHIBENS·IRACUNDIAMREPRIMEN
LVXVRIEPELLENS·SOBRIETATEMSVGGERENS·AMICITIASCONGREGANS·ADDUCENS
INCONCORDIAMDISCREPANTES·RECONCILIANSINIMICOS·QVISENIMVLTRAIN
IMICVMDVCATEVM·CVMQVOVNAMADDMPSALMIEMISERITVOCEM·
EXQVOINTELLEGITVR·QVIAETQVODBONORVMOMNIVMMAXIMVMESTCARI
TATEM·PSALMVSINSTAVRAT·CONIVNCTIONEMQVANDAMPERCONSONANTIAM
VOCISEFFICIENS·ETDIVERSVMPOPVLVMVNIVSCHORI·PERCONCORDIAMCONSO
CIANS·PSALMVSDAEMONESFVGAT·ANGELOSINADIVTORIVMSALVTISINVITAT·
SCVTVMINNOCTVRNISTERRORIBVS·DIVRNORVMREQVIESESTLABORVM·
TVTELAPVERIS·IVVENIBVSORNAMENTVM·SOLAMENSENIBVS·MVLIERIBVS
APTISSIMVSDECOR·DISSERTAHABITAREFACITORBIS·SOBRIETATEMDOCET·
INCIPIENTIBVSPRIMVMEFFICITVRELEMENTVM·TOTIVSECCLESIAEVOXVMNA·
PSALMVSSOLLEMNITATESDECORAT·PSALMVSTRISTITIAMQVAESECUNDUM
DMESTMOLITVR·PSALMVSETIAMEXCORDELAPIDEOLACRIMASMOVET·
PSALMVSANGELORVMOPVS·EXERCITIVMCAELESTIVM·SPITALETYMNIANA·
OVEREADMIRANDIMAGISTRISAPIENSINSTITVTVM·VTSIMVLETCANTARE
VIDEAMVR·ETQVODADVTILITATEMANIMAEPERTINETDOCEAMVR·
PERQVODMAGISNECESSARIADOCTRINANOSTRISMENTIB·INFORMATVR·
PROEOQVODSIQVAPERVIM·ETDIFFICVLTATEMALIQVAMANIMISNOSTRIS
FVERITINSERTA·CONTINVODILABVNTVR·EAVEROQVAECVMGRATIAETDI
LECTIONESVSCIPIMVS·NESCIOQVOPACTOMAGISRESIDEREINMENTIBVSACME
MORIAEVIDENTVRINHERERE·QVIDAVTEMESTQVODNONDISCATVREXPSALMI
NONOMNISMAGNITVDOVIRTVTIS·NONNORMAIVSTITIAE·NONPVDICITIAE
DECOR·NONPRVDENTIAECONSVMMATIO·NONPAENITENTIAEMODVS·
NON PATIENTIAEREGVLA·NONOMNEQVICQVIDDICIPOTESTBONVM
PRO CEDIT·EXIPSISDISCIENTIAPERFECTA·PRAENVNTIATIOXPIINCARNE
VENTVRI ETCOMMVNISRESVRRECTIONISSPES·SVPPLICIORVMMETVS·
GLORIAE POLLICITATIO·MYSTERIORVMREVELATIO·

103 *Rustic script;* Vespian Psalter, *8th century. (British Library; Department of Manuscripts; Cotton Vesp. A.1, f.31)*

104 Details from the Moutier-Grandval Bible, *written at Tours* c. 834–43.
The text on this page is written in capitals, uncials and Carolingian minuscules.
(British Library; Department of Manuscripts; Add. 10546, f.26)

some of the earliest *codices*. Alongside it a more narrow and condensed variety, the rustic script (fig. 103), appeared in inscriptions as well as in manuscripts.

Already at the beginning of the Christian era the Romans had developed a large variety of styles to accommodate the various aspects of everyday life; besides those suitable for inscriptions, there were the still quite formal book hands as well as more cursive styles appropriate for notes of a personal, administrative or commercial nature. The main book scripts of the late Roman period, uncial (fig. 104) and half-uncial, favoured a reduction in the size of individual letters and a tendency towards greater cursiveness. They also introduced the four-line system (in place of the old two-line system) to accommodate the formation of individual ascenders and descenders:

$$\text{ABCFG abcfg}$$

After the collapse of the Roman Empire and with the spread of Christianity uncials became the preferred script of Christian literature. In the 6th century, half-uncial was

in scecla. anima mea dnm . & exul
tauit spс meus In do saluatore meo;

Anno quintodecimo impe
rii tiberii cesaris. procu
rante pontio pilato iu
deam . tetrarcha autem
galilee herode . philip
po autem ffre eius tetrarcha
iturie & traconitidis regionis.
& lysaniae abiline tetrarcha . Sub
principibus sacerdotum anna &
caypha; Factum est uerbum dni
super iohem zacharie filium Indeser
to; Et uenit Inomem regionem ior
danis; predicans baptismum peni
tentie. Inremissionem peccatorum;
Sicut scriptum est Inlibro sermonum
esaye prophe. uox clamantis In

106 Sacramentum Gelasianum. *This fragment, one of several removed from a binding, shows the rather difficult to read Merovingian hand of the pre-Carolingian period; 8th century. (Bodleian Library, Oxford; Ms Douce f.1, f.1v)*

◁ 105 Gospel Lectionary Dalmatia *(Zadar) written in the Beneventan script which remained in use in southern Italy for nearly 500 years; late-11th century. (Bodleian Library, Oxford; Ms Canon Bibl Lat 61, f.7v)*

introduced to Ireland. From there, as a result of missionary foundations by Irish monks, the New Irish script was brought to Germany (Fulda), France (Tours), Italy (Bobbio) and Switzerland (St Gallen). In Britain (see Plate VI), where Christianity had been introduced by Irish and Roman missionaries, the resulting combination of styles led, in the 8th century, to the evolution of the Anglo-Saxon hand, a script which prevailed until well after the Norman conquest. Because of their geographical isolation Britain and Ireland were able to maintain a certain overall uniformity as far as the more formal book hands were concerned, but on the continent of Europe a large number of local styles developed, such as for example the South Italian Beneventan (fig. 105), the Frankish Merovingian (fig. 106), the Spanish Visigothic, and many other scripts. This process of disintegration was eventually brought to a halt by Charlemagne (742–814 AD) whose newly-won Empire

107 Bede: Expositio in Lucam. *Like the page from the* Moutier-Grandval Bible *(fig. 104) a good example of what came to be known as 'the hierarchy of scripts'; in this case Rustic capitals (for the major headings), uncials for the first line of the* Liber tertius, *and Carolingian minuscule for the rest of the text; Tours c.820, with late 10th-century additions.*
(Bodleian Library, Oxford; Ms Bodl. 218, f.62r)

brought a measure of unity to Western Europe. Under his guardianship and that of his successors there emerged a new style of writing, the Carolingian minuscule (fig. 107), which was to serve courtly and monastic establishments alike.

The Carolingian minuscule was a script of great clarity and overall harmony, which used the four-line system, few ligatures and abbreviations, and often artistically embellished capital or uncial letters for initials (figs. 104, 115) and headings. This clarity of graphic design was partially lost later with the creation of the other major script, the Gothic

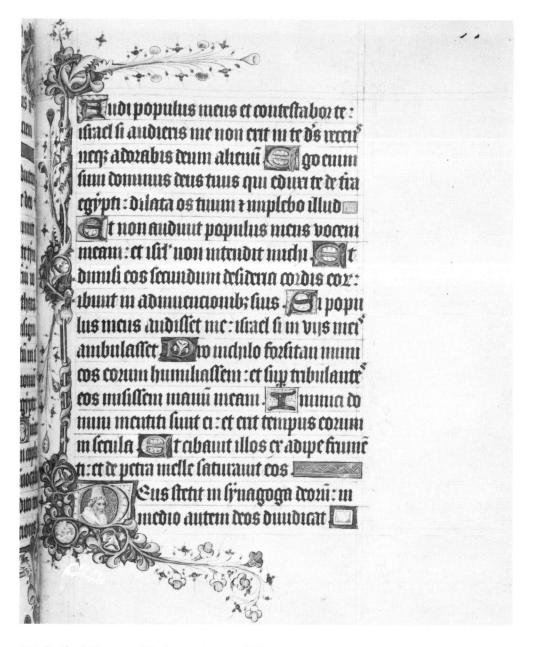

108 Bedford Hours and Psalter, *written (and illuminated) in fine Gothic style for John, Duke of Bedford, brother of Henry V, between 1420–1422. (British Library; Department of Manuscripts; Add. 42131, f.152)*

minuscule (and its various sub-divisions and later developments) which came into its own in the 12th and 13th centuries (fig. 108). This script 'broke' the curved elements of the letters into angular combinations of strokes, added decorative little feet and heads, and introduced fine hairlines to join individual script signs.

The 14th century, which saw the heyday of the Gothic script, was also, for much of Europe, a period of great devastation. The Black Death, endless dynastic quarrels, marauding *condottieri* and a rival Pope at Avignon greatly undermined people's faith and

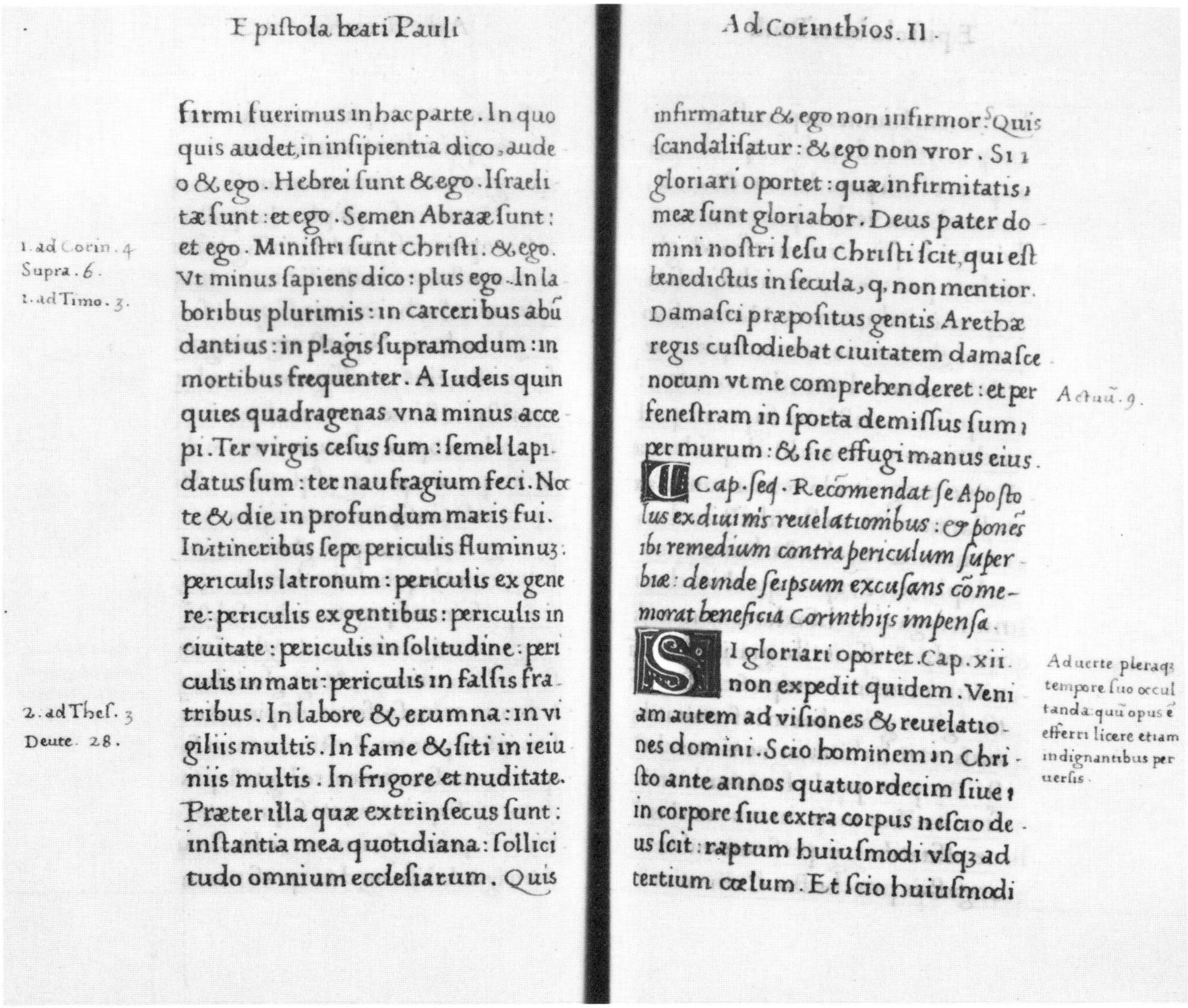

Epistola beati Pauli   Ad Corinthios. II.

firmi fuerimus in hac parte. In quo
quis audet, in insipientia dico, aude
o & ego. Hebrei sunt & ego. Israeli
tæ sunt: et ego. Semen Abraæ sunt:
et ego. Ministri sunt christi. & ego.
Vt minus sapiens dico: plus ego. In la
boribus plurimis: in carceribus abu
dantius: in plagis supramodum: in
mortibus frequenter. A Iudeis quin
quies quadragenas vna minus acce
pi. Ter virgis cesus sum: semel lapi
datus sum: ter naufragium feci. No
te & die in profundum maris fui.
In itineribus sepe periculis fluminuȝ:
periculis latronum: periculis ex gene
re: periculis ex gentibus: periculis in
ciuitate: periculis in solitudine: peri
culis in mari: periculis in falsis fra
tribus. In labore & erumna: in vi
giliis multis. In fame & siti in ieiu
niis multis. In frigore et nuditate.
Præter illa quæ extrinsecus sunt:
instantia mea quotidiana: sollici
tudo omnium ecclesiarum. Quis

(left margin:) 1. ad Corin. 4 / Supra. 6. / 1. ad Timo. 3.

(left margin:) 2. ad Thes. 3 / Deute. 28.

infirmatur & ego non infirmor? Quis
scandalisatur: & ego non vror. Si i
gloriari oportet: quæ infirmitatis,
meæ sunt gloriabor. Deus pater do
mini nostri Iesu christi scit, qui est
benedictus in secula, q. non mentior.
Damasci præpositus gentis Arethæ
regis custodiebat ciuitatem damasce
norum vt me comprehenderet: et per
fenestram in sporta demissus sum,
per murum: & sic effugi manus eius.
Cap. seq. Recommendat se Aposto
lus ex diuinis reuelationibus: & ponens
ibi remedium contra periculum super
biæ: deinde seipsum excusans comme
morat beneficia Corinthijs impensa.
Si gloriari oportet. Cap. xii.
non expedit quidem. Veni
am autem ad visiones & reuelatio
nes domini. Scio hominem in chri
sto ante annos quatuordecim siue,
in corpore siue extra corpus nescio de
us scit: raptum huiusmodi vsqȝ ad
tertium cœlum. Et scio huiusmodi

(right margin:) Actuu. 9.

(right margin:) Aduerte pleraqȝ tempore suo occultanda qui opus e efferri licere etiam indignantibus peruersis.

109 Epistles *(French), c. 1500; written in Antiqua and Italic. (Victoria and Albert Museum; K.R.P.C. 30, f.76v)*

confidence in the established order. In northern Italy, under the influence of rich city-states such as Florence and Venice, there arose a nostalgia for the past which paved the way for the coming of the Renaissance. Artists, scribes, scholars and patrons turned their attention to the study of classical subjects. In the early 15th century a new style of writing arose — the Antiqua (fig. 109), based on the old Carolingian minuscule and a vague memory of round classical lines. This new style was widely used by professional scribes. Eventually the carefully rounded and separately written letters became, no doubt in the interest of speed and economy, more cursive, creating yet another style, the Italic (fig. 109).

This is only an abbreviated and condensed account of some of the major developments of Western calligraphy, but it shows the elements which were responsible for the creation and dissemination of such styles: the Church first and foremost, but also secular institutions such as courts, chancelleries, scribal workshops (see p.157) and to some extent 'national' trends. The Church, by taking over the mantle of Rome, had inherited a sound worldly appreciation of practicalities and a deep respect for law and orderliness. The monks working in the *scriptoria* of the great monasteries, for example, saw their labour more as a practical way of safeguarding Christianity than a means of direct communication with the absolute; they were devout men but not necessarily mystics.

CHINESE CALLIGRAPHY

Writing materials and writing implements have always played a major role in the development of calligraphic styles. There is still an element of permanence and imposing dignity, so characteristic of Roman stone inscriptions, from which they ultimately derive, in the shape of present-day capital letters. The way the pen was cut and held became responsible for the shaping of calligraphic trends. This intimate interaction between style, writing material and the tools used for writing is nowhere more apparent than in the case of Chinese calligraphy.

Chinese calligraphy begins with the invention of the brush. The earliest style — the 'script of antiquity' — was either engraved in stone, incised with a metal stylus or knife in bamboo, wood and bone, or (later) applied with a bamboo stick dipped in lacquer on to wooden slips or bamboo tablets; some scholars claim that quite early on some form of ink was also in use (HTT, p.168). Under the Zhou emperor, Xuan Wang (827–781 BC), some elements of standardization were introduced, and the resulting style became known as the 'great seal' script. In the centuries that followed, a number of simplified variations developed in the provinces, which by the 3rd century BC led to the formation of the 'little seal' script. These early styles have a certain archaic beauty (see fig. 48). The original pictographic elements of many characters are still clearly visible, and the individual characters are bold, well-proportioned within themselves and in relation to each other; but they are not yet calligraphy.

Traditional sources credit Meng Tian (*d.* 209 BC) with the invention of the brush (HTT, p.159), but it is possible that at least a form of it was known and used much earlier; characters inscribed on Shang and Zhou bronze vessels, for example, often appear to have been formed after writing-brush patterns. The full effectiveness of the brush depended on the use of soft writing materials, which became available mainly during the Han period (206 BC–220 AD) — materials such as silk, 'silk-paper' (see p.42) and, after 105 AD, paper (see p.44). Paper, brush, ink and the ink-slab — the 'four precious things' of a scholar's study — changed the appearance of Chinese writing. A new style called *li shu*, the 'official' or 'clerical' script, arose, only to be superseded in the 4th century by the 'model' or 'normal' script, *kai shu* (fig. 110). The latter underwent hardly any further change, and is still the authoritative medium for the writing and printing of Chinese.

Quite early on, a number of elegant and sophisticated cursive forms developed alongside the more formal styles, such as the 'running script' or the 'grass script' (fig. 111); the latter is rather difficult to read, and looks, at least to those not conversant with Chinese writing, visually entirely different.

The Chinese brush, about 30 centimetres in length according to ancient measurement, consists of holder, hairs and sheath. The hairs are a mixture of rabbit, deer and goat hairs, bound with a silk or hemp string at one end, covered with lacquer to stiffen them, and

夢五陰集散我不得如嚮如影如炎如化五陰
以是故是字不住尒不不住世尊我不得如
是字不住尒不不住何以故是字无所有故
八不共法集散云何當作字言是菩薩世尊
共法集散世尊我若不得六波羅蜜乃至十
息念死集散我尒不得佛十力乃至十八不
念佛念法念僧念戒念捨念天念善念入出
相无作集散四禪四无量心四无色定集散
集散四念處集散乃至八聖道分集散空无
耶見集散皆尒如是世尊我尒不得六波羅蜜
得老死盡集散世尊我尒不得婬怒癡集散諸
老死集散世尊我尒不得无明盡集散乃至不
故是字不住尒不不住何以故是字无所有故以是
乃至意爾眼爾囙緣生受乃至意爾囙緣生
受尒如是世尊我尒不得无明集散乃至不得
當作名字言是菩薩世尊是色字乃至法字
不住尒不不住何以故是字无所有故以是
无所有故以是故是字无所
得云何當作名字言是菩薩世尊乃至法字
故世尊我尒不得眼集散乃至意集散若不可
故是字不住尒不不住何以故是字无所有
集散若不可得云何當作名字世尊是囙緣
不住尒不不住世尊我不得色集散乃至識

110 Kai shu *script. (British Library; Oriental Collections; S 5130)*

inserted in the holder, usually a bamboo tube. The sheath which is designed to protect the delicate hair tip is also made of bamboo. The mixture of rabbit, deer and goat hairs, which gives a soft centre, makes the brush more responsive to changes in pressure and to manipulation. For writing, the brush is held between the thumb and index finger, with the middle finger and the ring finger resting on the holder as guides. The scribe holds it vertically and unsupported over the paper; effects are achieved by lowering and raising it, drawing it towards, and flicking it away from oneself. Not only the fingers, but the hand, the arm, the whole body, indeed the whole personality of the scribe are involved in the process of writing. To achieve mastery of the brush is no mean feat. The deceptive speed with which the actual writing is executed is the result of discipline, much training and practice, long periods of concentration and a deep understanding of the characters, the lines of each character, their relationship with each other and their correct position in space. The first treatise on calligraphy, written by Lady Wei Shao about 320 AD states that a character must neither have too much 'bone' (structure) nor 'flesh' (consistency) nor 'sinew' (composition) but that all three must be in the right relationship to one another.

111 The Wang Xizhi *copy, a fragment from Dunhuang written in the so-called 'grass-script'.*
(British Library; Oriental Collections; S. 3753)

The pictorial heritage of the characters is never entirely lost. The individual strokes are related to natural objects (GB, p.382). Excessive symmetry is avoided, each character seeming to be suspended in an imaginary square.

Chinese calligraphy is closely connected with Chinese painting: painter and scribe use similar material (paper), similar implements (brush and ink) and, to a large extent, have the same technique. In traditional China, to be 'master of the three arts' — calligraphy, painting and poetry — was the hallmark of a truly educated, truly cultured, if not to say superior, person.

Illustration, illumination and picture-writing

A written text can be made aesthetically more pleasing in a number of ways. Calligraphy is one possibility; but there are several others. Some of them are well within the scope of an accomplished scribe, others need the assistance of craftsmen and artists.

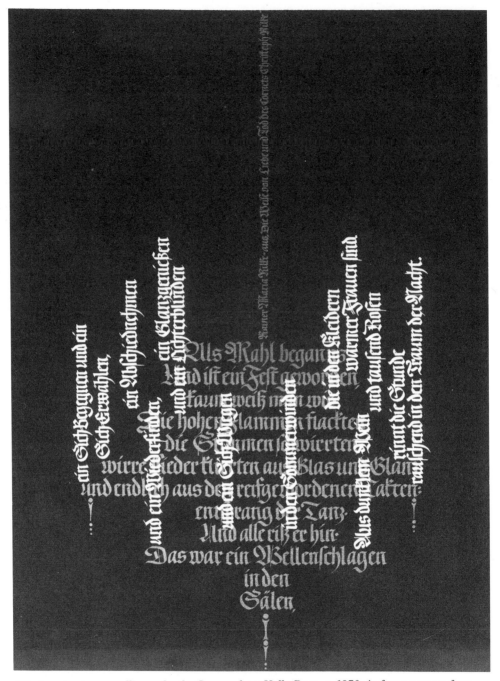

112 *A contemporary calligram by the German-born Hella Basu, c.1970; in fact a passage from Rainer Maria Rilke's* Die Weise von Liebe und Tod des Cornets Christoph Rilke. *(Property of the author)*

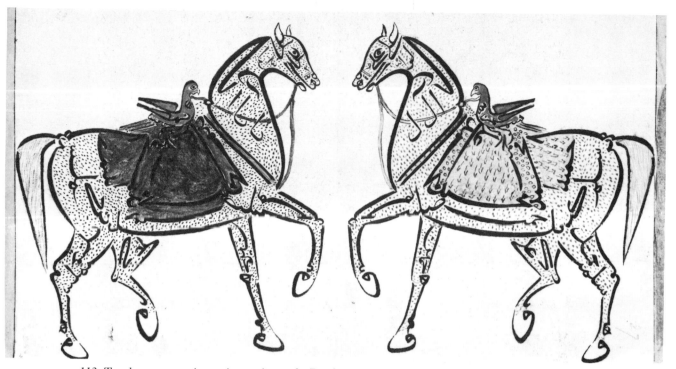

113 Two horses composing an invocation to the Prophet. Persian in Arabic script. (British Library; Oriental Collections; Add. 5660 F, f.27)

The simplest form of ornamentation, arising naturally from the process of writing, is the embellishment of letters, especially initial letters (see figs. 36, 104 and Plate VI). Or the text can be written in the shape of objects, geometric and abstract patterns, animals or human beings. Picture writing as such has always found a place in magic and in the preparation of amulets, but as a distinct literary art form it can be traced back to the Greek poet Simias, who in the 4th century BC wrote poetry in the shape of an egg, a double axe, and the wings of a bird. Simias was not the only Greek poet who used this art form; the tradition continued and was eventually, in the 6th century, introduced into Christian Europe by the Bishop of Poitiers, Venatius Fortunatus, who wrote his poem *De Sancta Cruce* in the form of a cross. Calligrams (text pictures, where the shape of the object or layout of the text is determined by the subject matter of the writing itself) remained popular throughout the Middle Ages, the Baroque period, indeed right up to the present time (fig. 112) — as such practitioners as George Herbert, the Dadaists, Hans Arp, Dylan Thomas, Robert Herrick and many other poets testify. The Concrete Poetry movement, much talked about in the 1960s, revived and popularized the tradition. The term 'calligram' was first introduced by the French poet Guillaume Apollinaire to describe his own works, published in 1918. Calligrams are, in the words of the French concretist Jean-François Bory, 'writing writing itself'.

Calligrams are not confined to the West. Arabic calligraphers were especially skilful in twisting and stretching the lines of elongated Arabic letters into elegant animal shapes (fig. 113) or imposing architectural patterns; and Chinese and Japanese scribes created human figures, even portraits, in this fashion.

Another branch of picture-writing is micrography. Here the script can be reduced to minute size: the whole text of the Koran, amounting to 77,934 words, has been written on the shell of one single egg (YHS, p.30). In addition, the individual lines of writing are used to 'draw' a picture. Micrography is known in most parts of the world — in the Far East, Southeast Asia, India (fig. 114) and in Western Europe; some of the most splendid examples are found in Hebrew writing, especially in the representation of the masoretic notes (fig. 115).

Picture-writing is without doubt already a form of illustration, but illustration still entirely under the control of the scribe. In a colophon of the (7th-century) Lindisfarne Gospels four persons are named as contributors: Bishop Eadfrith of Lindisfarne, who is said to have written the text; Bishop Ethelwald, who is given credit for the binding; Billfrith the Anchorite, who provided ornaments of gold and silver and the jewels for the outer casing; and finally Aldred, who inserted the Anglo-Saxon gloss (see Plate VI). It is generally assumed that Eadfrith not only wrote the text — a task he is supposed to have completed in no more than two years — but that he was also responsible for the lavish and intricate illustration which forms such an integral part of the whole manuscript. Though this is by no means the only case where writing and illustration were the work of one and the same individual, more often the task was done by different specialists.

Manuscript and text illustration was not an invention of the Christian Middle Ages. The Egyptian Books of the Dead, papyri placed in tombs with other offerings, were lavishly illustrated. Illustrations accompanied stone carved inscriptions in Egypt (see fig. 38), Mesopotamia and many other parts of the world. It could be argued that at a certain stage

◁ *114 The goddess Annapurna giving rice to the mendicant Siva, composed of repeated invocations to Durga written in the Bengali script; mid-19th century. (Victoria and Albert Museum; D. 422-1889)*

115 Pentateuch with Masorah; the masoretic notes have been written in the shape of a dragon; early 14th century. (British Library; Oriental Collections; Add. 21160)

illustration is writing: the Mide song-boards, notices, wintercounts (see p.26) — in fact, all truly pictographic scripts. Sometimes the balance between writing and illustration changes dramatically: whereas we are used to a lengthy written passage supplemented by an (explanatory) illustration, in the case of some Southeast Asian or Indian picture-albums, or certain types of Chinese and Japanese scrolls, prominence is given to the painting, and the text — short and sparse and often moved to one corner or to the outer edge of the composition — takes on the tenor of an (illustrative) explanation.

Illustrations are not always directly related to the text. Sometimes the illustration is a portrait, an ikon or the representation of a deity, and as such a focal point of meditation for the not yet fully initiated or those unable to read; sometimes it can take on magical properties and become an amulet, a protector of the text, the donor, the scribe or the person using the text.

Illumination is a rather specialized form of illustration (in popular usage the two terms are often interchanged) which was used with dazzling effect on the pages of Korans, medieval Christian manuscripts and, equally, Jewish manuscripts (quite often prepared in the same workshops). The illuminator (from *illuminare* – to light up, throw light upon) works not only with colours but also with precious metal, applying thin leaves of beaten gold to initials or to the background of a miniature.

Politics, religion and writing

For the non-believer and the non-partisan the difference between proselytizing, prophetic religions and political ideologies seems minimal. Both aim at unification for the purpose of control, both demand sacrifices in return for promises to be realized in some non-verifiable future: heaven, another life, the next generation. Both depend on propaganda, on effective information storage and information dissemination to increase their ranks by new converts while at the same time preventing heresy. Often religious and political ideologies combine to support each other's imperialistic tendencies towards maximum expansion. For all this, writing is the ideal tool. Written information can easily be controlled and verified; if heretic tendencies are discovered they can quickly be eliminated. (It is more difficult to change the minds of men than it is to burn a book.) Oral traditions leave too much to the discretion of the individual, and thoughts are less easily controlled than written texts. Writing has a further advantage: it multiplies information and by doing so makes the (right kind of) information more readily available to a much larger audience. Printing is even more effective, and has indeed been eagerly seized upon by all those anxious to promote their particular version of the truth. The process of (religious and political) conversion removes the individual from the security of his previous environment, negates most of what has so far served as background for his identity. If the conversion is to be successful and permanent, this sudden vacuum must be filled, quite speedily, by new visions, new concepts, new cultural possessions. Apart from the abstract reality of the new faith, the convert needs something more concrete to compensate him for what he has lost: a new social order, new moral aims, a new language, a new script.

For well over a millennium Islam and the Arabic script have maintained a wide sphere of influence at times stretching from Spain to Southeast Asia. For an even longer period Christianity and the Roman alphabet have dominated first Europe, then the Americas, Africa, Asia and the Pacific. Though this domination has been predominantly religious in nature it could on occasion provide the nucleus for the establishment of substantial empires. In Soviet Russia, Communism and the Cyrillic alphabet have in the course of the last sixty years formed a similar alliance and successfully eliminated most other forms of writing (see p.126).

A common script is a strong tool for unification. Neither China nor Mesopotamia would have survived and prospered without it. Mesopotamia has always been, throughout its history, an area of conflict where the centre of power fluctuated between ethnically and linguistically unrelated groups. But the economic survival of Mesopotamia, linked with irrigation, depended on a continuously effective system of administration which transcended temporary allegiances. Kings were expendable — they could easily be replaced by other kings, but communal agriculture and trade could not function without a minimum level of stability. Continuity and stability were largely provided by the scribe-administrators who, for over 3,000 years, irrespective of political changes, used the cuneiform script first created by the early Sumerians (see p.65).

In China the situation was more complex. Since the Chinese script does not depend on the spoken language, it was in itself (and after 4,000 years still is) the best tool for administration in a vast country inhabited by different linguistic groups. In the early part of the first Christian millennium Buddhist texts, written in Chinese, spread Chinese writing and Chinese influence further east, to Korea and Japan. In other words, Buddhism was the medium for the transmission of the Chinese script and the Chinese language, not the other way round. But then Buddhism in its purest form is neither a religion (there is no god, no soul, no final judgement, in fact nothing to bind — *religare* in Latin — the soul to its creator) nor a political ideology (each individual is truly an island; there is no causal connection between this generation and the next). Not that Buddhism was hostile to writing. In fact the first literary evidence of a more widespread use of writing in India comes from 5th-century BC Buddhist sources. Buddhism was anxious to promote a casteless society in which all had access to the same central core of information — towards the achievement of which committing the essential texts to writing (in Pali, the language of the people) was an important step. Though to some extent a revolutionary movement, Buddhism was certainly not a prophetic religion in the Mosaic tradition. Like Christianity, Islam and Communism, it grew by adding new recruits, but unlike them Buddhism did not want to change the world; its aim was to encourage the individual to withdraw from its contradictions into the realization of a more absolute harmony. Any language, any script, any form of information storage was adequate for its purpose.

The attitude of tribal/traditional societies to writing is radically different. Tribal societies are by nature exclusive; they have no message to spread and see outside influences mainly as a threat to their own integrity. Survival is a group effort, and depends largely on the preservation of the *status quo*. As we have seen, writing is both a means of unificaton and a tool for disruption; it can enlarge (by converting outsiders to one's creed) and diminish (by introducing alien ideas). Written information cannot be monopolized and protected as easily as information that is memorized.

Hindu society, which assigns special privileges and special duties to each caste, had little use for writing. The memorizing and the recitation of the sacred Vedic hymns which ensured the well-being of the community and the continuation of the universe was in the custody of Brahmins, whose position at the apex of the hierarchy depended on the retention of this monopoly. They knew how, when and in the presence of whom the hymns could be recited — and who was fit to share this information. Dilution of knowledge often means dilution of power. According to the *Manusmirti*, the classical treatise on Hindu law (which did much to fossilize Hindu society by reinforcing the sanctity of the caste system, especially the supremacy of the Brahmins) a Shudra who heard even by accident the recitation of the hymns should have his ears filled with molten lead, the tongue torn from his mouth to prevent him from repeating what he had heard, and his body split in twain. This is exclusiveness bordering on paranoia. It is thus hardly surprising that Hindu society was either hostile or at best indifferent to writing, and long after writing had, of necessity, been accepted, great care was taken to prevent this knowledge from falling into the hands of those who had most reason to rebel against the established order, namely women.

There is another interesting point. Since writing was never an integral part of (Hindu) Sanskrit culture, the powerful combination of language, script and religion which we have witnessed in the case of Arabic language/Arabic script/Islam, and Latin/Roman script/ Christianity, never occured. To this day Sanskrit, the classical language of Hinduism, can be written in any Indian script except Tamil (see p.111).

Certain similarities exist between traditional Hindu and traditional Jewish societies. Both are strictly exclusive (one is born a Jew or a Hindu, one cannot become one); both discourage contact with outsiders. Yet during the 2,000 years of the Diaspora, Hebrew writing and the Hebrew script spread to all corners of the world, for very special and quite different reasons. Hebrew writing did not go out to spread any new message, or attract new converts; it followed its own widely scattered people to reassure them of the validity of their own tradition in an alien and, more often than not, hostile environment.

Apart from possible connections with religious and political ideas, the written word has power of its own. *Verba volant, scripta manant* ('the spoken word passes, what is written remains') can be reassuring or it can be a threat, depending on where one stands. Because of its implied permanence and the fact that understanding depends on a period of initiation (the time it takes to master a particular script) the written word can take on the power of an amulet. The Egyptian hieroglyph for *ankh* was looked upon as a symbol of eternal life and good fortune long after its original meaning had been forgotten. There are the phylacteries with sacred writing which devout Jews wear during prayer, and the inscriptions on the doorposts of Jewish houses which are supposed to protect the inhabitants from misfortune. Even Muslims carry amulets which enclose passages from the Koran. Christians ascribe equal power to the Bible, laying it on the body of the dead, fanning sick persons with leaves taken from it, or using it as the ultimate protection against all evil emanating from the devil, the great adversary of the Lord.

Such power creates fear. Hostility to writing has never been restricted to tribal/traditional societies. Throughout history there have been sudden periodic outbursts of book-burning, of the destruction of whole branches of literature, or of a temporary turning away from literary learning. In 213 BC Shi Huang Di, the first emperor of Qin, for example, asked that 'all books in the historical archives, except the records of Qin, be burnt; that all persons in the Empire, except those who hold a function under the control of the official scholars, daring to store the classical literature and the discussions of various philosophers, should go to the administrative or military governor, so that these books may be indiscriminately burnt'. In 15th-century Mexico, Spanish priests, in part under the guidance of Bishop Landa, a great expert and to some extent admirer of indigenous culture (see p.145), indulged in a similar and unfortunately much more effective destruction of Maya literature. In Spain the Inquisition, when sending Jews to the pyre, burnt them together with their Talmud; in other Christian countries the same fate awaited heretics from time to time. Christian and Muslim rulers have periodically destroyed the libraries of their predecessors. In our own century we have witnessed the book-burning programmes initiated by Communists and Nazis, and after the Second World War a similar destruction of all Nazi-tainted literature was carried out. In China the Cultural Revolution showed its distrust of literary education, which it associated with the continuation of unwarranted privilege, by closing universities and printing presses, and sending all intellectuals to work in the fields. What all totalitarian movements (political or religious) fear most is not so much writing itself as the fact that writing encourages critical thinking, thus opening the door to heresy and dissension. To the Zen saying, 'if we are silent we are one, if we speak we are two' one could add, 'if we (are able to) write we may become many'.

Writing for special groups

Up to a point all writing is writing for special groups — those which have mastered a particular script. In some societies and under certain circumstances such groups will by necessity be small (we remember the meticulously trained professional scribes of Egypt and Mesopotamia); in other societies the knowledge of writing can be so widely dispersed as to foster illusions about the universal nature of writing as such, and of one script in particular. Sometimes the wide use and the sheer popularity of a script can overshadow this inherent element of exclusiveness: few people brought up in our Western civilization will consciously think of the alphabet as a limited form of information storage. Such natural exclusiveness, inbuilt in the very process of writing, is however different from that created on purpose and meant to serve special needs, such as shorthand and speed-writing for commerce and legal practices; Braille for the use of blind people; hobo and gypsy signs for minority groups outside the normal range of society; cabbalistic practices related to religious speculation and to magic; morse, codes and ciphers which play a part in war and in diplomatic intercourse, and all forms of secret and enigmatic writing. In the latter case a particular script is specially created to enhance and protect the exclusiveness of a particular group, or at least to provide such a group — which would normally be excluded from the use of writing for reasons of either physical or social handicap — with its own mode of information storage.

Memory aids have strong elements of exclusiveness, since very often they can only be understood or read with the aid of additional orally-supplied information. Australian message sticks (see fig. 1) for example are cut in the presence of the actual messenger, who has the various notches and incisions carefully explained to him. The *pustahas* of the Batak medicine men of Sumatra (see fig. 22) are private notebooks which contain the sum total of personal knowledge acquired during a long period of apprenticeship. They are primarily for the use of just one person — the one who wrote them in the first place. Similarly the Moso script (see p.87, and fig. 51) of the Nakhi people of south-western China can only be read with the help of a trained priest; and the same holds true for the script used in the Aztec *codices* (see Plate I) of Central America. None of these are truly secret scripts, however; they were not specifically created for the purpose of guarding a special type of information, and in most cases both the script and the interpreter are closely integrated with the rest of society.

SECRET SCRIPTS

Various elements can lead to the creation of secret, or at least enigmatic, scripts. Both the Ogham script (see fig. 85) and the Runes (see fig. 84) are connected with secret writing. The Nsibidi script of the Uyanga of Nigeria was in principle only used by members of the Nsibidi secret society, though some signs were also understood by outsiders. Nsibidi, which was unknown until 1905, is a purely ideographic script, using already highly conventionalized picture signs and also purely symbolic representations:

A man and a woman sleeping together on a bed; it is very hot and they put their arms outside. The short strokes at the bottom of the picture sign represent the legs of the bed.

A boy kept a girl as his friend until they both grew up. Then he married her and they lived together and made their bed with pillows for the feet and also for the head.

A man and his friend went to town to find two girls; one found a girl and took her to his home; the other could not find a girl so the two men parted company. (DD, p.150)

Nothing is known about the origin of this form of writing, but there exists a charming local legend which describes how the Uyanga learned it from the baboons who came and sat round their camp fire. Some scholars have speculated about possible connections with Egyptian hieroglyphs since the Nsibidi sign for house is (like the hieroglyphic sign for house — see p.63) of rectangular shape, whereas all the local huts are round; but this seems a rather tenuous connection.

Belief in the special significance of the letters of the Hebrew script is central to cabbalistic thought. Certain esoteric knowledge can be expressed and communicated by seemingly unintelligible combinations of letters and the use of their numerical value. Thus the Torah can be read simply as a text written in Hebrew script, but there also exists another mystical reading which perceives the Torah as composed of the secret names of God.

Abulafia, who was born in Spain in 1240, when looking for an absolute object to meditate upon — one capable of stimulating the deeper life of the soul by freeing it from ordinary perceptions — believed he had found it in the letters of the Hebrew script. Starting from the abstract and non-corporeal nature of script he developed a theory of mystical contemplation of letters and their configuration as the constituents of the name of God. His *Hokhmath ha–Tseruf* (science of the combination of letters) shows how the adept engages in combining and separating the letters in his meditation, how he deeply enjoys each combination in every direction, how he composes motifs on separate groups, and so forth. Each letter represents a whole world and the mystic must abandon himself to its contemplation (fig. 116). Abulafia equates his meditation with mystical logic, which moves the adept towards a realization of the secret name of God and into a world of true bliss. But it is a way not without danger, a journey that must be undertaken with proper control and discipline, for as each letter is also coordinated with a special member of the body 'one has to be most careful not to move a consonant or vowel from its position for if one errs in reading the letter commanding a certain member, that member may be torn away and may change its place or alter its nature immediately or be transformed into a crippled shape so that in consequence that person may become a cripple.' (GGS, p.138)

In the realm of practical Kabbalah belongs the tradition of the *kalmosin*, the angelic pens, thought to have been created by archangels such as Metatron, Michael, Gabriel and Raphael. Some of these scripts are probably derived from early Hebrew or Samaritan scripts, but there are others which bear a strong resemblance to cuneiform writing. In cabbalistic literature they are also known as *ketav ainayim* – eye-writing, because

שער סדר עמידתן פרק א

פרק א

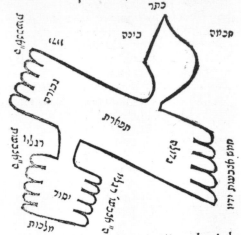

individual letters are composed of lines and small circles (the wedge of the cuneiform script?). Sometimes such letters are used in a text, otherwise written in normal Hebrew characters (fig. 117), for writing the Tetragrammaton or the divine names Shaddai and Elohim. Because of their magical properties they are also used in amulets. Some scholars have suggested that they are imitations of cuneiform signs created by persons who knew cuneiform writing without understanding it.

◁ *116 Moses Cordovero* Pardes Rimmonin*; Cracow, 1592. The letter* alef, *representing the harmonic unity of the ten* Sefirot *contained in it. (British Library; Oriental Collections; 1968, f.4)*

117 Book of Adam and Raziel; Amsterdam, 1701. Text in Hebrew script intermixed with kalmosin *(angelic pens). (British Library; Oriental Collections; 1967, e.5)*

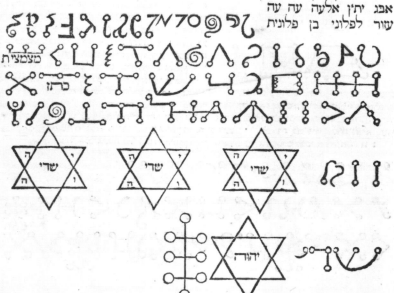

The term cryptography (from the Greek *kryptos*–hidden, and *graphein*–to write) refers mostly to the use of script(s) for the purpose of secret communications in connection with governmental, military, diplomatic and to some extent also commercial and industrial information. In practice this means that a written text can be converted into a cryptogram, with the help of a cipher or code, or both. Though basically there exists little difference between the two (up to a point a code is simply a more complex cipher), the two are usually regarded as separate. Broadly speaking, in a cipher textual units of constant and equal length — usually one letter, sometimes two, rarely three — are replaced either by a process of transposition (rearrangements of the letters in the actual text) or by substitution (replacement of the letters in the actual text by other letters or symbols without a change in sequence) in such a manner as to create a new text which will be meaningless to all but those who possess the same key as the person who enciphered the text in the first place. Various refinements are possible, and either one or more cipher-alphabets can be used. In the case of a code, the textual units which undergo cryptographic treatment are of varying and unequal length — letters, entire sentences, phrases, syllables or numbers. It is a more complex system, more difficult to work, more time-consuming to use and up to a point more effective.

Cryptography has been in use since ancient times. Towards the end of the Ptolemaic period and increasingly so during the time of the Roman emperors, Egyptian hieroglyphs could be used in this fashion. Certain signs were deliberately substituted by similar-looking ones, creating a wholly bizarre form of spelling, unintelligible to all but the initiated. Altogether three different cryptographical systems seem to have been in use, much to the confusion of those who have worked at the decipherment of the hieroglyphs. The Greeks similarly used cryptography, mainly for communications between commanders in the field and their superiors back home. The same can be said about Rome; in fact the first treatise on cryptography was composed in the 3rd century BC by Aeneas 'Tacticus'. The beginning of modern cryptography however, like that of modern diplomacy, goes back to Italy, to the Papal courts and those of the early Italian republics. From 1400 onwards ciphers became increasingly more complex and in the 16th century important improvements were made in France which soon reached England and other European countries. In the middle of the 19th century the increasing use of electromagnetic telegraphy stimulated an extension in both content and repertory, and by the end of the century large codes containing 100,000 and more words and phrases were compiled for governmental, and from now on also for commercial, communications. As technology advanced, codes and ciphers became increasingly more sophisticated, especially after the introduction of automatic cipher machines around 1925. But the same new technology which improved the effectiveness of codes and ciphers could also be used for breaking them, and overall the balance between the protection of secrecy and the possibilities for the penetration of cryptographic communication remained more or less the same.

WRITING FOR THE BLIND

Blind people read by touch, by running their fingers over a script specially devised for their use. The first authentic record of such a system comes from the beginning of the 16th century. It was the invention of a Spaniard, Francesco Lucas, and its basis rested on the idea of engraving letters upon wood. About a century later a French notary by the name of Pierre Moreau cast movable leaden type for the same purpose. A number of similar attempts were made, until eventually Haüy succeeded in embossing paper with such a script.

The basis of nearly all the early systems was a variation of the normal alphabet, and though this meant that at least people who had not been born blind could learn to master the script without undergoing yet another radical shift in perception, they had one serious disadvantage: they could not easily be written by blind persons. In the first half of the 19th century Louis Braille, a blind teacher in the Institut National des Jeunes Aveugles, developed a new system based on combinations of dots which could be written, and later also printed, with relative ease. In 1932 a universal Braille code for the English-speaking world was adopted by representatives of agencies for the blind of Great Britain and the United States.

The Braille alphabet consists of varying combinations of one or more raised dots in a six-dot oblong known as a Braille cell, which is three dots high and two dots wide. There are sixty-three possible combinations which provide for all the letters of the alphabet and also for punctuation, contractions etc. Combinations of dots have also been worked out to signify mathematics, music and other specialized fields. Braille is written with the aid of a metal slate or on a specially-constructed Braille typewriter.

SHORTHAND

The need to write with sufficient speed to record human speech has been responsible for a form of writing commonly referred to as shorthand. Until very recently shorthand was essential for reporting the proceedings of parliamentary and legislative bodies, the trials of cases in courts of law and above all for the smooth and speedy execution of business correspondence. Shorthand is however not an invention of modern times. An efficient form of shorthand, based on orthography, was used by both Greeks and Romans (see fig. 15); in fact an example has been found on a marble slab from the Acropolis in Athens dating from the 4th century BC. The earliest record of an organized system comes from 58 BC and is attributed to Marcus Tullius Tiro, a freedman and friend of Cicero. The Tironian *notae*, originally designed to record speeches in the Senate, were taught in Roman schools and outlived the fall of the Roman Empire; in 625 AD they appeared for example in the royal diploma of the Merovingian king, Clotaire II, and the early Christian church too made extensive use of them both for recording the words of important church leaders and for taking down accurate accounts of trials. In England shorthand, still based on orthography and the alphabet, staged a revival in Tudor times, when in 1588 Dr Timothy Bright published his *Characterie: an Arte of Shorte, Swifte, and Secrete Writing by Character*. It was not before the 18th century that the idea of shorthand based on sound instead of orthography began to gain favour, until eventually, in 1837, Isaac Pitman published his *Stenographic Sound Hand* which marked a new era of sound-based systems.

ROGUES' CODES

There is finally one more section of society which needs its own, and as far as possible secret, form of information storage. This comprises the groups which either by birth or from choice function, at least in part, outside normal society: criminals, terrorists, thieves and all types of social drop-outs. Since theirs is neither a particularly literate nor language-conscious sub-culture the necessary information can comfortably be expressed through pure pictography. Into this category fall the *Gaunerzeichen* or *Gaunerzinken*, criminal codes which give warning, mark victims and advertise insufficiently protected property. Such signs are documented from at least the early part of the 16th century. The most complete collection (17,000 signs) is perhaps that published by J. Gross in 1899 (HJ, p.46). Paul Scott in his *A Division of the Spoils* describes how during the disturbances which followed the partition of India, railway compartments carrying Muslims were marked with crescent moons — and thereby singled out when a train was attacked. Gypsy and hobo signs also fall into this category, but the information they store is mostly designed to help and advise, and to prevent other travelling members of the community from coming into unnecessary conflict with the rest of society. For example (EL, p.215):

1. abstract concepts

nothing   *spoilt*   *very good*   *danger*

2. warnings/advice

unsafe place   *man with gun*   *bad dog*   *dishonest man*

3. directions

in   *out*   *stop*   *go*

4. helpful information

kind-hearted woman   *you can camp here*   *tell pitiful story*   *if you are sick you will be cared for —*

V Moves towards the future

Mechanization and printing

Printing did not begin with Gutenberg. Some 600–700 years earlier a number of Far Eastern nations had already mastered the art of block printing, and at the beginning of the second Christian millennium they knew how to handle movable type; but the basic components of printing were known earlier still.

What then is printing? Disregarding superfluous technical terms we could say that printing is the multiplication of graphically stored information by mechanical means. The last two words are crucial. Multiplication on its own can be achieved equally well by hand (by copyists in medieval times, for example), but every time such a copy is made, almost exactly the same amount of time, effort and skill must be invested as when the text is written (not composed) for the first time. This brings us to another highly significant factor which distinguishes printing from copying; since, in the case of printing, the multiplication is done mechanically, no further alterations are possible. The printing press can neither correct mistakes nor make mistakes. (The copyists could do, and frequently did, both.) Thus information once stored can be multiplied in its original and true form almost indefinitely (whereas the more often a text is copied by hand the more mistakes are likely to creep in). Such incorruptibility becomes important the moment information storage relates to property and trade. This takes us back another 6,000 years to ancient Mesopotamia and to the use of property marks in the form of seals.

Not only by intent but also in practice a seal does exactly the same as the printing press: it reliably copies and multiplies information by mechanical means — in this case information of ownership. This information can consist of a picture (illustration), one single sign (movable type) or a short text (block print). We have here in embryo all the basic elements of printing. The reason for the long hiatus between the first Mesopotamian seal, the first Far Eastern block print and Gutenberg's Bible must not be sought in a lack of creative ability; it is a direct result of the way society functioned in the intervening millennia. As has been said before, every society develops or chooses the type of information storage essential for its survival. Printing is not a new form of information storage; it is simply a means of (identically) multiplying already-stored information. As such it becomes useful and essential only after a certain stage of social and economic complexity has been reached, and after the information which has to be multiplied relates to subjects more complex than the claim to just one piece of property. As a rule seals multiply statements, printing mutiplies texts.

Did xylography (block printing) precede printing with movable type? From the evidence so far available — and there are a great many gaps in our knowledge of the development of printing — this seems to be the case. With perhaps one exception: the already mentioned and highly mysterious Phaistos disc (see p.144 and fig. 90) found in Crete at the beginning of this century and generally dated 17th century BC. Here seals seem to have been used exactly like movable type to print what to all extents and purposes looks like a text. The fact that we can neither read this text nor identify the individual signs used for its composition, and that in addition nothing similar has so far come to light, puts us at a distinct disadvantage as far as meaningful interpretation, or even meaningful speculation, is concerned; it does not however alter the facts. Somewhere, for reasons we cannot yet comprehend, more than 2,000 years before experiments with movable type were made in the Far East, the basic principles of typography were understood and used by somebody in the ancient Mediterranean world.

Apart from the inherent mystery (why should so many types have been cut, either in wood or metal, to produce just one text?), the Phaistos disc poses another interesting question — the question of the true nature of invention. As we have seen before, the fact that a particular discovery has been made, and particular possibility comprehended, does not mean that it will be developed or even used beyond a very limited sphere. The twenty-four single consonant signs of the Egyptian script did not lead to the development of a purely phonetic form of writing. In the same way the wheel was known in pre-Columbian Mexico, but only used for toys; and the scholarly élite of Alexandria knew that the earth moved round the sun, they had comprehended the possibility of using steam for the creation of mechanical movements, but their knowledge remained largely abstract. It was not applied in a practical fashion for the purpose of transforming contemporary society, in the way that the steam engine transformed 18th- and 19th-century England or, to return to our immediate subject, in the way the Greeks, after two unsuccesful attempts at writing their language in a syllabic script, used and transformed the Phoenician consonant script into the alphabet. Inventions become effective only if existing social and economic conditions have already created a need for them, if society is ready for their use. The Greek democracies needed literate citizens to participate in affairs of government — and therefore a form of writing which could be learned without a lengthy period of apprenticeship. England in the 18th century, on the eve of a tremendous expansion in social, economic and political terms, needed new sources of energy. Horse-power and human labour alone no longer sufficed. Society was ready for mechanization and for the practical application of mechanization. Revolutions (political and economic) are in most cases only the, sometimes spectacular, end-product of a long period of development and evolution. Whoever made and used the matrices for printing the text on the Phaistos disc had already understood not only the basic principle of printing, but also that of typography; but the ancient Mediterranean world had simply no further use for it.

Much of our knowledge concerning the beginning of printing in the Far East is based on circumstantial evidence, but it is fairly certain that the technique originated in China either during the Sui dynasty (581–818 AD) or during the early Tang dynasty (618–907 AD). Attempts towards a mechanical multiplication of writing were however made much earlier. The use of stamping seals cut in relief, and the practice of obtaining duplicate inscriptions from moulds or matrices, were already in evidence during the 1st millennium BC. Once paper had been invented the technique of making impressions (by rubbing or ink squeeze) from stone began to develop. By the 6th century AD this method had been perfected to such an extent that copies of high calligraphic quality and, most important, perfect fidelity could be produced not only from stone but also from wood, metal and baked clay. The principle involved was already remarkably close to block printing. Since repeated copying was likely to damage the original text the next step was to prepare, on wooden blocks, a faithful copy of the original, at first with negative characters and later with positive characters cut in relief. The result was black script on white paper — a print.

Another element which contributed vitally to the invention and spread of printing was without doubt the rapid diffusion of Buddhism in the middle of the first Christian millennium, which dramatically increased the demand for Buddhist literature. Apart from being strongly motivated, Buddhist monks had at their command two important commodities: time and free labour. Whereas copying by hand is a somewhat solitary

118 *Chinese translation of the* Diamond sutra, *a Buddhist work originally composed in Sanskrit. The scroll, dated 868 AD, is generally considered the oldest complete and dated printed book in existence.*
(British Library; Oriental Collections; Or. 8210. P.2)

process, printing needs team effort: trees have to be felled, wood cut, the text has to be written, transferred to the block, the block has to be cut, the paper must be made and prepared — all this before printing can even commence.

None of the early Chinese imprints have so far been discovered and it is exceedingly doubtful whether any substantial number of them has survived. There exists however a good deal of indirect evidence, such as the report of the Japanese monk Ennin who in 839

119 Buddhist charms printed by order of the Empress Shotoku; Japan, 8th century. (British Library; Oriental Collections; Or. 78, a.11)

had seen, according to his own account, 1,000 printed copies of a *sutra* on the holy mountain of Wu tai shan, and a petition to the throne dated 835 which recommended the prohibition of the printing of calendars. The earliest printed text of decidedly Chinese origin, complete and dated, and showing a remarkable level of sophistication and technical skill, was found by Aurel Stein at the beginning of this century in Dunhuang. This is a copy of a Chinese translation of the *Diamond Sutra*, printed on seven sheets of paper glued together, and dated 868 AD; the text is now in the British Library (fig. 118). The *Diamond Sutra* is however not the earliest surviving example of a block-printed text. In 1966 in the course of excavation at the Pulguk-sa temple in Korea a single wood-printed *dhāraṇi* (Buddhist incantation believed to possess magical properties) was discovered in a *stupa* known to have been sealed in the year 751; quite obviously the *dhāraṇi* must have been printed before this date, and speculations have been put forward ranging between 704 and 751. In Japan the Empress Shotoku, in fear of a rebellion raised by one of her ministers, ordered the printing of one million *dhāraṇi* (fig. 119), which were placed into specially designed miniature pagodas and distributed throughout the country. This massive printing operation, which must have strained the resources of the court, took six years to complete (from 764–770 AD) and stands in odd contrast to the crudeness of the printing which betrays an almost complete lack of previous experience. Some vague suggestions have at times been made about the possibility of Korea or Japan (or even Tibet) being the place where printing originated, but there exist no records which suggest that printing was carried out in these countries either before, or for at least another two to three hundred years afterwards. In addition, China had for long dominated the cultural life of the Far East and both Korea and Japan had accepted, and had greatly benefited from, this influence. In fact the art of writing had reached both countries in just the same way.

   For almost 1,200 years the wood block (fig. 120) remained the principal vehicle of printing in China, Korea and Japan. The technique changed little. The first step was the writing of the text on a thin sheet of paper. This sheet was then attached, face down, to the block and left to dry. The upper surface of the paper was rubbed off and oil applied to make the remainder transparent, so that the engraver could see the characters more clearly. The wood surrounding the characters was cut away, and, once the block was dry, Indian ink was applied with a brush. Then paper, which had been kept moist for several hours, was placed on the block; the actual impression of the imprint was obtained by rubbing the paper with a tool made from a fine cord of bamboo sheath fibre wrapped round a circular card (DC, p.34).

Though block printing (from wooden blocks but also from metal plates) was without doubt the most important method used in the Far East, it was not the only one. Four hundred years before Gutenberg, movable type is supposed to have been used in China in a methodical and coherent manner. According to traditional sources the credit goes to the smith and alchemist Bi Sheng, who in 1045 AD produced movable type made of baked clay; in the course of time other materials such as wood, metal and even porcelain were used. During the 15th century printing with metal type was practised with great skill in Korea, and by the end of that century the royal court could boast its own type foundry. In Japan movable type was introduced almost simultaneously in the latter part of the 16th century from Korea and from Portugal. Although typography was short-lived in Japan, lasting not more than some fifty years, during this time Japanese printers did some exceedingly fine work (fig. 121).In the 17th century typography all but disappeared in the Far East, until it was reintroduced from Europe.

120 Wood block for printing from China. (British Library; Oriental Collections; Or. 78. a.11)

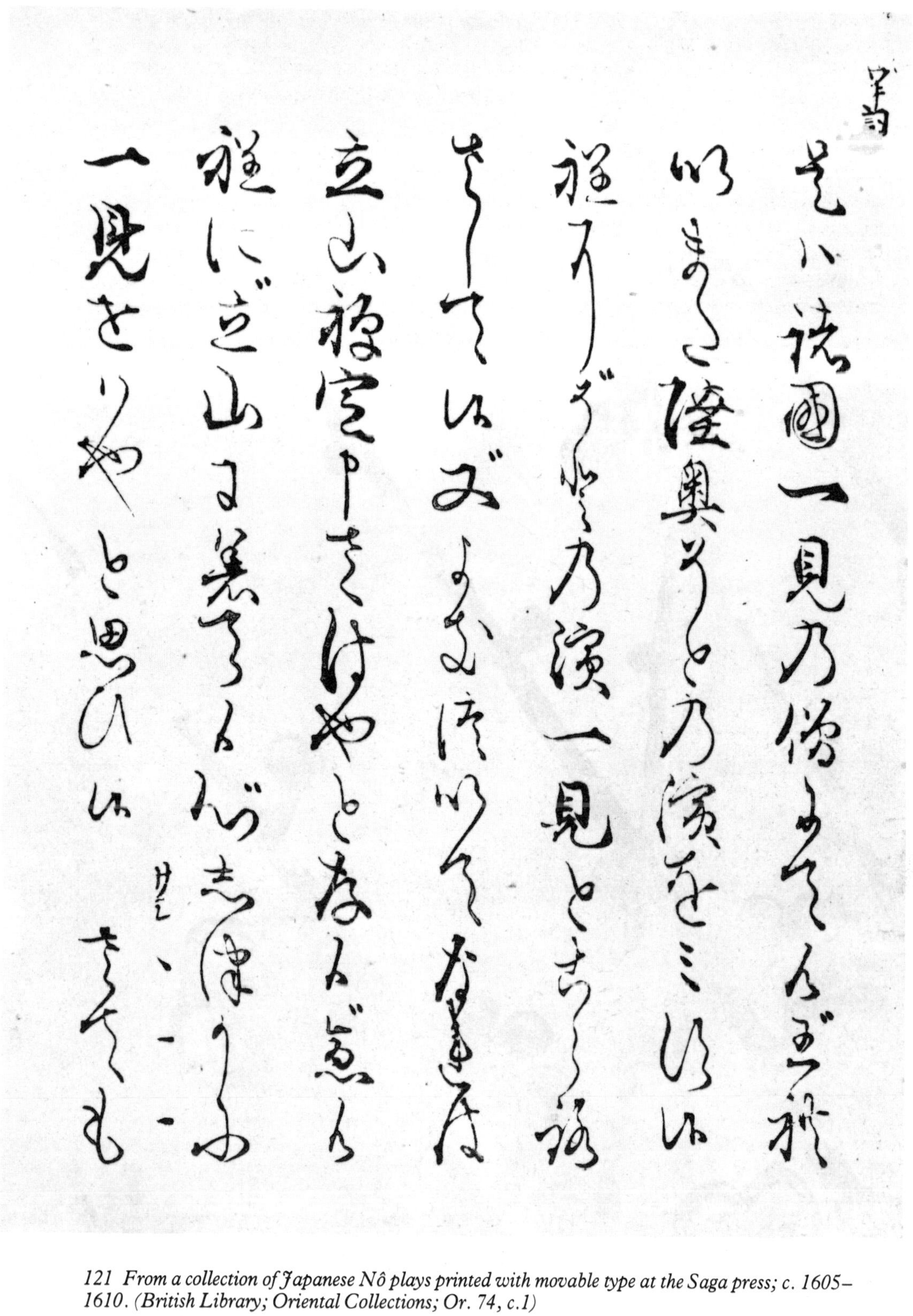

先ハ此画一見乃傍ゑ…
…陸奥うと乃演をミ…
…乃演一見とちく…
…てゐ…
立山祷宣…けやとなん…
枕に立山日美…
一見をりやと思ひ…

121 From a collection of Japanese Nô plays printed with movable type at the Saga press; c. 1605–1610. (British Library; Oriental Collections; Or. 74, c.1)

It has never been possible to ascertain just how much was known in Europe about the existence of printing in the Far East. A good deal of knowledge and many 'curiosities' travelled along the ancient caravan routes which connected East and West, but fragments of printed text or travellers' tales about the wondrous process of printing are conspicuously absent. As far as Europe was concerned the 15th century was the century of printing — or one should perhaps say that the century was ready for printing, and for the mechanical multiplication of written texts. Multiplication itself was nothing new and had indeed already reached as high a level of efficiency as was possible within the confines of available means. The growth of secular education, the interests of wealthy private book collectors and the needs of the Church had created a flourishing book market which made copying by hand a lucrative and already well organized trade (see p.157). But however well organized and numerous the scribes, copying by hand was still laborious and time-consuming. What was needed was a quicker, more reliable (hard-pressed scribes were liable to make mistakes and even the best scribes could not produce identical copies), and above all a cheaper, method of multiplication.

Much controversy surrounds the question of how far printing from wooden blocks played a role in the 15th century. Whereas some scholars are convinced that 'block books' were produced during the first half of the century, others (and they are by far in the majority) do not accept any dates prior to Gutenberg's invention. In the context of this study the controvesy is largely irrelevant, but it is perhaps safe to say that block printing was known and practised in the 15th (and also the 16th) century, but only in a rather limited fashion and more or less simultaneously with printing from movable type. The reason for this lay not only in the speed with which, in the 15th century, the use of typography was perfected and disseminated throughout Europe (and by the middle of the 16th century also outside Europe), but in the very nature of the script used for printing. The alphabet with its twenty-six or so letters lends itself more readily to the use of movable type than did the Chinese script, which could necessitate the use of up to 50,000 different characters.

Some of the early block prints, like the Buxheimer St Christopher, dated *c.* 1423 (fig. 122), show a high level of artistic and technical accomplishment, but are still rather crude if compared with the frontispiece of the *Diamond Sutra* (fig. 118). Of the same period are the chiroxylographic books, which intermix printing and handwriting, as for example the *Biblia Pauperum*, now in the library of the University of Heidelberg, where the Latin text (and colouring) have been added by hand (see Plate VII). In all likelihood such books originated from the printing of single sheets, which were meant to provide cheap tracts for the semi-literate to whom the picture was more important than the text.

This then brings us finally to Gutenberg's invention. It can safely be said that the two decades Gutenberg spent on the perfection of typography signalled the start of the modern period and that all subsequent scientific, political, ecclesiastical, sociological, economic and philosophical advances would not have been possible without the use and the influence of the printing press. This being the case, remarkably little is known about Gutenberg himself. No authentic portrait of him exists. The one often used is an engraving made in

122 Buxheimer St Christopher; first dated wood block print; 1423 AD. *(John Rylands University Library of Manchester; M. 13. 9PP)*

Cristofori faciem die quacumque tueris·:· Millesimo cccc°
Illa nempe die morte mala non morieris·:· xx° anno :ſt·

123 The earliest known portrait of Johann Gutenberg; engraving on copper, 1584 AD. (Gutenberg Museum, Mainz)

1584, some 116 years after his death (fig. 123). The date of his birth too is uncertain, but it is generally agreed that he was born Johann Gensfleisch zur Laden zu Gutenberg (Gutenberg being the house name) at Mainz sometime between 1400 and 1406. Few details of his life and work are clearly established. It is known that he was a goldsmith by profession and that he spent the most decisive part of his life, the twenty years between 1440 and 1460, first in Strasbourg and then later in Mainz. His experiments with typography in Strasbourg have left no tangible results. After his return to Mainz he borrowed a considerable sum of money from a wealthy lawyer by the name of Johannes Fust, an arrangement which facilitated the creation of the first printing press, but which was to rebound disastrously on Gutenberg. In the autumn of 1455 the now-famous 42-line Bible was ready, but Gutenberg himself seems to have reaped little benefit from his creation. Before the copies were sold, Fust demanded the repayment of his loan and Gutenberg lost the Bible, his workshop, his presses and type, and very nearly all claim to his invention. Fust not only had the necessary capital, but in the person of his son-in-law Peter Schöffer (a scribe who had been a foreman in the Gutenberg–Fust firm) he also had an accomplished and highly imaginative printer. Thus for the time being most of the credit, and most of the financial reward, went to the newly established Fust–Schöffer printing house (see Plate VIII).

In the last decade this version of events had been challenged as a rather romantic interpretation of available data (GDP, pp.292–322). The partnership between Fust and Gutenberg, it is argued, had simply been formally dissolved on 6 November 1455. The court which provided for the division of assets, equipment and profits had left Gutenberg with some capital, some equipment and a type he could call his own; he may even have continued to work as a printer. But this new interpretation barely alters the fact that Fust emerged from the partnership very much better off than Gutenberg.

How far then did Gutenberg's concept of printing differ from that of the Far East? How much of it was wholly new and how much was simply a brilliant synthesis of already existing elements? As we have seen, both the need for a more speedy reproduction of the written text and the means of providing it already existed — albeit in limited form. By the 15th century, paper — the ideal material for printing — had become readily available in Europe. As a goldsmith Gutenberg was familiar with some of the most basic concepts of typography: goldsmiths and kindred artists were used to cutting punches for their trademarks and for the lettering on cups, bells, seals and other articles of metalware. In addition his work as a manufacturer of pilgrim badges (*spiegel*) had introduced him to the concept of mass-production and the principle of shallow casting of (soft) metal in a mould. Another important component, the screw press, had been used in Europe for at least a thousand years. Suggestions have been made that Gutenberg took his inspiration from the heavy wine press, but it is much more likely that he adapted the smaller domestic presses used for the flattening of linen or the extraction of oil from olives. The screw press was important; it could produce an imprint more efficiently and, most important, more quickly than rub-printing (see p.198). There were two further innovations without which printing as we know it would never have been possible. One was replica-casting (SHS, p.24) from matrices which assured that in one and the same fount of type the same letters were not just similar but identical to each other, and that all letters could be set, evenly, on the level bed of the press so as to provide an absolutely flat printing surface. The second innovation was the preparation of an (oil-based) ink which would adhere to the metal type. Overall Gutenberg achieved a state of technical efficiency, as far as punch-cutting, matrix-fitting, type-casting, composing and printing were concerned, not to be surpassed in the West before the 19th century.

At first printers tried hard to imitate the scribe as closely as possible. Gutenberg himself had spent a good deal of time studying manuscripts before designing his founts. The mixture of mechanical and manual multiplication which we have already encountered in the case of chiroxylographic books lingered on, though somewhat in reverse: space was left by the printer for initials, ornamentation and illustration to be added, either by hand or with the aid of a printing block. To begin with a profusion of different (calligraphic) styles

ue maria
gra plena
dominus
tecū bene
dicta tu in mulierib'
et benedictus fruct'
ventris tui : ihesus
christus amen.

Gloria laudis resonet in ore
omniū Patri genitoq� proli
spiritui sancto pariter Resul
tet laude perhenni Labori
bus dei vendunt nobis om
nia bona. laus:honor: virtus
potētia: �4 gratia� actio tibi
christe. Amen.

Uiue deū sic �4 vines per secula cūn
cta. Prouidet �4 tribuit deus omnia
nobis. Proficit absque deo null'in
orbe labor. Illa placet tell' in qua
res parua beatū. Ose facit �4 tenues
luxuriantur opes.

Si fortuna volet fies de rhetore consul.
Si volet hec eadem fies de cōsule rhetor.
Quicquid amor iussit nō est cōtēdere tutū
Regnat et in dominos ius habet ille suos
Uita data ē vtē dā data ē sine fenere nobis
Mutua: nec certa persoluenda die.

Usus �4 ars docuit quod sapit omnis homo
Ars animos frangit �4 firmas dirimit vrbes
Arte cadunt turres arte leuatur onus
Artibus ingenijs quesita est gloria multis
Principijs obsta sero medicina paratur
Cum mala per longas conualuere moras
Sed propera nec te venturas differ in horas
Qui non est hodie cras minus aptus erit.

Non bene pro toto libertas venditur auro
Hoc celeste bonum preterit orbis opes
Pecuniis animi est bonis veneranda libertas
Seruitus semper cunctis quoque despicienda
Summa petit liuor perflant altissima venti
Summa petunt dextra fulmina missa iouis
In loca nonnunquam siccis arentia glebis
De prope currenti flumine manat aqua

Quisquis ades scriptis qui mentem forsitan istis
Ut noscas adhibes protinus istud opus
Nosce: augustensie ratdolt germanus Erhardus
Litterulas istos ordine quasꝗ facit
Ipse quibus veneta libros impressit in vrbe
Multos �4 plures nunc premit atꝗ premet
Quique etiam varijs celestia signa figuris
Aurea qui primus nunc monumenta premit
Quin etiam manibus proprijs vbicunꝗ figuras
Est opus:incidens dedalus alter erit

Nobis benedicat qui i trinitate vinit
ꝗ regnat Amen: Hono: soli deo est tribuendv
Aue regina celor mater regis angelo
rum o maria flos virginum velut rosa
vēlilum o maria : Tua est potentia tu
reginꝗ domine tu es super omnes gen
tes da pacem domine in viebv nostris
mirabilis deus in sanctis suis Et glori
osus in maiestate sua oth panthon kyr

Quod prope sacre diem tibi sum conuiua futurus
forsitan ignoras atfore ne dubites
Ergo para cenam non qualem stoicus ambit
Sed lautam sane more cirenaico
Nanque duas mecum florente etate puellas
Adducam quarum balsama cunnus olet
Vernula sola domi sedeat quam nuper habebas
Si nondum cunnus vepribus horruerit
Sunt quin simulent �4 auari crimen amici
O biciant facto rumo: utiste cadat Hec Philelphus

Hunc adeas mira quicunꝗ volumina queris
Arte vel er animo pressa fuisse tuo
Seruiet iste vbi:nobis iure sorores
Incolumem seruet usꝗ rogare licet

Est homini uirtus fuluo preciosior auro: aeneas
Ingenium quondam fuerat preciosius auro.
Miramurꝗ magis quos munera mentis adornāt:
Quam qui corporeis emicuere bonis.
Si qua uirtute nites ne despice quenquam
Ex alia quadam forsitan ipse nitet

Nemo suꝗ laudis nimium letetur honore
Ne uilis factus post sua fata gemat.
Nemo nimis cupide sibi res desiderat ullas
Ne dum plus cupiat perdat & id quod habet.
Ne uc cito uerbis cuiusquam credito blandis
Sed si sint fidei respice quid moneant
Qui bene proloquitur coram sed postea praue
Hic erit inuisus bina ꝗ ora gerat

Pax plenam uirtutis opus pax summa laborum
pax belli exacti precium est precuumque pericli
Sidera pace uigent consistunt terrea pace
Nil placitum sine pace deo non munus ad aram
Fortuna arbitris tempus dispensat ubi
Illa rapit iuuenes illa ferit senes

κλίω Τευτερπιη τε θαλεία τε μελπομένη τε
Περψιχορη τερατω τε πολυμνεία τουρανιη
τε καλλιόπη θεΔη προφερεσατη εξ ινατα
σαων ιεσνς Χρισονό μαρια τελοσ.

Indicis characteꝝ diuersaꝝ mane
rieruū impressioni paratarū: Finis.

Erhardi Ratdolt Augustensis viri
solertissimi:preclaro ingenio �4 miri
fica arte:qua olim Venetijs excelluit
celebratissimus. In imperiali nunc
vrbe Auguste vindelicoꝝ laudatissi
me impressioni dedit. Annoqꝗ salu
tis. M.LLLL.LXXXVI.Kalē.
Aprilis Sidere felici compleuit.

was used, but after 1480 printers started to become more conscious of the intrinsic autonomy of their craft (fig. 124); fifty years after Gutenberg's death (in 1468) two styles had gained prominence — the humanistic Antiqua and the Gothic, or Fractur.

As far as the overall economic situation of Europe was concerned, printing introduced a number of new and quite revolutionary concepts. First of all it shifted the emphasis from patronage to capital; the new printing centres which developed so rapidly during the hundred years after Gutenberg were mainly situated in commercial centres. With the loss of patronage the printer also lost the scribe's ready-made clientele. He no longer worked for a small circle of *cognoscenti* who had similar tastes and a similar level of education, but for a largely anonymous general public. To hold the attention of this new readership the printer had to make sure that the language of the text was sufficiently standardized to be understood in different parts of the country and by different classes of people; he had to find subjects of a more universal apeal; and last but not least he had to make the product, the book, attractive enough to invite sales.

124 Erhard Ratdolt's type-specimen, dated Augsburg 1 April 1486, but probably printed in Venice. (Bavarian State Library, Munich)

Industrialization and new technology

It is not, indeed it cannot be, the subject of this study to discuss either industrialization or what is often loosely termed new technology as such. What must interest us however is the effect each one had, or is likely to have, on writing as a form of communication and information storage. Whereas in the case of industrialization most of us are able to perceive a more or less clearly defined picture, as far as new technology is concerned we have to rely heavily on speculation. Such speculation is made more precarious by the sheer speed with which everything connected with new technology is liable to change, and by the fact that as far as social implications are concerned we have no definite models on which to base our speculations. 'New technology', 'electronic technology', the 'computer revolution', or whatever one may like to call it, is not a logical continuation of industrialization. The Industrial Revolution made use of machines and increasingly more sophisticated mechanical processes to support human labour (in relation to output); for new technology to function effectively, human labour has to be organized around it. If we return to the first sentence of this study, namely the statement that 'all writing is information storage', we must add that in the up-to-date history of information storage three distinct phases can be observed: (1) information storage by memory (oral tradition); (2) information storage by writing; and (3) information storage by technological, that is non-human, means. Indeed as we are repeatedly told, new technology is to a large extent information technology. Information technology cannot be compared with the invention of writing. Equally it is not an advance on printing. But it is a step away from writing as we know it.

What then were the effects of the Industrial Revolution on writing and on the use and status of literacy? Before looking for an answer to those questions we should perhaps return briefly to Gutenberg and the principle of replica-casting from matrices. This had been an invention of great importance; it had introduced to Europe, long before its general acceptance by industry, the 'theory of interchangeable parts' which was to form the basis of modern mass-production technique. In other words, as far as writing is concerned the long shadow of the Industrial Revolution made itself felt more than 300 years ahead of time. Printing fostered other elements usually associated with industrialization: dependence on capital (as Gutenberg had learned to his cost); mass-production, which stimulates the market and thus in turn increases demand; and the tentative beginning of a consumer society, which ultimately feeds on itself. Though none of this of course happened at once (there were the licensing laws which severely limited the number of master-printers in the kingdom and the presses they were allowed to use, censorship and many other restrictions), a beginning had most certainly been made.

Without doubt the Industrial Revolution encouraged the spread of literacy — not so much from ulterior motives, but because of an inherent and, as time went by, growing need for it. Even the most elementary and superficial list of just some of the components which made up the new pattern of economic life will illustrate this: overseas expansion (territorial and political as well as commercial), improved communications, banking, the growth of large-scale farming, the growing size of wholesale trade — all depended to a quite noticeable degree on paper, pen and an army of industrious clerks. By the end of the 19th century the new industrial techniques made possible by the practical application of scientific discoveries (such as electricity) necessitated the creation of large-scale companies and with them a concentration of the population into ever-growing urban areas. Steel, for example, could not be produced profitably by any of the small family businesses typical of the first stage of the Industrial Revolution. To illustrate this point: Krupp in Germany employed 122 men in 1848, 16,000 in 1873 and 70,000 in 1913. Such undertakings depended heavily on administration, and administration in turn depended as we have seen on literate coordinators and recorders (scribes/clerks).

If the first stage of the Industrial Revolution had destroyed the old cottage industries, the second stage drastically reduced the number of small business firms and to a large extent did away with domestic outworkers. Centralization became an important factor. Advances in medicine were, at least in part, responsible for an increasing population, and by the 20th century the old 'estate' democracy was beginning to be replaced by the new mass democracy. Universal franchise, when eventually it did come, was an additional inducement for the spread of literacy; as in classical Athens, the new form of democracy needed citizens of at least elementary literacy. This challenge to inherited privilege in turn encouraged not just literacy, but real education, which could stimulate curiosity and talent. Since, at least in theory, all were equal, the way to the top became possible through personal achievement.

If at the beginning the quality of education had been poor (the 18th-century Sunday and Charity schools did not want to encourage upward mobility but to teach the children of the poor how to be industrious and above all amenable citizens in a carefully graded society), by the end of the 19th century a note of genuine enthusiasm crept in. The growing prosperity and the political power of Western countries, where the majority of people knew how to read and write, was a further incentive. Educators and missionaries alike began to look upon literacy as the key to better health, a better character, greater sensibility and, as far as the colonies were concerned, political freedom. During the first half of the 20th century literacy became the norm in most Western countries: a child unable to master reading and writing might be suspected of being mentally retarded, a case for help and treatment — or, if all else failed, contempt. In the 1972 edition of Gustav Barthel's *Konnte Adam schreiben: Weltgeschichte der Schrift* we still read 'im einundzwanzigsten Jahrhundert wird es auf Erden kaum noch Analphabeten geben'–'in the 21st century there will be hardly anybody left who is unable to read' (or, to translate the German word *Analphabet* literally: 'who has not mastered the alphabet'). Yen ten years later we read in a British daily paper (*Daily Telegraph*, 22 July 1983): 'researchers who were shocked to discover that ten per cent of 23-year-olds cannot read or write properly, say in a report published today that Britain could have a literacy problem of unimaginable proportions . . . 3,500,000 adults may be functionally illiterate'. What went wrong? Or, better, what happened?

When computers first emerged in the 1940s they were mainly used for the manipulation of numerical data. This in itself was nothing particularly new: the Incas had used *quipus* (see p.77) and the Chinese the abacus, for exactly the same purpose. What was new was the speed with which computers could perform this task, and the volume of data they could handle. As technology advanced, the quite considerable size of the early computers decreased; in almost direct relation to this decrease in size their storage capacity grew, and the ability to retrieve stored information and to modify instructions (as to the manipulation of information) was further developed. In other words not only could computers store vast quantities of information — infinitely more than one could hold in one's memory or cope with on paper — but they could also provide, on request, just those pieces of information which were needed at a given moment, and provide them in exactly the form in which they were needed. Between 1950 and 1975 increasingly more sophisticated ways of using computers were designed. An important development was that of pattern recognition: the ability of a computer to correlate data in its memory bank with a given situation, rather as a physician compares a patient's symptoms with the sum total of knowledge stored in his own memory. The new expert systems which developed out of this ability made use, for the first time, of what is often referred to as artificial intelligence (the intelligence of one or more human beings which has been fed into the computer by an experienced knowledge engineer).

Expert systems allow a dialogue between user and database — between persons and a computer — as opposed to a simple interrogation of the database. As the dialogue continues, the computer can add new information to its memory bank; in other words, both the user and the computer (the reader and the book!) learn from each other. In addition the increasingly more sophisticated telecommunication links can transmit information from one computer to another — just as we speak to one another over the telephone, so computers can speak to one another over specially established networks. If calligrams (see p.178) were 'writing writing itself', in the new era of information storage writing can now write and read itself.

Whether we are aware of it or not, computers are already an integral part of our lives. In the so-called 'developed' countries there will be few homes which do not make use of electronic technology in one way or another — not just in the more obvious fields of television, video-recording or electronic games, but also in household appliances such as washing machines, cookers, watches, electric irons, calculators, sewing machines, central heating, and so forth. Micro-computers (DC/MJ, p.209) are used at work, for recreation and in schools: children are not only taught by computers, they have to learn how to be 'computer-literate' to function in today's, and most certainly tomorrow's, world (fig. 125). In the words of Murray Laver, the three Rs are being replaced rapidly by the three Ps: push-button, picture and program.

Basically a computer translates written language into positive and negative electrical impulses and, on demand, retranslates those impulses stored in its data bank back into written language, which is then made visible on paper (but also, increasingly, on a video-screen, on microfilm or microfiche). But electronic information storage does not stop at this point; there are videodiscs which store and communicate sound and picture, and there are machines with the ability to recognize, visually, a whole page of text without the need of a human intermediary to feed this text letter by letter into the data bank. Some computers have the ability to recognize voice patterns and to reply in an artificially-constructed 'human' voice. This is an enormous departure, a step forward which in a curious way takes us back some 6,000 years. Information is again stored in memory (this time the electronic memory of a computer) as it was once stored, before the evolution of systematic writing, in the memory of a specially chosen person or priest. There are indeed strangely ritualistic elements in the logistics of computer usage: the need for a password to enter a particular system (which proves that one belongs to the circle of initiates), the formality of address and answer, the limitations of the subject that can be discussed. Any dialogue with a computer is a dialogue based on computer rules, or rather on the rules programmed into the computer by somebody else. The result is increased efficiency in a specific area accompanied by a loss of overall independence. The risk is that of a divided society, divided not only into the 'information-poor' and the 'information-rich' (ML, p.20) — with the latter mainly to be found among the technologically affluent nations — but also the creation of a new class system among the information-rich; those who know how to handle, manipulate, select and create information, and those who passively accept information.

125 British Library staff working with a computer

In the ancient world the evolution of systematic writing had devalued, and eventually all but eliminated, oral tradition. At first writing had mainly been used for the storage of information related to commerce and administration, but slowly, sometimes reluctantly, it was deemed suitable also for the preservation of religious and secular literature. The parallels between those early days and our present situation seem uncomfortably close. There is the (perhaps still unconscious) decrease in the importance given to literacy and numeracy (an electronic calculator is so much more efficient than human memory) which we can observe all around us — except perhaps in 'developing' countries not yet blessed with a high level of new technology. There is the capacity, already used in certain areas, of electronic printing which commits information — literary information — directly into a machine-readable form without the help of scribes, publishers and booksellers, and makes this information directly available on demand. It is now possible to have a dialogue, visually or acoustically or both, with an electronic memory. A recipe for doom? Something to be regretted and feared? Not necessarily. The ancient world survived the transition from oral tradition to writing: even the Indian Brahmins did eventually commit their sacred texts to palm-leaf, and later on to paper, without the cataclysmic destruction of the universe they had been taught to expect and fear. There must have been stress, just as there is stress now — all periods of transition are stressful — yet without it the pictures on the walls of Altamira would never have been painted, and Plato, Maimonides, St Augustine, Dante, Shakespeare and Kant would never have become a possibility. Just as thousands of years ago a point was reached when the sum total of available knowledge had become too large to be stored in human memory, so the sum total of information necessary to sustain contemporary society is becoming too vast and is growing too quickly to be stored efficiently in a traditional form of writing. All writing may be information storage, as we have said at the beginning of this study, but it has now become increasingly obvious that information can once again be stored, quite effectively, without writing.

Select Bibliography

ABBOT, NABIA, *The rise of the North Arabic script and its Ku'ranic development.* Chicago, 1939

ALICHIN, BRIDGET *and* RAYMOND, *The birth of Indian civilisation.* 1968

ANDERSON, D.M., *The art of written forms.* 1969

ANDREWS, CAROL, *The Rosetta stone.* London, 1981

ARNTZ, H., *Die Runenschrift.* Halle, 1938

BACKHOUSE, JANET, *The Lindisfarne Gospels.* London, 1981

BANKES, GEORGE, *Moche pottery from Peru.* London, 1980

BANKES, GEORGE, *Peru before Pizarro.* Oxford, 1977

BARTHEL, GUSTAV, *Konnte Adam schreiben: Weltgeschichte der Schrift.* Köln, 1972

BARTHEL, THOMAS S., *Das Geheimnis der Kohau-rongorongo.* 'Urania' 19.5., 1956

BASHAM, A.L., *The wonder that was India.* London, 1954

BENSON, ELIZABETH P., *The Mochica.* London, 1972

BOWLER, BERJOUHI, *The word as image.* London, 1970

BURNEY, CHARLES, *From Village to Empire.* Oxford, 1977

CARCOPINO, JEROME, *Daily life in Ancient Rome* (transl. by E.O. Lorimer). London, 1981

CARTER, THOMAS FRANCIS, *The invention of printing in China and its spread westwards.* New York, 1925

CASSEL, DON *and* JACKSON, MARTIN, *Introduction to computers and information processing.* Reston, Virginia, 1981

CHADWICK, J., *The decipherment of Linear B.* Cambridge, 1958

CHATELAIN, CP. E., *Introduction à la lecture des notes tironiennes.* Paris, 1900

CHIBBETT, DAVID, *The history of Japanese printing and book illustration.* Tokyo, 1977

CHILD, H., *Calligraphy today.* (2nd edition), 1976

CLAPPERTON, R.H., *Paper: an historical account.* Oxford, 1934

COE, MICHAEL D., *The Mayas.* (6th edition), London, 1980

COWLEY, A.E., *The Hittites.* London, 1920

CRESWELL, K.A., *Bibliography of the architecture, arts and crafts of Islam.* Cairo, 1961

DANZEL, T., *Die Anfänge der Schrift.* Leipzig, 1912

DEGERING, H., *Die Schrift.* Berlin, 1929

DELITSCH, H., *Geschichte der abendländischen Schriftformen.* 1928

DIRINGER, DAVID, *The alphabet: a key to the history of mankind.* (3rd edition), London, 1968

DIRINGER, DAVID, *A history of the alphabet.* (2nd edition), London, 1977

DIRINGER, DAVID, *The hand-produced book.* London, 1953

DIRINGER, DAVID, *The illuminated book, its history and production.* London, 1958

DREYFUSS, HENRY, *Signs, images, symbols.* New York, 1966

DRIVER, G.R., *Semitic writing: from pictograph to alphabet.* London, 1948

EVANS, ARTHUR, *Scripta Minoa.I.* Oxford, 1909

FAULMANN, KARL, *Die Initiale: ein Beitrag zur Geschichte der Bücher-Ornamentik.* Wien, 1886

FÉVRIER, J.-G., *Histoire de l'écriture.* Paris, 1959

FÖLDES-PAPP, K., *Vom Felsbild zum Alphabet*, Stuttgart, 1966

FRANKEL, DAVID, *The ancient kingdom of Urartu*. London, 1979

FROBENIUS, LEO *and* FOX, DOUGAL C., *Prehistoric rock pictures in Europe and Africa*. New York, 1937

FRIEDRICH, J., *Entzifferung verschollener Schriften und Sprachen*. Heidelberg, 1954

GAINES, H.F., *Cryptoanalysis, a study of cyphers and their solution*. New York, 1956

GARDINER, A.H. *and* PEET, T.A., *The inscriptions of Sinai*. (ed. J. Cerny). 1955

GAUR, ALBERTINE, *Writing materials of the East*. London, 1979

GELB, I.J., *A study of writing: the foundations of grammatology*. Chicago, 1963

GHIRSHMAN, R., *Iran*. (2nd edition), London, 1961

GOODY, JACK *and* WATT, IAN., *The consequences of literacy*. (Comp. study in Society and History v.5.no.3.), 1963

GORDON, C.H., *Ugaritic grammar*. Rome, 1940

GREEN, PETER, *A concise history of ancient Greece*. London, 1981

GRINSTEAD, ERIC, *Analysis of the Tangut script*. Lund, 1972

GURNEY, O.R., *The Hittites*. (Revised edition), London, 1961

HARRIS, ROY, *The origin of writing*. London 1986

HELLINGA, LOTTE, *Johann Gutenberg* and *The origin of printing* ('Dictionary of the Middle Ages', New York – in preparation)

HOSKING, R.F. *and* MEREDITH-OWENS, G.M. (*ed.*), *A handbook of Asian scripts*. London, 1966

HUNTER, G.R., *The script of Harappa and Mohenjo-daro*. London, 1934

IPSIROGLU, M.S., *Das Bild im Islam*. Wien, 1971

IRWIN, C., *The romance of writing*. New York, 1956

JACKSON, DONALD, *The story of writing*. New York, 1981

JAMES, T.G.H., *An introduction to ancient Egypt*, London, 1979

JENSEN, HANS, *Signs, symbols and script: an account of man's effort to write*. London, 1970

JOHNSTON, E., *Writing and illuminating and lettering*. 1906

KÉKI, BELA, *5000 Jahre Schrift*. Leipzig, 1976

KRAMISCH, STELLA, *Unknown Indian ritual art in tribe and village*, Philadelphia, 1968

KRISHNA RAO, M.V.N., *Indus script deciphered*. 1982

LAMB, C.M. (*ed.*), *The calligraphers handbook*. 1956

LANG, D.M., *Armenia, cradle of civilisation*. (3rd edition), London, 1980

LAVER, MURRAY, *Computers and social change*. New York, 1980

LEHNER, ERNST, *American symbols: a picture history*. New York, 1966

LINGS, MARTIN, *The Quranic art of calligraphy and illumination*. London, 1976

LOSTY, J., *The art of the book in India*. London, 1982

LÜLFING, HANS, *An der Wiege des Alphabets*. Leipzig, 1977

MALLERY, GARRICK, *Picture writing of the American Indians*. Washington, 1893

MARTIN, M.J., *The origin of writing*. Jerusalem, 1943

MASON, W.A., *A history of the art of writing*. New York, 1920

MASSEY, W., *The origin and progress of letters*. London, 1963

MCARTHUR, TOM, *Worlds of reference: lexicography, learning and language from the clay tablets to the computer*. Cambridge, 1986

MCLEOD, M.D., *The Asante*. London, 1981

MERCER, S.A.B., *The origin of writing and the alphabet*. London, 1959

MOORHOUSE, A.C., *The triumph of the alphabet*. New York, 1953

MORISON, STANLEY, *Selected essays on the history of letterforms in manuscript and print.* (D. McKitterick, ed.) Cambridge, 1981

MORRIS, IVAN, *The world of the shining prince: Court life in ancient Japan.* London, 1979

MORRIS, RONALD W.B., *The prehistoric rock art of Argyll.* Pool, 1977

NAVEH, JOSEPH, *Early history of the alphabet.* Jerusalem, 1982

NEWDIGATE, B.H., *The art of the book.* London, 1938

OGG, O., *The 26 letters.* (2nd edition). 1961

PAINTER, G.D., *Gutenberg and the B 36 group: a reconsideration.* In: 'Essays in honour of Victor Scholderer'; ed. by D.E. Rhodes. Mainz, 1970

PARPOLA, ASKO *(et al.), Decipherment of the Proto-Dravidian inscriptions of the Indus Civilisation.* Copenhagen, 1969

PATTIE, T.S., *Manuscripts of the Bible.* London, 1979

PETRAU, A , *Schrift und Schriften im Leben der Völker.* Leipzig, 1939

PETRIE, FLINDERS W., *The formation of the alphabet.* London, 1912

POSSEHL, GREGORY L. (*ed.*), *Ancient cities of the Indus.* New Delhi, 1979

POWELL, J.W., *Tenth annual report of the Bureau of Ethnology to the Secretary of the Smithsonian Institute.* Washington, 1893

PRIES, A., *Die ältesten, alten und neuen Schriften der Völker.* Leipzig, 1927

REED, R., *Ancient skins, parchments and leather.* London, 1972

REEFE, THOMAS Q., *Lukasa: a Luba memory device.* (Africa Arts. 10.p.49.)

ROBINSON, R., *Phonetic writing.* (ed. E.J. Dobson). London, 1957

ROY, A.K. *and* GIDWANI, N.N., *Indus Valley civilization: a bibliographical essay.* New Delhi, 1982

SAFADI, YASIN HAMID, *Islamic calligraphy.* London, 1978

SAMPSON, GEOFFREY, *Writing systems.* London, 1985

SCHMITT, ALFRED, *Entstehung und Entwicklung der Schriften.* (herausgegeben Claus Haebler), Köln, 1980

SCHMITT, ALFRED, *Untersuchungen zur Geschichte der Schrift.* Leipzig, 1940

SCHOLDERER, VICTOR, *Johann Gutenberg, the inventor of printing.* (2nd edition). London, 1970

SCHOLEM, GERSHOM G., *Major trends in Jewish mysticism.* (6th edition). New York, 1972

SELER, E., *Gesammelte Abhandlungen zur amerikanischen Sprach-und Altertumskunde.* Graz, 1960

SETHE, KURT, *Die neuentdeckte Sinaischrift und die Entstehung der Semitischen Schrift.* Göttingen, 1917

SETHE, KURT, *Vom Bild zum Buchstaben.* Leipzig, 1939

SMITH, M.E., *Picture writing from ancient Southern Mexico.* 1973

STEINBERG, S.H., *Five hundred years of printing.* (3rd edition), London, 1979

STREICHER, H., *Die graphischen Gaunerzinken.* Wien, 1928

TAUBE, M., *Tibetische Handschriften und Blockdrucke.* Wiesbaden, 1968

THOMPSON, J. ERIC S., *Maya hieroglyphs without tears.* London, 1972

THOMPSON, J. ERIC S., *The civilization of the Mayas.* Chicago, 1927

TOZZER, A.M. (*ed*), *Landa's relación de las cosas de Yukatán. A translation edited with notes.* Cambridge (Mass), 1941

TSIEN, TSUEN-HSUIN, *Written on bamboo and silk: the beginning of Chinese books and inscriptions.* Chicago, 1962

VAILLANT, GEORGE C., *Aztecs of Mexico.* New York, 1941

VENTRIS, MICHAEL G.F. *and* CHADWICK, JOHN, *The decipherment of Linear B.* London, 1958

VERVLIET, HENDRIK D.L. (*ed.*), *The book through five thousand years.* London, 1972

WELLARD, JAMES, *By the waters of Babylon.* London, 1972

WELLISCH, HANS H., *The conversion of scripts: its nature, history and utilization.* University of Maryland, 1978

WEULE, KARL, *Vom Kerbstock zum Alphabet*. Stuttgart, 1921

WHALLEY, JOYCE IRENE, *The pen's excellence: calligraphy of Western Europe and America*. 1980

WHEELER, MORTIMER, *The Indus civilisation*. Cambridge, 1960

WHORF, B.L., *The phonetic value of certain characters in Maya writing*. Cambridge (Mass), 1933

WIDMANN, H. (*ed.*), *Der gegenwärtige Stand der Gutenberg-Forschung*. Stuttgart, 1977

ZIAUDDIN, M., *A monograph of Moslem calligraphy*. Calcutta, 1936

Index

(*Figures in* **bold** *refer to page numbers of illustrations*)